Global Environmental Politics

D1584576

Global Environmental Politics is the perfect introduction to this increasingly significant area. The text combines an accessible introduction to the most important environmental theories and concepts with a series of detailed case studies of the most pressing environmental problems.

Features and benefits of the book:

- Explains the most important concepts and theories in environmental politics.
- Introduces environmental politics within the context of political science and international relations theories.
- Demonstrates how the concepts and theories apply in a wide variety of real world contexts.
- Case studies include the most important environmental issues from climate change and biodiversity to forests and marine pollution.
- Each chapter is written by an established international authority in the field.

This exciting new textbook is essential reading for all students of environmental politics and will be of great interest to students of International Relations and Political Economy.

Gabriela Kütting is a Professor at the Division of Global Affairs, Rutgers-Newark University, USA.

"The contributions in Gabriela Kütting's volume explore institutionalist and critical approaches to global environmental politics. The volume presents important insights for students on the future direction of research, and shows convincingly that justice plays an increasingly important role in global environmental policy making."

Ulrich Brand, *University of Vienna, Austria*

"This text reminds readers that global environmental politics is a vibrant and evolving field of study. The book surveys a diverse set of ideas even as it focuses deserved attention on some of the most interesting and pressing problems of the day, including climate change, deforestation, and biological diversity. Perhaps most impressively, even as the text examines the tangible ecological costs of poverty, overconsumption, and inequality, it does not dodge difficult ethical and political questions concerning social justice and legitimate governance."

Rodger A. Payne, *University of Louisville, USA*

"*Global Environmental Politics* is not just a wide-ranging and up-to-date survey of the most complex and significant environmental issues in an increasingly interconnected world. More importantly, it systematically addresses these issues through sophisticated theoretical lenses that are diverse yet complementary. This book will be an indispensable resource for understanding what is rapidly becoming the most crucial cross-cutting – global, regional, national and local – issue-area of 21st century world politics."

Philip G. Cerny, *Professor Emeritus of Politics and Global Affairs, University of Manchester, UK and Rutgers University, USA*

"This excellent book introduces students to an appropriate range of pressing issues in global environmental politics. Although most of the contributors start from a background in international relations, the range of topics they address is impressively broad. As a result, the book will serve the purposes not only of international relations students concerned with environmental issues, but of students of environmental politics more generally as they attempt to grapple with the transnational dimensions of environmental problems."

Christopher Rootes, *Professor of Environmental Politics and Political Sociology, University of Kent, UK*

Global Environmental Politics
Concepts, theories and case studies

Edited by
Gabriela Kütting

Routledge
Taylor & Francis Group

LONDON AND NEW YORK

First published 2011
by Routledge
2 Park Square, Milton Park, Abingdon, Oxon OX14 4RN

Simultaneously published in the USA and Canada
by Routledge
711 Third Avenue, New York, NY 10017

*Routledge is an imprint of the Taylor & Francis Group,
an informa business*

Transferred to Digital Printing 2011

Typeset in Times New Roman by
Book Now Ltd, London

British Library Cataloguing in Publication Data
A catalogue record for this book is available from the British Library

Library of Congress Cataloging in Publication Data
Global environmental politics: concepts, theories & case studies / edited by Gabriela Kütting.
p. cm.—(Global environmental politics)
Environmental policy—International cooperation. I. Kütting, Gabriela.
GE170.G5557 2010
363.7′0526—dc22   2010007957

ISBN: 978-0-415-77793-3 (hbk)
ISBN: 978-0-415-77794-0 (pbk)
ISBN: 978-0-203-84456-4 (ebk)

Contents

Contributors

Frederike Boll is a doctoral student at the Westfälische Wilhelms-Universität Münster, Germany.

Antje Brown is a research fellow at Stirling University and Teaching Fellow at Aberdeen University. Her research interests include International Relations, EU politics, multi-level governance and environmental politics.

Jennifer Clapp is Professor and CIGI Chair in International Environmental Governance at the University of Waterloo, Ontario, Canada. She is the author of numerous articles and several books, including *Paths to a Green World* (co-written with Peter Dauvergne; MIT Press, 2005), in the field of environment, development, and global governance

Shlomi Dinar is Assistant Professor at Florida International University and has written several articles on environmental security. He is also the author of *International Water Treaties: Negotiation and Cooperation along Transboundary Rivers* (Routledge, 2008) and has recently edited a volume on resource scarcity, conflict, and cooperation to be published by MIT Press.

Timothy Ehresman is a doctoral student in the Department of Political Science at Colorado State University.

Lucy Ford is Senior Lecturer at Oxford Brookes University and is the author of several articles on global civil society in an environmental context.

Doris Fuchs is Professor of International Relations and Development at the Westfälische Wilhelms-Universität Münster, Germany. She is the author of *Business Power in Global Governance* (Lynne Rienner, 2007) and has published extensively in the field of international political economy, environment, and consumption.

Paul G. Harris is Chair Professor of Global and Environmental Studies, Head of the Department of Social Sciences, and Director of the Social and Policy Research Unit at the Hong Kong Institute of Education, Hong Kong. He has published numerous books and articles on global environmental politics.

Peter Hough is Senior Lecturer at Middlesex University and the author of *The Global Politics of Pesticides* (Earthscan, 1998) and *Understanding Global Security* (Routledge, 2nd ed., 2008).

David Humphreys is Senior Lecturer in Environmental Policy at the Open University. He has written and edited several books and articles on deforestation and forest certification issues. In 2008 he was the recipient of the Sprout Award of the International Studies Association.

Peter Jacques is Associate Professor of Political Science at the University of Central Florida and the author of *Ocean Politics and Policy: A Reference Handbook* (ABC-Clio, 2003), *Globalization and the World Ocean* (Rowman & Littlefield, 2006), and *Environmental Skepticism: Ecology, Power, and International Relations* (Ashgate, 2009).

Gabriela Kütting is Associate Professor of Political Science at Rutgers, the State University of New Jersey, Newark. She has published extensively in the field of global environmental politics and is the author of *The Global Political Economy of the Environment and Tourism* (Palgrave Macmillan, 2010) and co-editor of *Power and Knowledge in a Local–Global World* (with R. Lipschutz, 2009).

Dimitris Stevis is Professor of Political Science at Colorado State University. He is co-editor of *Palgrave Advances in International Environmental Politics* (Palgrave Macmillan, 2006) and has published extensively in the field of labor politics as well as environmental politics.

John Vogler is Professor of International Relations at Keele University, UK, and chair of the BISA environment working group. He has published widely on aspects of international environmental politics and on the European Union and he is a member of the ESRC Centre for Climate Change Economics and Policy.

Marc Williams is Professor of International Relations at the University of New South Wales and has published extensively in the field of international political economy and environment. His most recent book is *Global Political Economy: Evolution and Dynamics*, 3rd ed. (Palgrave Macmillan, 2010), with Robert O'Brien.

Abbreviations

AIA	advanced informed agreement
BCSD	Business Council for Sustainable Development
CCPR	Codex Committee on Pesticides Residue
CEC	Commission on Environmental Cooperation
CEFIC	European Chemical Industry Council
CITES	Convention on International Trade in Endangered Species
CO_2	Carbon dioxide
COP	Conference of the Parties
CSD	Commission for Sustainable Development
CTE	Committee on Trade and Environment
DGD	decision guidance documents
DSD	Division on Sustainable Development
DTIE	Division of Technology, Industry, and Economics
ECA	export credit agency
EPA	Environmental Protection Agency
ETS	emissions trading scheme
EU	European Union
FAO	Food and Agriculture Organization
FSC	Forest Stewardship Council
G77	Group of 77 developing countries
GATT	General Agreement on Tariffs and Trade
GEF	Global Environmental Facility
GEP	global environmental politics
GMO	genetically modified organism
ICC	International Chamber of Commerce
IEJ	international environmental justice
IISD	International Institute for Sustainable Development
IMF	International Monetary Fund
IMO	International Maritime Organization
INGO	international non-governmental organization
IPCC	International Panel on Climate Change
ISMO	international social movement organization
ISO	International Organization for Standardization
ITTO	International Tropical Timber Organization
IUCN	International Union for the Conservation of Nature

LMO	living modified organism
MARPOL	International Convention for the Prevention of Pollution From Ships
MEA	multilateral environmental agreement
MNC	multinational corporation
NAFTA	North American Free Trade Agreement
NATO	North Atlantic Treaty Organization
NGO	non-governmental organization
OECD	Organization for Economic Cooperation and Development
OILPOL	Convention on Oil Pollution
PAN	Pesticide Action Network
PCB	polychlorinated biphenyl
PIC	prior informed consent
POP	persistent organic pollutants
ppm	parts per million
REDD	reducing emissions from deforestation and forest degradation
TBT	technical barriers to trade
TNC	transnational corporation
TNGO	transnational non-governmental organization
TRIPS	Trade Related Intellectual Property Rights
UN	United Nations
UNCED	UN Conference on Environment and Development
UNCTC	UN Center on Transnational Corporations
UNDESA	UN Department of Economic and Social Affairs
UNDP	United Nations Development Programme
UNEP	United Nations Environment Programme
UNFF	United Nations Forum on Forests
WBCSD	World Business Council for Sustainable Development
WSSD	World Summit on Sustainable Development
WTO	World Trade Organization
WWF	World Wide Fund for Nature

Introduction

Gabriela Kütting

The field of global environmental politics has formed an important subject in undergraduate courses for nearly twenty years. The environment has traditionally been approached from an institutional angle in international politics, which means studies have focused on international treaties, organizations, and other set-ups as the primary agent of environmental improvement. Thus, traditionally, political science researchers have focused most prominently on the field of regime theory and more recently on the field of global governance in general. As a result, both global environmental politics and global governance are concerned primarily with the relations between political actors and the structure within which they operate. They see institutions as the main social force both as causes of change and as prescriptions for solving problems (Young 2002: 3). But, more recently, many researchers have felt that such a focus is no longer enough. As Peter Haas puts it:

> What is needed is a clearer map of the actual division of labor between governments, NGOs, the private sector, scientific networks and international institutions in the performance of various functions of governance. Also needed is an assessment of ... how well they actually perform these activities.
>
> (Haas 2004: 8)

There is an emerging feeling that global environmental politics as a field of study is not concerned principally with the improvement of the problem studied except as a political, an institutional, or a policy issue. In this book, the contributors adopt a wider view of global environmental politics, one that takes account of a greater variety of environmental challenges that do not neatly fit either the pattern of existing institutions or the tendency of most environmental politics scholarship to focus on institutional case studies. So the analysis of conceptual questions underlying global environmental politics also includes discussions on consumption, social justice, and North–South issues, while the case studies are a mixture of examples focusing on instances in which institutions or environmental actors miss the main problem or examples where institutional analyses are extended to include other issues.

Most of environment-related international relations is centered around the notion of governance, either in its traditional neoliberal institutionalist regime theory form or in its transnational form. Global governance is an umbrella term covering different types of international or transnational regulation or institutionalization. So, for example, regimes are seen as a traditional form of global governance, as are international institutions such as the World Trade Organization (WTO) or the United Nations. Recently, transnational forms of governance have also been included in this definition, such as global codes of conduct used by multinational corporations or the development of norms by global civil society. Then there is global political and economic governance, the main focus of which is not the environment but which nevertheless has a decisive impact on environmental issues. The number of global governance institutions has risen dramatically in the past thirty years or so, and, with increasing trade and financial regulation, these areas have been both opened up for global institutionalization and removed from the domestic arena. As Rosenau and Czempiel (1992: 12) put it:

> Governance is a more encompassing phenomenon than government. It embraces governmental institutions but it also subsumes informal, non-governmental mechanisms, whereby those persons and organizations within its purview move ahead, satisfy their needs, and fulfill their wants ... Governance is thus a system of rule that is as dependent on inter-subjective meanings as on formally sanctioned constitutions and charters ... It is possible to conceive of governance without government – of regulatory mechanisms in a sphere of activity which function effectively even though they are not endowed with formal authority.

In the environmental field, the number of international agreements and voluntary arrangements is well in the hundreds, and they cover all sorts of regional and global issues ranging from the Climate Change Convention to forest stewardship councils. These form the main subject matter of the study of the environment in international politics.

In the field of global governance, a variety of actors, structures, and regulations converge and need to be separated for heuristic purposes, although they obviously form a coherent (or not so coherent) whole. There are a number of global governance organizations which are closely related to global environmental governance. The environmental institutions of the UN, but more importantly non-environmental organizations such as the WTO, the International Monetary Fund, and the World Bank, have a strong impact on environmental governance through their economic, trade, investment, and development policies.

The disillusionment with state policies and international organizations has led to the rise of transnational protest movements and non-governmental actors in both the civil society and corporate fields. (Although a strict definition of civil society includes the corporate sector, modern usage of the term suggests a distinction.) These civil society actors have been busy creating additional and alternative forms of global governance, which have become part of the global network of regulations, norms, and ethics. In some cases, they contribute to and shape international governance; in some cases transnational governance exists in addition to international governance (Keck and Sikkink 1998; Princen and Finger 1994).

Global corporate governance takes place on two levels. First of all, the rise of the multinational corporation has drawn after it the increasing liberalization of trade and finance institutionalized through international organizations (Newell 2001). These are structural changes leading to a different corporate climate and can thus be described as a type of corporate governance, although the corporate entity is obviously not the legitimator of this governance. Second, multinational corporations have set up among themselves certain rules by which they abide as a form of self-governance. There is a multilayered rationale to this self-governance. First of all, it delays or avoids the imposition of other rules which may be stricter, compulsory, or less convenient. Second, it facilitates standardization, which is good for expansion but also for monopolization. Third, it is good for image. A typical form of self-governance – not an international governmental organization – is the International Standards Organization (ISO). This develops voluntary standards, such as ISO 9001 and ISO 14001, which are procedural and environmental procedural standards, respectively.

Corporate codes of conduct, as found in the garment industry, are another form of self-governance. These were introduced as apparel companies came increasingly under attack for the atrocious working conditions under which their garments were produced, usually by subcontractors. Such voluntary codes, designed by the companies themselves, commit companies to patrolling working conditions in the factories where their garments are made, and the companies themselves are responsible for their implementation. Global corporate governance has thus facilitated the establishment of global markets but has so far avoided the regulation of social and environmental degradation.

There has been a very strong response to this increasing global corporate climate and market-based governance from global civil society quarters (Lipschutz 2001). Global civil society contributes to and tries to reform other forms of governance. The understanding is that the Northern or Western state has progressively given up on its social welfare role and become a representative or guardian of the interests of global markets, and the "policeman role" previously fulfilled by states has therefore been gradually taken over by non-state actors. Consequently, these actors are given a role in the international arena. Non-governmental organizations (NGOs) have an advisory role in the formulation and negotiation of international environmental agreements and are increasingly included in the advisory policy-making process of organizations such as the World Bank or the UN. They also have a role at the national level and feed into the policy process by advising foreign, development, and environment ministries. Non-governmental organizations involved in such formal channels are usually reformist rather than radical. Radical organizations do not participate in shaping global governance since they believe there are fundamental systemic shortcomings that cannot be addressed through a reform of existing forms of global governance. Radical movements can be found outside the policy process in the form of the landless movement, protests outside WTO ministerial meetings, and so forth (Goldman 2009). The increasingly vocal nature and huge numbers of people involved in such movements have led to a questioning of the legitimacy of some forms of global governance. All these issues will be discussed in detail in this book.

Political action is important, but we cannot lose sight of the fact that there are also challenges that need to be studied in their own right. One major challenge is the fact that we are not dealing with an ever increasing or at least stable amount of resource and sink capacity on this planet. Some resources are infinite, others are not. Clearly, for a sustainable future, the pressure on resources and sinks needs to ease up. At the same time, both resources and the access to those resources need to be divided up differently to provide entrée to those who have been excluded from the benefits of globalization. Clearly modern technology or ecological modernization can provide us with the tools to achieve this, but it does not supply the distribution mechanisms to allow more equal access to resources and sinks. These are questions of consumption and equity or social justice. Recent technological developments have shown that the availability of more sustainable technology alone is not enough to achieve more equity and sustainability or to eradicate poverty, because the cost and access to such technologies make them unattainable to the majority of people who need them most. Some would go much further – as, for example, David Harvey (2003: 137), who argues that the current international or global system can only be described as "accumulation by dispossession." Thus, the existence of a solution to a particular problem does not solve that problem. The notions of unequal distribution and a lack of social justice or structural inequality have been raised throughout history, and while this may not have been in an environmental context they are nevertheless familiar and important questions in the study of society. Likewise, environmental decline is a widely studied issue, even in the context of commodification, overaccumulation, overproduction, and so on. Even the notions of unequal wealth and environment have been analyzed together. However, they need to be recast in the face of the environmental challenges of the twenty-first century and in the context of the theoretical framework in which global environmental politics is usually looked at. This is exactly what this book is doing.

Chapter outlines

The book kicks off with a chapter on theoretical perspectives, placing global environmental politics within the discipline of international relations. Initially it was a relatively marginal concern, but the demands of the "real world" forced the environment onto the academic agenda. Inevitably, existing theories and approaches were deployed in the study of the novel problems of transboundary pollution and global environmental change but environmental specialists were soon making their own distinct contributions. In order to make sense of this, it is useful to consider the purpose of theory and its underlying assumptions. For example, the many theories discussed will all have a different starting point and a main focus which will lead them to prioritize different issues, values, and constructs and will also steer them toward different conclusions. This brings us to the basic questions of the role and significance of various actors, most notably the state, but it also prompts us to define the exact problem that we should seek to address. Are we interested primarily in actors such as the state or civil society and do we believe that change for the better will be initiated and pushed through by them? Are we more skeptical and do we want to focus on consumptive or equity issues? Do we believe that the environment is a security issue and the best way forward is to treat it as such? John Vogler addresses these questions in a theoretical context before they are followed up and discussed in more detail in subsequent chapters.

Lucy Ford explains and discusses transnational actors in global environmental politics. Transnational actors engage in international activities across national boundaries but do not do so on behalf of a state or an international organization. In fact, there are many non-state actors who contest this concentrated global power in the hands of political and economic elites. Non-state actors championing a particular issue such as the environment are challenging nation-states – and, by extension, interstate organizations – claiming they are failing to solve global issues. Their aim is to redefine the issues, agendas, and problems by pointing out where these institutions are failing, promoting their reform, sometimes working with them and bypassing the nation-state, and sometimes even calling for them to be abolished – as seen for example in the "WTO – Shrink or Sink" campaign that was organized and signed by a transnational, heterogeneous collection of networks, associations, and NGOs self-defined as transnational civil society. When defining transnational actors, then, we are referring to all those non-state actors – transnational corporations, NGOs, or social movements – that operate *across* the globe and form part of global politics. They are neither states nor international organizations, but they act alongside them, sometimes collaborating with and sometimes challenging them, and at other times ignoring them altogether. Many of the issues highlighted by NGOs have to do with North–South issues.

In her chapter on global political economy and development issues, Jennifer Clapp focuses on the linkages between globalization, the environment, and development. She analyzes the relationship between the economy and the environment in a global context, focusing particularly on the role of finance and trade and their connection with environmental degradation. On the one hand, advocates of the globalizing economy as a liberating force stress the positive impacts that this process has on the environment and push for policies that promote further international economic integration as a means by which to promote global sustainable development. Critics of globalization, on the other hand, see mainly negative environmental impacts as a result of growing international economic integration and push for environmental policies that rein in global economic transactions. Many see this debate as too polarized and focused on one-sided representations of the facts, and as a result a third view has begun to gain prominence. This "middle ground" perspective sees strengths and weaknesses in both arguments while acknowledging that, in some instances, global economic linkages can lead to environmental harm. However, it suggests that with proper management the global economy can be a force for environmental improvement.

Shlomi Dinar, in his chapter on environmental security, sees environmental improvement not in economic tools but in the way the environment is perceived as a security issue and the policy consequences arising therefrom. Environmental security is a contested concept. Generally, proponents of linking the environment with security point to the roots of resource scarcity and environmental degradation in promoting intra-state and interstate violent conflict and wars. The traditional definition of security, restricted to the polemics of state sovereignty, military affairs between states, and the threat of interstate war as a function of threats to territorial integrity, should be expanded to include other issues, such as the environment. These analysts have also regarded the linkage itself as important in elevating environmental issues to the forefront of national security affairs, creating the political urgency to resolve environmental problems. Yet critics of the linkage between the concepts of environment and security generally dismiss the relationship on several grounds. First and foremost, such thinkers (regarded as traditionalists) believe that expanding the definition of security, as it is conventionally regarded, waters the concept down to something too vague to be analyzed rigorously. Others criticize the link, claiming that the environment is antithetical to everything society often regards as security, and for that reason connecting the two concepts will prevent us from thinking critically about dealing with environmental problems. Specifically, the chapter contends that, if security is generally couched in the discourses of war, conflict, sovereignty, and traditional power dynamics, then associating it with the environment is not only misguided but also misleading. However, if the term is likewise associated with tenets of peace, cooperation, non-military strategies (i.e. bargaining), and interdependence, then linking it with the environment is very useful.

Chapter 5 introduces a fairly new concept to global environmental politics. Sustainable consumption has become a pivotal topic in recent years. Trends in resource depletion and environmental degradation caused by consumption levels and patterns, particularly in industrialized countries, combined with sharp rises in consumer demand in high-growth countries, such as China and India, highlight one of the most fundamental problems facing humankind today as well as its causes. Consumption deals with the household level and how consumer and citizen actions influence political and economic governance. Thus it is part of global political economy approaches but a subfield in its own right. The chapter describes the rise in importance of the study of consumption as well as identifying the actors of global sustainable consumption governance.

The last chapter in Part 1 brings environmental and ecological justice to the forefront of political concepts to be considered in global environmental politics. The topic of environmental and ecological justice has come to occupy a unique and useful place in the field. Some of the earliest attempts to study issues of justice related to the international environment arose in works by legal scholars attending to international environmental law. However, the field of international relations has itself come to embrace environmental justice issues as central to wider discourses on international justice and fairness and as integral to studies of global environmental politics. Scholars in the field of international relations have for some time raised concerns regarding the fairness and moral urgency of problems in global environmental politics. And, as scholarly work on global environmental issues, initiatives, and institutions has advanced over time, the concept of justice has become central to broader environmental policy debates. Motivated by the growing significance of justice and equity for global environmental politics, this chapter offers a historical and analytical overview of international environmental justice, covering concepts as well as the application of justice issues.

Part 2 offers case and policy studies which apply the concepts discussed in the first part of the book. The case studies are not all conceptually similar, and this is a reflection of the environmental problems faced by the global community, which do not neatly fit into analytical categories. For example, case studies based on institutions such as climate change or persistent organic pollutants have a different time frame than do those on food and agriculture or the marine environment, where the institutional aspects form a rather small part. The simple fact is that environmental issues are diverse and cannot be boxed neatly into either issues or sectors. Having a mix of case studies emphasizes the relational aspects and complexity of studying global environmental politics.

The case studies begin with the most prominent and pressing issue – climate change. It reflects all dimensions of global environmental politics, ranging from classical regime analysis to critical approaches, from state-centric analysis to transnational networks, addressing conflict and cooperation in the field of political economy, environmental justice, and dilemmas over consumption. In this chapter, the historical trajectory of institutional action on climate change is retraced from the Climate Change Convention to the Kyoto Protocol and its various Conference of the Parties meetings. The problem is then addressed in a wider framework, placing the dilemmas of equity, North–South divisions, civil society activism, economic constraints, and scientific consensus in perspective. Students will understand the full complexity of this multilayered challenge to global cooperation and the problems global society faces in the twenty-first century.

Marine pollution does not share the limelight of climate change as an environmental issue, but it is equally challenging. The World Ocean – the ensemble of oceans around the globe – is riddled with complex and persistent pollutants, most of which come from inland sources. These pollutants include, among many other contaminants, toxic chemicals, fertilizers, garbage, hydrocarbons, and carbon dioxide. However, most marine pollution regimes focus on ocean dumping – pollution added to the ocean deliberately from ships or land-based structures. This chapter explains the disconnect between most pollution that reaches the ocean and the policies the international community has devised to limit environmental damage to marine ecosystems. Peter Jacques highlights the central inconsistencies between institutional frameworks to deal with marine pollution and the social, economic, and structural origins of the marine environmental problems, thus showing precisely where the inconsistencies in and real challenges to global environmental politics lie.

Antje Brown addresses another vital issue, namely that of species protection. The term "biodiversity", though used widely and liberally by researchers and practitioners, refers to a complex and under-researched environmental policy area. Deforestation, habitat destruction, wildlife conservation, overfishing, species extinction, and the introduction of genetically modified organisms have all necessitated the adoption of a biodiversity regime at the UN level in the form of the Biodiversity Convention of 1992 and subsequent Biosafety Protocol of 2000. The chapter explores the different aspects involved in the biodiversity debate and identifies key actors and their motivations. It also provides an overview of the

UN policy to date and highlights unresolved issues that are likely to occupy stakeholders in the near future. Ultimately, biodiversity is positioned at the policy periphery and is not integrated properly into the political and economic paradigms of societies.

While biodiversity is dealt with by a weak institution that operates at the margins of political and economic life, agriculture is a sector that has not been institutionalized in an environmental context. Agriculture plays an important role in global environmental politics in a variety of ways. It shows the local–global linkages between Northern consumption and its social and environmental consequences in developing countries dependent on agricultural exports. Global trade policy has serious implications for food security and environmental security as well as raising equity considerations. The social and power relations underlying the structure of the global political economy are particularly visible in the agricultural sector, and this chapter assesses what lessons the agricultural case offers to those conceptualizing global environmental politics, but also vice versa – what concepts are particularly useful for capturing the complexity of the agricultural issue.

Forests are a political economy issue. Apart from playing such an important ecological role, they have been at the forefront of innovative institutional efforts to develop more inclusive policy tools. As the subject matter of deforestation is such an obviously fraught example of the point where economic needs and wants clash with scientific advice, it is an ideal study of exactly where the problems are located in this ambiguous relationship. It brings to the fore all the issues that are currently pertinent in global environmental politics and globalization in general: questions of governance, the role of transnational actors, the meaning of sustainable development, North–South relations, problems of development and poverty, the connection between poverty and environmental degradation, and the relationship between Western science and indigenous knowledge, to name but a few. This complex relationship is explained and analyzed here.

Agriculture is a case that illustrates the linkages between food production and the environment in its various guises which are too complex to fit into one governance system. Agriculture deals with food security, global political economy issues, and consumption issues, as well as a variety of environmental justice considerations. Marc Williams examines how different agricultural problems require different solutions and are approached with different policy sets.

The final case study is on persistent organic pollutants – chemical substances that persist in the environment, bio-accumulate through the food web, and pose a risk of causing adverse effects to human health and the environment. With the evidence of long-range transport of these substances to regions where they have never been used or produced and the consequent threats they pose to the environment of the entire planet, the international community has now, on several occasions, called for urgent global action to reduce and eliminate the release of these chemicals, and an international environmental agreement has been established on this matter. This chapter explores this new and relatively unknown yet crucially important environmental issue and how it fits into the study of global environmental politics.

References

Goldman, M. (2009) "Water for all! The phenomenal rise of transnational knowledge and policy networks," in G. Kütting and R. Lipschutz (eds), *Environmental Governance: Power and Knowledge in a Local–Global World*, London: Routledge.

Haas, P. (2004) "Addressing the global governance deficit," *Global Environmental Politics*, 4(4): 1–15.

Harvey, D. (2003) *The New Imperialism*, Oxford: Oxford University Press.

Keck, M., and Sikkink, K. (1998) *Activists beyond Borders*, Ithaca, NY: Cornell University Press.

Lipschutz, R. (2001) "Environmental history, political economy and change: frameworks and tools for research and analysis," *Global Environmental Politics*, 1(3): 72–91.

Newell, P. (2001) "Environmental NGOs, TNCs, and the question of governance," in D. Stevis and V. Assetto (eds), *The International Political Economy of the Environment: Critical Perspectives*, Boulder, CO: Lynne Rienner.

Princen, T., and Finger, M. (1994) *Environmental NGOs in World Politics*, London: Routledge.

Rosenau, J., and Czempiel, E.-O. (1992) *Governance without Government: Order and Change in World Government*, Cambridge: Cambridge University Press.

Young, O. (2002) *The Institutional Dimensions of Environmental Change*, Cambridge, MA: MIT Press.

Part 1

1 International Relations theory and the environment

John Vogler

This first chapter aims to situate the study of environmental questions within the broader context of International Relations (IR) theorizing. It then seeks to provide a brief review of the main theoretical strands in IR thinking about the environment, including the institutionalist study of international cooperation and regime formation, the emergence of ideas on global environmental governance, and the radical critique to which they have been subjected. The chapter concludes with a consideration of what may be regarded as the foundational security concerns of IR as a discipline and the ways in which the relationship between security and environmental degradation have been theorized.

Classical IR theory

The study of IR as a distinct discipline was essentially a product of the Great War of 1914–18, the experience of which prompted urgent questions about how the old European interstate system might be reformed in order to provide a new basis for security. European history had been punctuated by armed conflict, but it was the unprecedented scale of industrialized warfare that made any repetition appear unthinkable. International public law and functional international cooperation over such matters as the organization of railways, telegraphs, and postal services was already well established by the end of the nineteenth century, but it was the question of security and the avoidance of war that dominated all others. How was peace and order to be achieved in what was usually assumed to be an anarchical system of conflict-prone nation-states? The then dominant school of liberal internationalists (sometimes also described as idealists) proposed the strengthening of international law and the building of new international institutions for cooperation. If not providing for world government, this would at least serve to offer some insurance against a repetition of 1914 through the institutionalization of a collective approach to security in the newly formed League of Nations. The conditions for this experiment may not have been right, or the idea itself may been fatally flawed (Claude 1962), but disillusionment with the failure of the League and the onset of another world war gave rise to the ascendancy of a rival school of "realist" thought owing much to European traditions of *realpolitik*, in a process famously set out by E. H. Carr (1939) on the very eve of World War II. Realism, a label adopted to highlight the supposed inadequacy of the ideas of prewar "idealist" thinkers, became the dominant approach in the 1950s and arguably, with writers such as Kissinger (1970), Waltz (1979), and Mearsheimer (2001), along with hosts of similarly inclined practitioners and commentators, remains so until this day. Realism shared with its "idealist" protagonists a view of the world system constituted by sovereign states; where it differed was in its stress on the primacy of national interests, power politics, and the ultimate significance of armed force. If there was to be any security it would be achieved through deterrence and power balancing rather than through international cooperation and the pursuit of common interests.

Even twenty years ago it was possible to write an IR textbook without specific mention of the environment. Nowadays, if not impossible, it would be unlikely![1] In more traditional writing, natural resources were the object of competition and conflict between states or constituents of national power (Morgenthau 1948). The environment provided the (often overlooked) context of international politics. It did not constitute a subject in its own right and, significantly, was regarded as a constant rather than as a site of dangerous or destabilizing change. As Stevis (2006) notes, in his study of the trajectory of academic work on the international politics of the environment, most of the relevant research before the 1970s was conducted by economists, geographers, and others from outside the IR discipline, even if their focus was fixed upon the geopolitics of resource scarcity.[2] There were also some largely technical and legal studies of resource conflicts and transboundary legal problems, but it was not until environmental issues became firmly implanted on the actual agenda of international politics, around the time of the 1972 UN Conference on the Human Environment in Stockholm, that the growing problems of transboundary and then global degradation attracted substantial theoretical interest among IR scholars.

As the discipline of IR developed, these established approaches have been subject to waves of criticism, from positivists demanding scientific evidence for theories, from Marxist-inspired critical scholarship, and more recently from constructivists and postmodern theorists challenging some of the core assumptions of the established discipline. Since the late 1960s the study of IR has, thus, fractured in many ways, but it is probably true that, if they share little else, the majority of scholars have a core concern with security and peace, even if they now define them in rather different ways. A major criticism (Smith 1993) leveled at the work of those who came to specialize in the IR of the environment is that they continue to reside at the periphery of this theoretical ferment, failing to engage fully with the twists and "turns" of theoretical debate in the discipline. There may be some truth in this, as we shall see below, for there has been a dominant concern with building international environmental cooperation inspired by a largely liberal institutionalist perspective. However, as we shall also see, there is also work deriving from very different assumptions and traditions, which challenges the very notion of a state-centric world and calls for radical solutions. A useful distinction propounded by Cox (1981) is that between "problem-solving" and critical theory. "Problem-solvers" work within the prevailing assumptions of the international system trying to find ways in which interstate cooperation can be advanced, scientific findings better integrated into policy, and regimes made more effective in their implementation. As we shall see, this description covers the bulk of the work that has been done on the international politics of the environment. By contrast, "critical theorists" are not interested in solving what are regarded as intermediate and technical problems. They are concerned more with probing the underlying assumptions of prevailing practice, which may include the relations between the state and capital or the way in which accepted discourses implicitly privilege some groups and disadvantage others. Writers on international environmental politics also share with their counterparts elsewhere in the discipline a tendency to react to trends in world politics, a parallelism with events, and an inevitable concern with normative issues. This often, but not always, extends to a common problematic – the question of how global governance is to be achieved – and, increasingly, to questions of environmental security.

The study of interstate cooperation and regimes

When the international dimension of environmental problems was first being considered seriously, there was a dominant academic concern with international cooperation as a means to their solution. As a well-known text of the early 1990s put it, the problematic was:

> Can a fragmented and often highly conflictual political system made up of over 170 sovereign states and numerous other actors achieve the high (and historically unprecedented) levels of co-operation and policy co-ordination needed to manage environmental problems on a global scale?
>
> (Hurrell and Kingsbury 1992: 1)

It is noteworthy that the necessity for international cooperation in the "management" of the global environment and the primacy of state governments in this enterprise was usually taken for granted. Equally, this view rested upon the assumption of international anarchy and the need to provide some functional equivalent to a world government if transboundary and global problems were to be addressed. A "liberal institutionalist" approach came to dominate the field.

Those who studied the fast-developing network of multilateral environmental agreements (MEAs), such as the Montreal Protocol of 1987, were intellectually indebted to work that had been developed in the field of international political economy since the 1970s.[3] This was readily adapted to the emerging environmental problematic. The approach utilized the concept of a regime often attributed to a seminal article by Ruggie (1975) and developed and defined by Krasner (1983) and his collaborators as a means of describing and analyzing international institutions. It is important to realize that the term "institution" is here used in a sociological sense – as a pattern of human roles and rules – rather than in the more established international sense that would term an organization, such as the World Bank, an institution. The regime concept was first deployed to understand how "cooperation under anarchy" could occur in international economic relations, a specific case in point being provided by the travails of the world economy in the 1970s, when it appeared that an apparent loss of US hegemony, manifested by the ending of the dollar standard in 1971, would lead to the permanent unraveling of the international monetary order. The argument was advanced that such regimes could survive "after hegemony" (Keohane 1984) because there were very good self-interested reasons for nations to cooperate. Such cooperation, understood in regime terms, did not rest only upon the existence of international legal rules and formal organizations (which since the 1920s had been assiduously studied by IR specialists) but also upon sets of more intangible principles and norms, which were the key characteristics of a regime – constituting in effect an international-level institution. The central task was to analyze such sets of "principles, norms, rules and decision-making procedures around which actors' expectations converge in a given area of international relations" (Krasner 1983: 3) and then to comprehend the circumstances under which regimes were created and subject to change.

This regime-centred "liberal institutionalist" approach provided a readily available means to comprehend the very rapid development of MEAs during the 1980s and 1990s, when well over a hundred such agreements were negotiated at both regional and global levels. Managing the global environment posed many similar problems to those encountered in stabilizing the global economy. However, there were some significant differences. While self-interested behavior provides the dynamic for the operation of global markets, from an environmental perspective it can lead to a "tragedy" of the global commons. The global commons are areas and resources that do not fall under the sovereign jurisdiction of any state: the high seas, Antarctica, outer space, and the atmosphere. If users pursue their own short-term interest and access to the commons is unrestricted and resources are finite, then the probable result, according to Hardin (1968), would be ecological collapse and general ruin. There are many sobering examples of such behavior – for example, the fate of whale and fish stocks and the reckless pollution of the atmosphere. There has been extensive work on local commons demonstrating that the problem can be solved either through privatization (Hardin's solution) or by some form of collective agreement among users (Ostrom 1990). At the global level "privatization" has limited application (for example, in the extension of Exclusive Economic Zones at sea) and there is, of course, no central government to control and regulate access to the commons. It is here that regimes may provide the necessary institutional equivalent to the kind of commons governance that is exercised in a voluntary way at the local level (Vogler 2000).

It is also the case that, although its origins may lie elsewhere, the elaboration and development of regime thinking have been heavily influenced by the work of those concerned with international environmental cooperation (Underdal 1992; Young 1997). There has also been an attempt to build cumulative data on the characteristics of environmental regimes (Breitmeier *et al.* 2006). Environmental regime creation was investigated in terms of established models for the resolution of collective action problems relying in particular on game theoretical and micro-economic analysis. The use of such formal models to analyze strategic behavior and to account for cooperation has a long history in international relations (Schelling 1960; Rapoport 1974). The game of "prisoners' dilemma" has been particularly significant in that it highlights the difficulties of cooperation, from which both parties might benefit, under conditions of suspicion and imperfect information. If played on a "one-off" basis, the rational strategy is to avoid cooperation, but, as Axelrod (1990) has demonstrated, if the game is iterated, then parties will benefit from developing patterns of cooperation. It may be argued by analogy that regimes can provide a stable institutionalized setting within which governments can learn the benefits of cooperation. This important insight, encapsulated in Young's (1994) notion of "institutional bargaining" and marking a sharp difference from realist theorizing, is the understanding that institutions matter in themselves and serve to modify the behavior of the governments that participate in them. Alongside attempts to explain the formation of regimes, significant effort was directed to an understanding of regime effectiveness in solving transboundary and global environmental problems (Victor *et al.* 1998). Less attention has been directed at how regimes alter over their life-cycle as institutions, but there has been significant recent work on how various environmental and other regimes affect each other in what has become known as "institutional interplay" (Young 2002).

The critique of regime analysis

During the genesis of regime thinking, Susan Strange (1983) made the critical point that there really was no such thing as a distinct theory of regimes, rather a reuse and redirection of existing approaches in IR theory. The realist account termed "hegemonic stability theory" posited that international cooperation could be sustained only by the authority and dominance of a hegemonic power. This was hardly an attractive proposition for students of environmental politics, confronted with the abdication by the US of its previous leading environmental role from the 1980s onward (although it may retain some validity in discussions of whether the climate change regime can progress without US engagement and leadership). Instead, as we have seen, liberal institutionalism became the mainstream approach within which most of the work on international environmental cooperation has been conducted. Institutions or environmental regimes were seen as significant determinants of government behavior and sources of learning, leading to potential absolute gains for all concerned and most significantly to the joint management of a shared vulnerability to environmental change.

Yet it is also true that there have been more recent theoretical departures that would not fit with Strange's assertion. Again, none are specific to the study of international environmental cooperation. Realists and liberals share a rational actor model which tends toward fixed assumptions on the motivation of states. Indeed, the difference between the two schools of thought can perhaps be narrowed down to a dispute over whether gains are seen to be relative or absolute. In the realist world view there is always a struggle for power, achievable only at the expense of others, while, for those of a more liberal inclination, states pursue their interests which can often be realized through cooperation that serves to increase joint benefits. Game theorists characterize these two positions in terms of "zero-sum" conflict games or "positive-sum" cooperative gains. Other scholars have challenged the often unspoken assumptions that constrain this classic debate. They point out that interests are not "given" and cannot be assumed as the basis of rational policy strategies. Instead they are subject to those shifting perceptions of reality held by political actors. This is often described as a "cognitivist" position because the crucial variable is seen to be knowledge. Thus, regime change and development is not explicable solely in terms of the calculus of power and interests within an institutional setting. Here attention has been directed toward the important interface between scientists and policy-makers where, for example in an influential account by Haas (1990), knowledge-based, transnational "epistemic communities" determined the way in which the Mediterranean anti-pollution regime was constructed. In another important study, Litfin (1994) considered the discourses suffusing the complex relationships between scientific advice and policy-making that conditioned the negotiation of the 1987 Montreal Protocol on the restoration of the stratospheric ozone layer.

These "cognitivist" approaches reflect a broader trend in IR theorizing that has rejected strict positivistic social science explanation in favor of understanding based upon the analysis of discourse and meaning (Ruggie 1998). Wendt (1992) famously made the point that international anarchy was not an objective condition but "what states make of it." This constructivist view appeared to challenge rational choice accounts of state behavior, although Wendt (1999) and other writers have attempted to argue that it can be married to existing types of explanation in IR.[4] Constructivism has great potential for the study of international environmental cooperation because it is centrally concerned with the evolution of norms of behavior, the identity of actors such as the EU, and questions of compliance (Bernstein 2001; Checkel 2001; Vogler 2003). Potentially, it can surmount a key theoretical contradiction in regime analysis which, simply stated, is that, while regimes are made up of a sets of norms, principles, and rules which are essentially social constructs, regime analysts have applied the positivistic methods of social science to them. In more formal terms, there is a clash between the ontological status of regimes and the epistemology of those who study them. On the other hand, a wholesale adoption of a constructivist or "post-positivist" approach would have to grapple with the point that environmental regimes are predicated upon what Searle (1995) has called the "brute" physical facts of nature, such as deforestation or climate change, that exist independently of our observations. We may construct and interpret them in many ways, but the most authoritative and useful, in terms of bringing about the physical changes upon which human survival depends, must remain the method of positivistic natural science. Perhaps a distinctive feature of the study of international environmental politics is that it raises such fundamental questions in starker terms than in other areas of IR.

Global governance

As discussed in detail by Jennifer Clapp in Chapter 3, globalization can mean many things, but in essence it represents a move away from a world divided into distinctly separate national economies and societies, presided over by sovereign state authorities, toward economic and perhaps even social systems that transcend national boundaries and, by some accounts, operate on a global basis. One of the clearest examples is provided by the evident integration of what were national and regional financial markets into what now appears to be one single, tightly interconnected world system. Something similar has occurred with production processes, which are now seen to be globally distributed, although such globalization remains patchy with some sectors such as agriculture, still subject to extensive national control and protection. Although such processes of globalization were accelerated by the ending of the Cold War, they have been evident over a long period, and IR scholars responded to such trends by considering the threat that they posed to the prevailing "Westphalian" order of nation-states. John Burton (1972), for example, proposed a "world society" model of a complex overlapping "cobweb" of human systems that was radically different from the orthodox international politics conception of state-to-state interaction. Transnational processes were analyzed linking the international and the local as well as the emergence of a whole variety of supposedly "new actors" (Keohane and Nye 1972, 1977; Mansbach *et al.* 1976; Rosenau 1980). Such a pluralist view of international politics included international organizations, the European Union, and, most prominently, transnational business corporations and non-governmental organizations (NGOs). If these new types of actors did not supplant the state they might certainly rival it and provide alternative and appropriate forms of "global governance" over phenomena that seemed to have outrun the capabilities of states. There was, too, an element of wishful thinking. This harked back to an idealist "world government" tradition whereby nation-states would be replaced by a less war-prone and more rational form of political organization. Much of the discussion of NGOs and the possible emergence of a "global civil society" has this normative dimension, as Lucy Ford describes in detail in Chapter 2 in this book.

Environmental degradation often has a transnational character and is intimately associated with the processes of economic globalization, although the relationship between growth, increases in trade, and adverse environmental impacts remains a matter of academic dispute. Nonetheless, students of international environmental politics had good reason to pursue some of the trends in IR outlined above. Dissatisfaction with the environmental performance of governments and interstate institutions was typified by the disappointments of the "Rio process," where so many of the promises made at the 1992 Earth Summit failed to be realized and progress with the newly established climate and biodiversity regimes proved to be agonizingly slow. In particular, NGOs, many of which had achieved great prominence through their environmental actions, seemed to provide not only a significant focus for empirical study (Princen and Finger 1994; Newell 2000) but also a virtuous alternative to the self-interested machinations of state governments. There was, too, the empirical observation that non-state actors, whether regional entities such the EU, transnationally organized NGOs, or the private business sector, play an increasing role which has been particularly evident in environmental politics. Thus, for example, NGOs were significant in transmitting local protest at environmental destruction to the international level (Wapner 1996; Willetts 2008). The study of such "transnational advocacy networks" (Keck and Sikkink 1998) resonates with the work on "epistemic communities" by regime analysts. Both challenge the state-centric view of international politics, but the extent to which state governments continue to play a dominant role remains a source of lively dispute.

Although government spokespersons increasingly acknowledge "multi-stakeholder" involvement, it is often the case that, when they speak of "global governance," they frequently mean no more than a rearrangement of existing international organizations. The long debate over whether UNEP should be promoted from the status of a UN program to that of an independent specialized agency and whether there should be an overarching world environmental organization provides a case in point. This is far from what is understood by the term in academic discourse. The whole point of using the term "governance," rather than the more orthodox "government," is to capture the idea that, in an increasingly globalized system, many of the control functions traditionally the preserve of nation-states have been transferred elsewhere (Paterson *et al.* 2003). Thus global governance theorizing breaks with the state-centric focus of the regime analysts and puts NGOs or private actors at the centre of its analysis (Pattberg 2007). As demonstrated by the development of privately based rules on forest products, they can provide governance for sustainability where states have failed to engage in effective international cooperation (Humphreys 2006).

Radical ecopolitics

Realism and liberalism never entirely monopolized the study of International Relations. There were always other more radical approaches in the sense that they refused to accept the prevailing order of nation-states and market-based economies that provided the axioms upon which the dominant approaches in the field were founded. In the early twentieth century, radical approaches to IR often had a basis in Marxist historical materialism and the understanding that the state had an essentially class nature; Lenin referred to it as the "executive committee of the bourgeoisie." It followed that international conflicts arose from the contradictions within the world capitalist system. Thus Lenin ([1916] 1965) famously explained World War I as a conflict arising not from interstate anarchy and the breakdown of the balance of power system but from clashing imperialisms driven by the imperatives of capitalist accumulation and, in particular, a declining rate of return on investments. Other theorists in the Marxist tradition provided explanations similarly based upon the various crises of capitalism, notably underconsumption, to which states were bound to respond, often by engaging in aggressive behavior. Marxist approaches to international relations have been further developed in the study of global political economy. Here the focus has been on the underlying dynamics of capitalist accumulation in the world system and the patterns of dominance and dependency that arise – notably in North–South relations. Such dependency is not simply based upon disparities in the ownership and control of material wealth but also operates in the realm of ideas. Thus Marxists who have developed the ideas of the Italian theorist Antonio Gramsci on hegemony have been able to make some connection with those, such as the constructivists, who prioritize the role of discourse and "ideational" factors.

The environmental problematic was not a central concern of twentieth-century Marxist scholars of international relations. Advocating class-based revolution as the necessary basis for a new and fairer international order, they would have been hard put to establish that socialist societies were also environmentally virtuous societies. While there was ample evidence that the growth trajectory of the capitalist world gave rise to massive resource exploitation and ecological damage, this was rivaled by the malign environmental consequences of the policies pursued by the Soviet Union and other avowedly socialist states. Nonetheless, as environmental issues have risen to prominence, Marxist scholars have found that their fundamental critique of capitalist accumulation does provide a powerful means of analyzing the interconnected crisis of the world economy and environment (Paterson 2001). Various frameworks, including a neo-Gramscian one, can be deployed to understand how firms come to dominate an issue area such as forestry, biodiversity, and biosafety (Humphreys 1996 and Chapter 9 in this volume; Levy and Newell 2005). In this, market-based globalization is the driver of degradation, and states (acting as the agents of capital) are regarded as part of the problem rather than, as in mainstream work, the solution (Vogler 2005). It follows that the global ecological crisis cannot be regarded as a "collective action problem" between states and that international regimes are "epiphenomenal" in the sense that they merely give the impression that something is being achieved without affecting the underlying operations of global capitalism.

This rejection of the significance of the state and the whole enterprise of interstate cooperation in the solution of environmental problems represents a fundamental attack upon mainstream International Relations theorizing. Nor is such a critical approach exclusive to those who fully subscribe to Marxist ideas and historical materialism. There are many other types of significant radical scholarship which also insist that the roots of the problem cannot be addressed through the encouragement and development of international environmental cooperation – discussed further in Chapters 5 and 6 here. The feminist critique of existing IR theory seeks to expose the gender bias inherent in the state system and even in those NGOs and other actors associated with global environmental governance. This fundamental critique both relocates the sources of the problem and challenges mainstream approaches to environmental management (Bretherton 1998). Other writers (Laferrière and Stoett 1999; Saurin 1996) have proceeded by importing ideas derived from radical green political thought. With these approaches the study of global environmental politics has moved a long way from the mainstream preoccupation with interstate institutions. Kütting (2004), for example, delves into production and supply chains in the global economy that give rise to complex interactions at local and global levels, linking environment with development and thus providing the drivers of both economic growth and degradation. This may possibly help us to understand that the politics of the global environment has always depended not only upon the earnest attempts of developed country reformers to institute regimes for conservation but also, critically, upon the urgent demands of the South for development and redistribution.

The return to security

The achievement of security in a disorderly and anarchic system has historically been regarded as the overriding concern for international theory, as Shlomi Dinar outlines in Chapter 4. While the IR of the environment built upon the tradition of the study of international cooperation, it did not initially engage with questions of war and peace. These were implicitly understood to be separate from the concerns of students of environmental politics, except perhaps when it came to the environmental consequences of the nuclear arms race and the possibility, much debated in the 1980s, of a "nuclear winter" following a nuclear exchange. In retrospect it may seem strange that such a central concept as security was not subject to critical interrogation in the IR literature during most of the Cold War period. This may well have been because the threat of a collision between two nuclear armed superpowers was such an evident possibility that fear of the consequences of their involvement tended to prevent or limit the extent of other violent conflicts, at least in Europe. Security continued to be defined as the security of the state and to be assessed in terms of its ability to ward off armed incursions across its frontiers.

In the 1980s this neglect of the theorization of security began to change. Buzan (1983) made important distinctions between the referent objects of security. Whereas the orthodox referent object was the state, one could now also speak of "societal security" or even "environmental security." In some officially sponsored accounts, a focus on the security of the state and its borders was replaced with a new concept of "human security" (UNDP 1994). This multidimensional idea comprised a range of threats against which human beings should be secured. They included hunger, poor health, physical violence, and the destruction of the physical environment. In the academic world "critical security studies" burgeoned and connections were made between security and emancipation (Booth 1991). The so-called Copenhagen School adopted a constructivist-inspired approach in which what mattered was the attribution of the security label to an issue by means of a "speech act" (Buzan *et al.* 1998). "Securitizing" an issue involved raising its political profile, and in the wake of the ending of the Cold War there were numerous examples of such activities related to the environment. For activists, portraying environmental problems in terms of their relationship to national security had the advantage of raising their political salience and the amount of public expenditure likely to be dedicated to them. "Security" threats are usually judged by publics to have sufficient gravity and urgency to give them priority over other calls upon governmental expenditure. At the same time, elements of military establishments were under (what turned out to be) the mistaken impression that the ending of the Cold War would yield a "peace dividend" under which major cuts in military expenditure would be achieved. Environmental conservation was argued to provide a new and alternative role for the military, and organizations such as NATO began to discover a whole range of alternative threats to security, including environmental degradation. As Daniel Deudney (1990) pointed out at the time, there remained a profound antipathy between the methods and mindset of military establishments and those of the environmental movement; thus those who engaged with the securitization and militarization of the environment did so at their peril.

At this point it is important to make a crucial distinction. Scholarly work on environmental security falls into two broad categories. On the one hand, there is the question of how environmental change and degradation relates to violent conflict and the integrity of the state and its territory – the orthodox concerns of Strategic Studies and International Relations. As with the activity by military establishments referred to above, this merely extends existing ideas of security by adding a range of new triggers for violent conflict and corresponding analysis and action by the armed forces. The other category has more radical implications because, by incorporating the environment problematic, it seeks to redefine the very meaning of security. It is essentially part of the critical and human security movements discussed above. Thus the referent object of security ceases to be the state and becomes the survival of the biosphere. It is in this sense that reference is made, for example, to climate security. While the first category fits in well with established realist thinking and the concerns of policy-making elites, merely adding a new area of state security concern, the latter is firmly embedded in critical approaches to international relations and connects with the radical ecopolitics discussed above.

The ending of the Cold War and the rising international profile of global-scale environmental issues, as evidenced by the signing of the climate change and desertification conventions at Rio in 1992, helped to focus policy and academic attention on their potential to provoke conflict. In the longer term this may be regarded as a concern, dating back to the gloomy predictions of Thomas Malthus in the nineteenth century, with the problems of overpopulation, resource scarcity, and social collapse. It was, also, very much a developed-world perspective in that, faced with these challenges, "state failure" in the South might lead to a variety of undesirable consequences in the North, including terrorist attacks, migration pressure, and the interruption of supplies of raw materials. Accordingly, substantial and well-funded academic effort was directed beginning in the 1990s toward an empirical investigation of the connections between environmental degradation and armed conflict. Such research was generally framed within the orthodox concerns of realist IR. "Environmental security" was defined in terms of managing threats to the integrity of the state and its territory and the preservation of international stability in the face, for example, of the ill-understood consequences of climate change and desertification in Africa.

Extensive work in this area was undertaken by Homer-Dixon (1991, 1999) and his collaborators, who developed and attempted to test three hypotheses on environmental change, scarcity, and conflict. War and insurrection could arise from struggles over diminishing resources brought about by environmental degradation in ways that would instantly be recognized by realist students of international conflict. Alternatively, the loss of livelihood occasioned by ecological collapse could force large-scale population movements and armed confrontation over territory. Finally, internal insurrection and the collapse of the fragile institutions found in the developing world might also be triggered, leading to the transnational spread of conflict and intervention. Causal chains were complex and uncertain, but it did become clear that many current conflicts had their origins in a morass of poverty, underdevelopment, ethnic hatred, and ecological collapse. However, the finding of the research was that there was no clear and direct relationship between environmental change and conflict (Barnett 2001; Gleditsch 1998). In another important study by Baechler (1998), environmental change was seen as just one component of a syndrome of "maldevelopment" in which the developed North and its practices were deeply implicated.[5]

The uncertainties thrown up by these empirical studies did not prevent policy-makers from commissioning work that attempted to provide practical guidance to political and military elites on the management and, indeed, prosecution of environmentally induced conflicts. In the late 1990s, for instance, NATO produced a study (Lietzmann and Vest 1999) that endeavored to identify a set of syndromes and early warning indicators that would alert decision-makers to potential conflicts. Also, as the scientific evidence for climate change became more and more convincing in the first years of the twenty-first century, military analysts began to prepare scenarios for national security policy in the context of a radically altered world (Schwartz and Randall 2003). Environmental change was conceptualized as a "threat multiplier" but still in a fairly orthodox way. Events in the Arctic, as the ice receded, and national claims to territory and control of the Northwest Passage provide a graphic illustration (Solana 2008).

Of much greater theoretical significance was the re-evaluation of the key concept of security that was proceeding elsewhere in the discipline. In fact, as Swatuk (2006: 216) observes, "almost as soon as the 'environment' appeared on the policy map of state security apparatuses, dissenting and critical voices could be heard questioning the appropriateness of linking environmental issues to (national) security practices." By detaching the concept from the referent object of the state and its territory, space was opened up to consider whether environmental issues should be not just an extension of security, but part of a wholesale reconfiguration in which it was possible to think about environmental questions as security issues in their own right. Such thinking takes a holistic view of natural and human systems and is fully aware that pre-existing security debates, even when they take the environment into account, are constructed in such a way as to privilege the interests of the powerful and the "developed." The dire systemic consequences of climate change may be regarded as so devastating that they replace interstate war as the principal problematic facing the international system.

This analysis is not confined to radical scholars. Elements of it have entered mainstream discourse. For example, after the attacks on the World Trade Center in 2001, security issues tended to be narrowly defined in US and European policy-making circles as involving "terrorism, failed states, and weapons of mass destruction." However, this was soon challenged by assertions that in fact, in terms of the potential for destruction and loss of human life, climate change represented a greater threat than terrorism (King 2004). Followers of the Copenhagen School would recognize a securitization move here, with interested parties attempting to divert resources away from the "war on terror" to the mitigation of and adaptation to the effects of climate change. Much of this may simply have been rhetoric, but it was surely of some significance that climate security was placed on the agenda of the UN Security Council in April 2007. Were this to become widely accepted, it would denote not so much a "return to security" issues but a thoroughgoing redefinition of what it means to be secure – with the most profound implications for the study of international relations.

Conclusion

This chapter has described the ways in which the study of international environmental politics has evolved within the discipline of International Relations. Initially it was a relatively marginal concern, but "real-world" developments forced the environment onto the academic agenda. Inevitably, existing theories and approaches were deployed in the study of the novel problems of transboundary pollution and global environmental change, but environmental specialists were soon making their own distinct contributions in regime analysis, in the study of non-state actors, and in the redefinition of the central concept of security.

In order to make sense of this and to think through the ways in which the various theoretical approaches converge or contrast, it may be useful to ask four, often highly interrelated, questions that are relevant to any form of IR theorizing. They are:

- What is the purpose of theory?
- What are the underlying theoretical assumptions – both ontological (those things that are believed to exist) and epistemological (how we may know about them)?
- What is the role and significance of the state?
- What is the problem that we should seek to address?

Theories may simply be regarded as attempts to make explanatory generalizations about phenomena, following the example of the natural sciences (positivism). Such theorizing often has a political agenda other than enquiry for its own sake. Scientific investigation is directed to the solution of problems. This would provide a fairly accurate description of much of the work in international environmental politics that addresses the circumstances under which regimes may be built and developed. As we have seen, many other approaches in the field have a distinctly different critical approach which may be subversive rather than "problem-solving". Radical ecopolitics has this characteristic, but it is always worth remembering that such distinctions have a long pedigree. Thus, after World War I, some theorists were concerned with reform and institution-building while others, on the political left, sought the establishment of world peace through the overthrow of the prevailing economic and social order.

It is also necessary to tease out the assumptions that guide theoretical work. Mainstream regime analysis, and indeed the bulk of realist and liberal theorizing, is predicated on a model of human action, that people or indeed states are assumed to make rational choices among alternative courses of action in terms of a set of relatively fixed interests or preferences. As we have seen, a critical distinction between realist and liberal thinkers is whether the negotiation of these preferences leads to essentially conflictual or cooperative outcomes. Liberal institutionalism is founded upon the latter view. Quite different are those who adopt a constructivist approach. In their view preferences are never fixed but always subject to change, and this, rather than the distribution of power or the conjunction of interests, provides the key to obtaining international cooperation on environmental issues. A critical question is whether discourse or constructivist analysis can be combined with rational choice accounts or whether they have fundamentally different epistemologies. There are some interesting questions for environmental scholarship here because of the significance of natural science for policy-making alongside the socially constructed nature of the norms of behavior that are the essential characteristic of regimes.

International Relations in general, and the definition of security in particular, has prioritized the state. While regime theorists continue to focus upon interstate cooperation, much of the most innovative work in environmental politics has challenged its supremacy. In particular the study of global environmental governance has focused upon the advocacy and regulatory activities of non-state entities. There is a sense that the state, far from being regarded as part of the solution to global environmental degradation, is itself a major part of the problem. Analysts adopting the standpoint of radical ecopolitics would have no dispute with this characterization of the state. Although the tendency among environmental activists and green theorists has been to distrust the state and to seek alternative forms of governance, there is now a growing realization that, in any time frame that is relevant to the solution of pressing environmental problems, the state cannot be excluded. The critical question, not least for the future of interstate environmental regimes, is whether it is possible to "green" the state (Eckersley 2004) and whether interstate environmental cooperation can be an ecologically relevant activity (Vogler 2005).

A theme of this chapter has been that, whereas theories of International Relations and the growth of the discipline were predicated upon the problem of war and insecurity, in a conception that excluded environmental issues, the latter have become an integral part of a contemporary redefinition of security. The ending of the Cold War, the advance of globalization, and a growing understanding of the magnitude of the threat to human existence posed by global environmental change has led to a perceptible shift in the definition of security and hence the problem that policy-makers and IR theorists feel called to address. Environmental change is recognized as a significant driver of contemporary conflicts, which in themselves are very different from the large-scale interstate warfare that provided the impetus for early realist and liberal internationalist writing. But, more than this, the stability of the climate and the survival of ecosystems have in some ways replaced the integrity of the state as that which is to be secured in a world system that is far removed from that confronting international theorists in the first half of the twentieth century.

Notes

1   Despite the magnitude of the problem of climate change and the increasing salience of environmental and resource issues at high-level international meetings, such as the G8, it seems evident that such issues still have a relatively marginal status in the literature.

2 The major exception was provided by Harold Sprout and Margaret Sprout (1971).
3 A rather similar process may be observed in the way in which the very substantial work on monitoring and verification, which had arisen in response to the need for arms control during the Cold War, was adapted to meet the requirement to ensure the implementation of international agreements.
4 For an accessible treatment of this issue and refutation of Wendt's argument that rational choice and constructivist approaches can be combined in IR, see Smith and Owens (2008).
5 Homer-Dixon's work on environment conflict linkages is rather narrowly focused compared with the grand historical sweep of some of his other writing, notably *The Upside of Down* (2006).

Recommended reading

Barnett, J. (2001) *The Meaning of Environmental Security: Ecological Politics and Policy in the New Security Era*, London: Zed Books.
Betsill, M., Hochstetler, K., and Stevis, D. (eds) (2005) *Palgrave Advances in International Environmental Politics*, Basingstoke: Palgrave Macmillan.
O'Neill, K. (2009) *The Environment and International Relations*, Cambridge: Cambridge University Press.
Vogler, J., and Imber, M. F. (eds) (1996) *The Environment and International Relations*, London: Routledge.

References

Axelrod, R. (1990) *The Evolution of Co-operation*, London: Penguin.
Baechler, G. (1998) *Violence through Environmental Discrimination: Causes, Rwanda Arena, and Conflict Model*, Dordrecht: Kluwer.
Barnett, J. (2001) *The Meaning of Environmental Security: Ecological Politics and Policy in the New Security Era*, London: Zed Books.
Bernstein, S. (2001) *The Compromise of Liberal Environmentalism*, New York: Columbia University Press.
Booth, K. (1991) "Security and emancipation," *Review of International Studies*, 17(4): 313–26.
Breitmeier, H., Young, O. R., and Zürn, M. (2006) "The international regimes database: designing and using a sophisticated tool for institutional analysis," *Global Environmental Politics*, 6(3): 121–41.
Bretherton, C. (1998) "Global environmental politics: putting gender on the agenda," *Review of International Studies*, 24(1): 85–100.
Burton, J. W. (1972) *World Society*, Cambridge: Cambridge University Press.
Buzan, B. (1983) *People States and Fear: The National Security Problem in International Relations*, Brighton: Wheatsheaf.
Buzan, B., Waever, O., and de Wilde, J. (1998) *Security: A New Framework for Analysis*, Boulder, CO: Lynne Rienner.
Carr, E. H. (1939) *The Twenty Years' Crisis, 1919–1939: An Introduction to the Study of International Relations*, London: Macmillan.
Checkel, J. T. (2001) "Why comply? Social learning and European identity change," *International Organization*, 55(3): 553–88.
Claude, I. L. (1962) *Power and International Relations*, New York: Random House.
Cox, R. (1981) "Social forces, states and world orders: beyond international relations theory," *Millennium: Journal of International Studies*, 10(2): 126–55.
Deudney, D. (1990) "The case against linking environmental degradation and national security," *Millennium: Journal of International Studies*, 19(3): 461–76.
Eckersley, R. (2004) *The Green State: Rethinking Democracy and Sovereignty*, Cambridge, MA: MIT Press.
Gleditsch, N. P. (1998) "Armed conflict and the environment: a critique of the literature," *Journal of Peace Research*, 35(3): 381–400.

Haas, P. M. (1990) "Obtaining environmental protection through epistemic consensus," *Millennium: Journal of International Studies*, 19(3): 347–63.

Hardin, G. (1968) "The tragedy of the commons," *Science*, 162: 1243–8.

Homer-Dixon, T. (1991) "On the threshold: environmental changes as causes of acute conflict," *International Security*, 16(2): 76–116.

—— (1999) *The Environment, Scarcity and Violence*, Princeton, NJ: Princeton University Press.

—— (2006) *The Upside of Down: Catastrophe, Creativity, and the Renewal of Civilisation*, London: Souvenir Press.

Humphreys, D. (1996) "Hegemonic ideology and the International Tropical Timber Organisation," in J. Vogler and M. F. Imber (eds), *The Environment and International Relations*, London: Routledge.

—— (2006) *Logjam: Deforestation and the Crisis of Global Governance*, London: Earthscan.

Hurrell, A., and Kingsbury, B. (eds) (1992) *The International Politics of the Environment: Actors, Interests and Institutions*, Oxford: Clarendon Press.

Keck, M. E., and Sikkink, K. (1998) *Activists beyond Borders: Advocacy Networks in International Politics*, Ithaca, NY: Cornell University Press.

Keohane, R. (1984) *After Hegemony: Cooperation and Discord in the World Political Economy*, Princeton, NJ: Princeton University Press.

Keohane, R., and Nye, J. S. (eds) (1972) *Transnational Relations and World Politics*, Cambridge, MA: Harvard University Press.

—— (1977) *Power and Interdependence: World Politics in Transition*, Boston: Little, Brown.

King, D. A. (2004) "Climate change science: adapt, mitigate or ignore?," *Science*, 303 (9 January): 176–7.

Kissinger, H. (1970) *The White House Years*, Boston: Little, Brown.

Krasner, S. D. (ed.) (1983) *International Regimes*, Ithaca, NY: Cornell University Press.

Kütting, G. (2004) *Globalization and the Environment: Greening Global Political Economy*, Albany: State University of New York Press.

Laferrière, E., and Stoett, P. J. (1999) *International Relations Theory and Ecological Thought: Towards a Synthesis*, London: Routledge.

Lenin, V. I. ([1916] 1965) *Imperialism, the Highest Stage of Capitalism: A Popular Outline*, Peking: Foreign Languages Press.

Levy, D., and Newell, P. J. (eds) (2005) *The Business of Global Environmental Governance*, Cambridge, MA: MIT Press.

Lietzmann, K. M., and Vest, G. (eds) (1999) *Environment and Security in an International Context*, Brussels: NATO Committee on the Challenges of Modern Society.

Litfin, K. (1994) *Ozone Discourses: Science and Politics in Global Environmental Co-operation*, New York: Columbia University Press.

Mansbach, R., Ferguson, Y., and Lampert, D. (1976) *The Web of World Politics*, Englewood Cliffs, NJ: Prentice-Hall.

Mearsheimer, J. (2001) *The Tragedy of Great Power Politics*, New York: W. W. Norton.

Morgenthau, H. J. (1948) *Politics among Nations: The Struggle for Power and Peace*, New York: A. A. Knopf.

Newell, P. (2000) *Climate for Change: Non-State Actors and the Global Politics of the Greenhouse*, Cambridge: Cambridge University Press.

Ostrom, O. (1990) *Governing the Commons: The Evolution of Institutions for Collective Action*, Cambridge: Cambridge University Press.

Paterson, M. (2001) *Understanding Global Environmental Politics: Domination, Accumulation, Resistance*, Basingstoke: Palgrave.

Paterson, M., Humphreys, D., and Pettiford, L. (2003) "Conceptualizing global environmental governance: from interstate regimes to counter-hegemonic struggles," *Global Environmental Politics*, 3(2): 1–10.

Pattberg, P. H. (2007) *Private Institutions and Global Governance: The New Politics of Environmental Sustainability*, Cheltenham: Edward Elgar.

Princen, T., and Finger, M. (eds) (1994) *Environmental NGOs in World Politics*, London: Routledge.

Rapoport, A. (1974) *Fights, Games, and Debates*, Ann Arbor: University of Michigan Press.

Rosenau, J. N. (1980) *The Study of Global Interdependence: Essays on the Transnationalisation of World Affairs*, London: Frances Pinter.

Ruggie, J. G. (1975) "International responses to technology: concepts and trends," *International Organization*, 29(3): 557–83.

—— (1998) *Constructing the World Polity: Essays on international Institutionalization*, London: Routledge.

Saurin, J. (1996) "International relations, social ecology and the globalisation of environmental change," in J. Vogler and M. F. Imber (eds), *The Environment and International Relations*, London: Routledge.

Schelling, T. (1960) *The Strategy of Conflict*, New York: Oxford University Press.

Schwartz, P., and Randall, D. (2003) *An Abrupt Climate Change Scenario and its Implications for National Security*, San Francisco: Global Business Network. Available: www.gbn.com/consulting/article_details.php?id = 53 (accessed 18 October 2009).

Searle, J. R. (1995) *The Construction of Social Reality*, Harmondsworth: Penguin.

Smith, S. (1993) "The environment on the periphery of international relations: an explanation," *Environmental Politics*, 2(4): 28–45.

Smith, S., and Owens, P. (2008) "Alternative approaches to international theory," in B. Bayliss, S. Smith, and P. Owens (eds), *The Globalization of World Politics: An Introduction to International Relations*, 4th ed., Oxford: Oxford University Press.

Solana, P. (2008) *Climate Change and International Security: Paper from the High Representative and the European Commission to the European Council*, S113/08, Brussels: Council of the European Union.

Sprout, H., and Sprout, M. (1971) *Toward a Politics of the Planet Earth*, New York: Van Nostrand Reinhold.

Stevis, D. (2006) "The trajectory of the study of international environmental politics," in M. M. Betsill, K. Hochstetler, and D. Stevis (eds), *Palgrave Advances in International Environmental Politics*, Basingstoke: Palgrave Macmillan.

Strange, S. (1983) "*Cave! Hic dragones*: a critique of regime analysis," in S. D. Krasner (ed.), *International Regimes*, Ithaca, NY: Cornell University Press.

Swatuk, L. A. (2006) "Environmental security," in M. M. Betsill, K. Hochstetler, and D. Stevis (eds), *Palgrave Advances in International Environmental Politics*, Basingstoke: Palgrave Macmillan.

Underdal, A. (1992) "The study of international regimes," *Journal of Peace Research*, 32: 227–40.

UNDP (United Nations Development Programme) (1994) *Human Development Report 1994*, Oxford: Oxford University Press.

Victor, D., Raustiala, K., and Skolnikoff, E. (eds) (1998) *The Implementation and Effectiveness of Environmental Commitments*, Cambridge, MA: MIT Press.

Vogler, J. (2000) *The Global Commons: Environmental and Technological Governance*, Chichester: John Wiley.

—— (2003) "Taking institutions seriously: how regime analysis can be relevant to multilevel environmental governance," *Global Environmental Politics*, 3(2): 25–39.

—— (2005) "In defense of international environmental cooperation," in J. Barry and R. Eckersley (eds), *The State and the Global Ecological Crisis*, Cambridge, MA: MIT Press.

Waltz, K. (1979) *Theory of International Politics*, Reading, MA: Addison-Wesley.

Wapner, P. (1996) *Environmental Activism and World Civic Politics*, Albany: State University of New York Press.

Wendt, A. (1992) "Anarchy is what states make of it: the social construction of power politics," *International Organization*, 46(2): 391–425.

—— (1999) *A Social Theory of International Politics*, Cambridge: Cambridge University Press.

Willetts, P. (2008) "Transnational actors and international organizations in global politics," in B. Bayliss, S. Smith, and P. Owens (eds), *The Globalization of World Politics: An Introduction to International Relations*, 4th ed., Oxford: Oxford University Press.

Young, O. R. (1994) *International Governance: Protecting the Environment in a Stateless Society*, Ithaca, NY: Cornell University Press.

—— (ed.) (1997) *Global Governance: Drawing Insights form the Environmental Experience*, Cambridge, MA: MIT Press.

—— (2002) *The Institutional Dimensions of Environmental Change: Fit, Interplay and Scale*, Cambridge, MA: MIT Press.

2 Transnational actors in global environmental politics[1]

Lucy Ford

Introduction

Traditionally, the question of "who" acts in international politics has received the answer: "Why states of course!" In traditional realist international relations theory, the nation-state has been seen as the unit of analysis and key actor involved in international politics, including the politics of the environment. Liberal and critical approaches to IR, on the other hand, want to highlight that beyond the realm of interstate politics there is an array of actors such as transnational social movements, non-governmental organizations (NGOs), and transnational corporations (TNCs) – sometimes referred to collectively as *non-state*, *transnational*, or *civil society* actors – that have a bearing on politics and political outcomes. Questions about "who acts and how" are fundamentally about what constitutes "the political" in global environmental politics.

This chapter is concerned with transnational actors in global environmental politics. The first section starts by locating transnational actors in IR, defining more clearly some of the key concepts and both how these have evolved over time and how they relate to developments within the discipline of IR. It further provides some conceptual tools for analyzing the role of transnational actors in global environmental politics, including contested theoretical approaches and challenges to explaining their significance. In particular it examines the sphere of global civil society, where transnational actors are said to be located. The second section then focuses on a variety of transnational actors, among them transnational environmental movements, NGOs, and transnational corporate actors. It asks what motivates them and how they act and engage in global environmental politics.

Locating transnational actors in international relations

The discipline of IR is notorious for a confusing variety of concepts that are sometimes used interchangeably and sometimes mean different things. So, for example, while IR in its origin was concerned with analyzing the international relations between nation-states as well as their interactions with international organizations such as the United Nations or NATO, more recent scholars now often understand it to be about social, economic, cultural, or political interactions across the globe. They might want to talk about transnational politics, world politics, global politics, or indeed global political economy. Similarly, the term non-state actor can be confusing. Although strictly it appears to be referring to any actor that is not a state or a government, the boundaries between what constitutes state and non-state are not always clear. For example, the UN might be seen as a non-state actor in that it stands alone as an institution. However, it is clearly an international – indeed intergovernmental – organization and a channel through which states (and other actors) operate. The UN claims moral authority over world politics. It is, as it were, the closest body to a world government. Some would argue that international organizations, such as the UN, the World Bank, the International Monetary Fund (IMF), or the World Trade Organization (WTO), embody a quasi-world state that holds a lot of power to direct world affairs (see, for example, Shaw 2000).

However, there are many non-state actors who contest this concentrated global power. Non-state actors championing a particular issue such as the environment are challenging nation-states and, by extension, interstate organizations – claiming they are failing to solve global issues. Their aim is to contest the agenda, to point out where these institutions are failing, to promote their reform, to work with them (sometimes bypassing the nation-state), and sometimes even calling for them to be abolished, as seen for example in the "WTO – Shrink or Sink" campaign organized and signed by a transnational, heterogeneous collection of networks, associations, and NGOs self-defined as transnational civil society (see, for example, Third World Network, n.d.). When defining transnational actors, then, we are referring to all those non-state actors such as TNCs, NGOs, or social movements that operate *across* the globe and form part of global politics. They are neither states nor international organizations, but they act alongside them, sometimes collaborating with and sometimes challenging them, and at other times ignoring them altogether.

The evolution of some of the key concepts to do with understanding transnational actors can usefully be related to the historical development of the discipline of IR in general and global environmental politics in particular. Within IR the study of transnational actors came to the fore during the 1970s with the theoretical developments of pluralism and complex interdependence (Keohane and Nye 1977). Out of this developed the study of international regime theory, which focuses on the importance of institutions and shared norms among actors (see Chapter 1 in this volume). The emphasis in this body of literature is on the effectiveness of international institutions that deal with transboundary issues and the institutional settings and arrangements as well as power structures that enable or constrain international cooperation. In the field of the environment, this literature looks particularly at international environmental regimes – or Multilateral Environmental Agreements (MEAs), as they are referred to most often. While much of regime theory stands accused of state-centrism, there is within this school of thought acknowledgement of the role of non-state actors, known as epistemic communities. They are transnational networks of knowledge-based experts from the world of science, NGOs, or business that contribute expertise to the policy-making process in particular issue areas, such as the environment, trade, or security, which fosters wider institutional learning (for example Vogler 2003).

From international regimes to global governance

The analytical framework of international regimes has tended to be replaced by that of global governance. The concept of governance has become prominent in IR since the end of the Cold War. No longer was the world seen as divided into a simple bipolar system maintaining international order. A lot of the literature has focused on how processes of globalization are generating a more complex, multilevel world political system which implicitly challenges the old Westphalian assumptions about the nation-state. Questions about how to govern the new world order have become prominent, not least in relation to transboundary issues, such as environmental degradation. Governance as a concept is distinguished from government. A government is backed by formal authority, by police powers to ensure implementation of policies. Governance, on the other hand, is more encompassing than government, including institutions as well as non-governmental mechanisms. Held and McGrew (2003: 8) describe governance as

> the structures and processes of governing beyond the state where there exists no supreme or singular political authority … it constitutes a broad analytical approach to addressing the central questions of political life under conditions of globalization, namely: who rules, in whose interests, by what mechanisms and for what purposes?

It is thus a vision of a global institutional architecture that is multilayered, pluralistic, and structurally complex, with national governments still acting as strategic sites for enmeshing global governance. The shift from regimes to governance is also visible in global environmental politics, and much of the literature now talks about global environmental governance as the sphere of global environmental politics (Lipschutz et al. 1996; Paterson *et al.* 2003). A move away from state-centric analysis has also occurred, with the focus on analyzing transnational environmental movements and NGOs as well as TNCs as actors in global environmental politics (see, for example, Princen and Finger 1994; Lipschutz *et al.* 1996; Wapner 1996; Keck and Sikkink 1998; Betsill *et al.* 2006).

There are a variety of theoretical approaches to global governance. The universalizing liberal language of global governance, as seen for example in *Our Global Neighbourhood*, the report of the UN Commission for Global Governance, claims we are entering a new era of democratization, economic transformation, multilateralism, and collective responsibility (UNCGG 1995:1). While international governance was once played out in intergovernmental relationships, *Our Global Neighbourhood* claims this new global era is marked by the involvement of NGOs, citizens' movements, TNCs, and the global market alongside states and intergovernmental organizations (ibid.: 3). In the liberal academic literature, too, this inclusion of transnational actors in the policy-making process is what is perceived to be new about global governance (Young 1997).

Increasing transnational activism is attributed to the perceived powerlessness of the state in a globalizing world, particularly when it comes to so-called global issues, such as environmental degradation. Alongside the forces of globalization, pressure from grassroots movements is seen as a challenge to the power and authority of states (UNCGG 1995: 10–11). The response, according to the report, is for the states-system – organized around a reinvigorated UN – to welcome these challenges in the form of a widened global governance. Non-governmental actors, according to the report, have brought about a "global associational revolution" (ibid.: 253) consisting of "a multitude of institutions, voluntary associations, and networks … [which] channel the interests and energies of many communities outside government, from business and the professions to individuals" (ibid.: 32).

Alongside NGOs, global business is considered to be an "even more clearly identifiable sector with a role in global governance" (UNCGG 1995: 255). Business is seen as being "in the forefront of 'futures' research, mapping out long-range global scenarios and assessing their implications for corporate responsibility," following the lead of the Business Council for Sustainable Development (BCSD), which is "illustrative of this new role" (ibid.). In this liberal, pluralist account, this wide range of non-governmental actors is seen as standing alongside states. Moreover, it is viewed as enabling the democratization of global governance.

Critics of the liberal discourse caution that there is a danger of overemphasizing the diffusion or even loss of state power. The importance and centrality of state sovereignty does not disappear. The key institutions remain intergovernmental ones. Despite claims that environmental issues, because of their global nature, challenge the sovereign, interstate system, and despite liberal claims to be creating some global civil space, the political framework of the liberal global political economy has not fundamentally altered. While states may appear to have lost autonomy, juridically their claim to sovereignty is not undermined (Paterson 1997: 175). Critical voices in the global governance debate draw connections to Foucauldian and neo-Gramscian discourse. Here global governance marks not the retreat of the state, but rather the ultimate form of government rationality or, as Foucault termed it, "governmentality," the "unspoken rationality of neoliberal globalization" (Douglas 2000: 116). Neo-Gramscians similarly liken global governance to a strategy of global capitalist hegemony, a process of institutionalization that stabilizes and perpetuates world order (Cox 1981: 136; Ford 2003: 122). In these views, global environmental governance is not so much about managing global environmental problems as about perpetuating dominant capitalist structures and practices.

The space of global civil society

Within the literature on global governance, transnational actors are often said to be located within the sphere of global civil society. The concept of civil society itself is an old and complex one that has seen shifts over time in its boundaries with state and market, also varying theoretically from liberal to critical positions. However, as some authors have pointed out, there are problems with constructing bounded spheres on account of the often transnational dimension of social relations (Shaw 1994). The extrapolation of civil society to global civil society is open to different interpretations. Predominantly, it is claimed that changing circumstances under conditions of globalization have affected non-state actors and the way they organize as well as who and what they target. The sphere in which they are said to be operating has also become globalized. If national social movements were located in civil society, now transnational and global social movement activism is growing in a sphere of global civil society (see, for example, Shaw 1994; Lipschutz *et al.* 1996).

The term "global civil society" is now widely used among social movements, NGOs, and business, as well as government representatives and the institutions of global governance. It is actively shaping a political sphere and creating new transnational political identities and subjects (Drainville 2004). Lipschutz sees it as consisting of "self-conscious constructions of networks of knowledge and action, by decentred local actors, that cross the reified boundaries of space as though they were not there" with the aim "to reconstruct, re-imagine, or re-map world politics" (Lipschutz 1992: 390). In his view, global civil society is a *parallel sphere* that seeks to bypass the states-system and construct "new political spaces" (ibid.: 393).

This leads to questions about what the sphere of global civil society adds to our analysis of transnational actors. Different theoretical viewpoints have different takes on the meaning and importance of global governance and global civil society.

The dominant liberal view, as depicted in documents such as *Our Global Neighbourhood*, envisages a pluralistic, relatively harmonious, emancipatory political sphere (see also Lipschutz *et al.* 1996; Wapner 1996; Kaldor 2003). Liberals refer to it as that "domain that exists above the individual and below the state but also across state boundaries, where people voluntarily organize themselves to pursue various aims" (Wapner 1996: 66). In this view, global governance is constituted by the addition of global civil society to international society, made up of both NGOs and business actors. It is portrayed as a space of "civility" and not as a potential site for conflicting interests.

On the other hand, traditional IR theorists are skeptical about the importance of global governance or global civil society (for example, Grieco and Ikenberry 2003). They see any institutional mechanisms above the state level as inevitably subject to distortion and abuse by the most powerful nation-states, who will further their interests through these institutions or ignore and bypass them.

Critical voices agree partially with some of the realist analysis about the abuse of such institutional mechanisms by powerful states, but they locate the whole scenario within global capitalism, seeing powerful states as seeking to expand their control over global capitalism, not just for the sake of political power in and of itself. Neo-Gramscians, for example, emphasize the role of ideology as well as institutions in maintaining capitalist hegemony. Here the sphere of global civil society is in danger of contributing to the enclosure of the global public sphere, by creating an elite space that legitimizes global governance. However, the neo-Gramscian view also sees global civil society as a site for potential contest to hegemony, and thus a site of struggle and resistance. They view global civil society as the terrain where progressive forces are challenging the increasing power of capital and seeking to create transnational links and new political spaces for mobilizing on global problems such as social injustice and environmental degradation (for example, Gill 2003).

In line with the perceived transformative potential of global civil society, sections of social movements – in particular established NGOs – consciously define themselves as members of global civil society, invoking the language of democratization and participation. They see the sphere of global civil society as a political space for engaging with the institutions of global governance in an attempt to make up for the democratic deficit that these non-transparent and unaccountable institutions create.

On the other hand, less institutionalized grassroots movements with radical agendas are suspicious of a politics of engagement, which they view as a form of cooptation (Ford 2003). In the neo-Gramscian view, the establishment of an enlarged liberal sphere of global civil society where people can participate in the management of the environment is consistent with the notion that civil society is a mechanism of hegemony. By this is meant that civil society's involvement and perceived contribution to policy-making is a concession to the people in return for their acquiescence in preserving the dominant social, political, and economic capitalist model. Further, they see such discourses of global civil society as strategies for absorbing and neutralizing potentially counter-hegemonic ideas (Cox 1993: 55). However, they also stress that civil society is the space for change, the space where hegemony is challenged. It is where the struggle over environmental policy is played out. Global civil society thus is not only a sphere of action, but it has *agency*, as do the actors operating from the sphere, be they transnational environmental movements, TNCs, or transnational business networks.

We saw that there are different interpretations of the phenomenon of global civil society and its democratizing potential. While one can argue that there has indeed been an increase in the activity of transnational actors in the sphere of global civil society and therefore increased *participation* of these actors in global governance, that does not necessarily translate into democracy – although some maintain it could potentially enhance democracy within global governance (for example, Held and McGrew 2003). Reports such as *Our Global Neighbourhood* may be slightly exaggerating the claims of democratization because participation does not necessarily equal representation. Here NGOs are situated in the same sphere as business actors, competing for participation in global institutions. Previously, the UN's *Agenda 21* had for the first time ever called upon the global population to participate in the saving of the planet (United Nations 1992). However, the locus of authority remains entrenched in the interstate system, with a growing recognition of the role of business as by far the dominant section of this so-called global civil society. Critical scholars view environmental issues as being depoliticized through the orthodox discourse of global environmental governance building within the liberal global political economy (for example, Paterson 2000). That is to say that environmental issues are separated out from those to do with economy and politics and seen as discrete problems that are capable of being fixed through institutions, market-based mechanisms, or changed behavior, yet without challenging the parameters of the current system.

At heart the study of the role of transnational actors in global environmental politics is about power relations. As we saw above, global environmental governance is the arena of global environmental politics. It is here that the global management of transboundary environmental issues is fought out. Global civil society is now most readily identified as the space in which transnational actors operate. It is portrayed in the dominant liberal literature as a democratizing force for global governance. However, critical scholars want to deconstruct this space and make the power relations explicit. Ultimately, we might want to ask in what way an analysis of transnational actors challenges conventional approaches to understanding political outcomes in global environmental politics. For this we now turn to an illustration of a variety of transnational actors.

Transnational actors in global environmental politics

The previous section has illustrated the context and space of transnational activism. Traditionally, the role of transnational actors in the policy-making process, as in the discipline of IR more generally, has not been at the center of analysis. Although regime theory in its analysis of environmental regimes and MEAs acknowledges epistemic communities as contributors to global environmental politics, the emphasis has been on the role of scientists and technical experts contributing expertise to the understanding of environmental issues (Vogler 2003). This has been particularly important where controversy or uncertainty has been under discussion, notably with issues such as climate change. The presence of epistemic communities, however, has not radically unsettled the state-centricity of regime analysis. While it has introduced actors other than states, these have been limited to elite experts. These types of elite actors must not be confused with the broader transnational environmental movement and might better be described as part of broader advocacy networks (Keck and Sikkink 1998).

This section will focus on transnational environmental movements, NGOs, and transnational business/TNCs as actors in global environmental politics. It will use the concept of NGOs generally, although they are sometimes also referred to as international NGOs (INGOs) or transnational NGOs (TNGOs). Although this book's focus is on global environmental politics and the focus of this chapter is on the transnational actors in global environmental politics, this is not to say that environmental issues can be seen in isolation. Indeed, focusing on single issues can be counterproductive because it may fail to challenge the fragmented, disciplinary technical-rational discourse that is a key contributor to environmental degradation and current global environmental governance. If environmental issues are separated out of their social, political, and economic context, the root causes are rendered invisible, leading to techno-fix solutions that may exacerbate the problem (Ford 2003). Indeed, concerns among transnational actors are rarely limited to discrete environmental problems. The analysis of global environmental change and issues of sustainability is mostly couched in a much broader framework, looking at the relationship between the environment and human economic, social, cultural, and political development.

Transnational environmental movements and NGOs

Particularly since the 1960s, global environmental movements have proliferated with the awareness and politicization of environmental degradation and its relationship to the wider organization of modern societies in their economic, political, and cultural aspects. Increased awareness around the connection between globalization and environmental degradation has led movements to take their struggle out of a purely national context. The 1992 UN Conference on Environment and Development (UNCED) is usually quoted as the watershed for transnational actor involvement in global environmental politics, where close to 1,500 NGOs organized a parallel conference and many more movements and NGOs rallied from across the globe. Twenty years later, over 6,000 officially registered NGOs gathered in Johannesburg for the 2002 International Summit on Sustainable Development, alongside countless "unofficial" groups and movements. Movements and organizations across the world also campaigned on climate change in the run up to the UN Climate Change Conference in Copenhagen in December 2009.

It is hard to find a consensus among social movement theorists as to how a social movement might be defined. Scholars have challenged the literature that has tended to see social movements as bounded by nation-states, or geographically limited to regions or cultures, particularly the North (see, for example, Walker 1994; Stammers and Eschle 2005). Broadly, social movements, including environmental movements, are heterogeneous groups that share collective identity, solidarity, and common purpose (for example, Diani 2000). They vary in size, issues, and tactics, and the environmental movement itself spans various shades of green. Despite the diversity of identities and experiences, these movements do identify commonalities in the experience of late capitalist modernity and connections are sometimes forged across space and place.

Transnational movements, then, are movements that are building transnational cooperation around common goals and purposes (Smith *et al.* 1997: 59–60). Sydney Tarrow defines them as: "socially mobilised groups with constituents in at least two states, engaged in sustained contentious interactions with power-holders in at least one state other than their own, or against an international institution, or a multinational economic actor" (Tarrow 1994: 11).

Thus transnational environmental movements are movements that are creating links and acting transnationally because they perceive the root causes of environmental degradation to be tied up with the forces of globalization, such as the increasing globalization of capital and with it the globalization of governance structures. That said, there are many movements that campaign solely on national, regional, or local issues. But, increasingly, there is an awareness of the relationship between the local and the global. Indeed, "think global act local" became a prominent slogan within the green movement, linking global awareness with the importance of connectedness to place and rooted action, as seen for instance in the Transition Movement (Griffiths 2009).

While many movements campaign on specific issues, it is important to note that the boundaries between issues are not necessarily always rigid. Transnational movements campaigning on human rights abuses, gender inequality, or labor issues often share similar concerns and goals to environmental movements, in that their individual causes may all in some ways stem from the nature of the current global economic and political system. Indeed, many environmental movements would not want to separate the environment and human development. They argue that sustainability and social justice go hand in hand.

The terminology for describing transnational movements has varied enormously: for example, INGOs, international social movement organizations (ISMOs), international pressure groups or interest groups, or transnational advocacy groups or networks (Keck and Sikkink 1998; Stammers and Eschle 2005). Within the field of the environment more specifically, they have been described as environmental transnational coalitions (Princen and Finger 1994). More broadly they have been identified as world civic politics (Wapner 1996), global citizen action (Edwards and Gaventa 2001), or people's movements (Shiva 2005). Many movements have identified globalized capitalist structures and distant, unaccountable governance structures as part of the problems they care about and have identified themselves as anti-globalization movements, anti-capitalist movements, pro-democracy movements, global justice movements, or, more boldly, the "movement of movements" (Mertes 2004).

There is a danger of conflating organizations with movements (Stammers and Eschle 2005). The environmental movement broadly conceived contains a wide variety of groupings. While some NGOs could be seen to be located on a spectrum within the environmental movement, it is not the case that all NGOs are *part of* the movement as such. Some large, established NGOs, such as the IUCN (International Union for the Conservation of Nature) or the WWF (World-Wide Fund for Nature), have a high degree of cross-fertilization with established institutions of governance. These large, bureaucratic, professional environmental NGOs are far removed from the grassroots of the environmental movement, though they may share common concerns.

Others, such as the pressure groups Friends of the Earth or Greenpeace, are financially independent of governmental institutions and sometimes take an anti-state position as well as lobbying at the state and interstate level. As such they have a two-pronged approach. On the one hand, they have been involved, along with organizations such as the IUCN and WWF, in setting and monitoring the implementation of institutional responses, in the context of international environmental regime formation and maintenance and within the United Nations as well as within national governments or at the EU level. On the other hand, they are working in solidarity with grassroots environmental movements sometimes taking direct action (Young 1999; Ford 2003).

Grassroots movements are largely marginalized from institutional processes, often by choice. They might not fit neatly into a "transnational" category, because they may be campaigning on a particular local issue and may lack resources to network transnationally. However, they clearly identify transnational structures as the root cause of environmental destruction. Movements such as Via Campesina, Climate Camp, or Earth First! are challenging the top-down governance process through direct action. They are highly critical of the institutional channels available and their responses to environmental problems. They are also critical of institutionalized environmental NGOs that they see as coopted by the dominant powers of global governance. These grassroots activist movements perceive themselves to be engaged in an emancipatory struggle for freedom from dominating discourses to pursue alternative, equitable, and sustainable ways of living, working for a redistribution of power, and carving out political space. Their strategy is not necessarily to influence the agenda of the global governance process but rather to take direct action to increase awareness about issues and to challenge and confront the state and economic powers that be directly. Although they may be active in specific places and localities, they are forging transnational links through networks such as the Peoples' Global Action or the World Social Forum (Williams and Ford 1999; Ford 2003; Mertes 2004). The movement of movements could be seen as the transnational heart of a large variety of groups and movements across the globe. Within this, diverse groups are campaigning for the preservation of economic, political, cultural, and ecological diversity, which they perceive to be under threat from a globalizing monoculture (see Shiva 1993; Gill 2003).

The intention here is not to measure which movements have been most successful, in for example lobbying the institutions of global governance or attempting to shut them down. Rather, the emphasis is on the political and cultural process of activism and the impediments which may be preventing successful outcomes, and on the portrayal of these movements as agents of change. Indeed, instrumentally, these movements may be relatively powerless compared with large business lobby groups. However, there is a powerful, cultural element to the movements for social change, which through global action and the global media are spreading new discourses and challenging existing ones.

Importantly, movements do not just arise as a means to an end, but are actively engaged in processes of socio-cultural change, bringing forth alternative ways of knowing and doing. Progressive movements are thus not just challenging the organization of the global political economy but actively showing what an alternative could look like. This cultural aspect of social movements is something that has been largely ignored in social movement theory, which focuses on the reasons for mobilization of collective behavior. Alberto Melucci (1996: 2) has warned that social movements must not be reduced purely to a political dimension, for this would deny the communicative role they play. His project is concerned with analyzing the actors' *construction* of their own action (ibid.: 16), the actual processes of cultural change. Yet such an approach must not lose sight of the context, which remains the global political economy. Social movements need to be reflexive about their position within this hegemony as well as about the dangers of cooptation. As seen above, they need to be able to contextualize their agency within the global matrix.

TNCs and business advocacy groups

Like transnational environmental movements and NGOs, TNCs have mushroomed in the last three decades, and they constitute important players in the modern capitalist world economy, responsible for large amounts of investment and trade. A TNC is a corporation that is active in more than two countries – that is, it may have a host state, but it operates subsidiaries in various other locations and involves the movement of capital, resources, and people across national boundaries. Examples might include oil corporations such as Shell or BP, or food giants such as Unilever or Nestlé. Apart from TNCs, though, there are also related business advocacy groups which act in the interests of transnational business, such as the International Chamber of Commerce (ICC), the World Business Council for Sustainable Development (WBCSD), or the European Chemical Industry Council (CEFIC).

TNCs and business advocacy networks are clearly important transnational actors in global environmental politics because of the close link between the global economic system and global environmental degradation. Unlike transnational movements and NGOs, they are pursuing instrumental goals rather than acting on principled beliefs (Keck and Sikkink 1998; Clapp 2005a). They are motivated by profit, which leads to the growth imperative and resulting increased demand on resources that can contribute directly to environmental degradation, given that many TNCs are operating in environmentally sensitive sectors, such as natural resource extraction. While some TNCs invest in and produce environmentally benign goods and services, generally trade and investment patterns within the capitalist global economy tend to exacerbate rather than mitigate environmental degradation on account of the growth imperative. The distanciated processes of global capitalism, including the activities of TNCs, contribute both directly and indirectly to processes of environmental degradation. This leads to a tension between global environmental governance as pursued through MEAs and the freedom to do business. TNCs and transnational business advocacy networks acting on their behalf are eager to minimize regulation designed to limit environmental (and social) degradation. Fundamentally, then, there is a conflict of interest between their aims and those of global environmental policy. Like NGOs, they are involved in lobbying within the global environmental policy-making process, though they are often pursuing very different outcomes from those of NGOs. While NGOs and social movements may be seeking to challenge the very culture of capitalist relations that *systematically produce* environmental degradation and social injustice, TNCs are attempting to influence the agenda to prevent measures that could be harmful to business. There is no denying the power of TNCs, as some have greater assets than nation-states. However, not all commentators see them as necessarily an obstacle to sustainable development. Some argue that these assets can be used to contribute positively to sustainable development, such as through the transfer of innovative and clean technology and the investment in infrastructure and job creation (Murphy and Bendell 1997). In this way, the world has seen a greening of some businesses.

The greening of business or greenwash?

Apart from official lobbying in opposition to global environmental policy, business has been very busy re-creating itself as a vanguard of sustainable development (Schmidheiny 1992; ICC 1991). The institutionalization of this concept is not limited to governments and international organizations. In addition to UN documents and government policies, the concept of sustainable development has entered the corporate world. However, business is not blind to the environmental movement's criticisms and in the concept of sustainable development has found a way to discursively integrate environmental problems without substantially changing its social and material productive practices. The link between economic growth and environmental degradation remains solid despite the corporate sector's promotion of sustainable development (ICC 1991).

During the 1992 UNCED conference, business was brought on board and the WBCSD (formerly the BCSD) was born. This lobby group managed to ensure that during official negotiations the role of business in environmental degradation was played down. *Agenda 21*, signed at UNCED as a comprehensive blueprint for global action on sustainable development (United Nations 1992), mentions corporations only in order to emphasize their role in sustainable development and eschews any mention of the need for business to be regulated. More fundamentally, at the same time as UNCED was being held, UN reforms were underway that dismantled the UN Centre on Transnational Corporations (UNCTC) (Clapp 2005b: 25). Attempts by the UNCTC to include corporate accountability measures within *Agenda 21* had been rejected by industrialized countries during preparatory meetings. The controversy over the lack of provisions in *Agenda 21* regarding corporations was further enhanced by the fact that corporations such as ICI and ARCO, major environmental polluters with a track record of funding anti-envrionmental lobby groups, were found to be contributing to the funding of UNCED itself (Doran 1993; Chatterjee and Finger 1994).

Critical voices would argue that business is using the discourse of sustainable development as a way of subverting environmental concerns through greenwash (Beder 1997). As far back as 1984, UNEP and ICC organized the World Industry Conference on Environmental Management (WICEM), which three years before the Brundtland Report's promotion of sustainable development was discussing the possibility of achieving economic growth and sound environmental management. The position was a distinctly corporatist one. At WICEM it was recommended that industry should become more strongly involved in formulating environmental policy in general as well as in formulating national environmental regulatory frameworks (Trisoglio and ten Kate 1991). By 1991, in the run up to UNCED, WICEM II was clearly carving out the niche for industry in defining and spearheading their particular model of sustainable development.

As part of this quest, WICEM II further called on business and industry to foster harmonious relations with local communities in order to gain their confidence and to become better integrated into the community and wider society. The result of WICEM II was *The Business Charter for Sustainable Development: Principles for Environmental Management*, adopted in 1990 and first published in 1991. This states, for example, that

> economic growth provides the conditions in which protection of the environment can best be achieved, and environmental protection ... is necessary to achieve growth that is sustainable ... In turn, versatile, dynamic, responsive and profitable businesses are required as the *driving force* for sustainable *economic* development and for providing managerial, technical and financial resources to contribute to the resolution of environmental challenges. Market economies, characterised by entrepreneurial initiatives, are essential to achieve this ... making market forces work in this way to protect and improve the quality of the environment – with the help of standards such as ISO 14000, and judicious use of economic instruments in a harmonious regulatory framework – is an ongoing challenge that the world faces in entering the twenty-first century.
>
> (ICC 1991; emphasis in original)

It is clear from this passage that business, in line with conventional economic orthodoxy, perceives environmental degradation to be something *outside of* economic processes. The environment is something that is separate from and that impinges on and challenges economic and corporate structures and processes. Business and growth cannot be questioned in themselves; the task is to "manage" the challenges within the given framework. Business is clearly bidding for its narrow view of sustainable development to be implemented and for business to take on a major role in the implementation. While on the one hand aiming to become more closely integrated with community and society, business is actually lobbying for autonomy and self-regulation or at most market-based instruments such as carbon-trading.

The privatization of global environmental governance

Another key dynamic in the provision of global public goods has been that of public authority versus private power. Global governance has sometimes involved a shift away from public authority to private agencies, as seen for example in the public–private partnerships such as Global Compact, which involves more than 4,700 corporate participants as well as stakeholders from over 130 countries. At heart it advocates responsible corporate citizenship to the challenges of globalization in the areas of human rights, labor, environment, and anti-corruption, contributing to a more sustainable and inclusive global economy (UNGC n.d.).

Likewise, business advocacy groups such as WBCSD, and the institutions such as the International Organization for Standardization (ISO), promote voluntary codes of conduct that, as well as safeguarding the autonomy of business, are implicating business in environmental management. The growth in voluntary codes of conduct is blurring the boundary between public and private and leading to what has been called "mixed regimes," involving states and private authorities in the "creation and maintenance of international principles, norms, rules and decision-making procedures" (Clapp 1998: 295).

There has been a tension between the general liberalization and deregulation trend in the globalized political economy and the growing need for environmental regulation, which has led to a search for "new and private forms of (environmental) regulation, such as (environmental) standards ... as a way out of this *tension* between deregulation and re-regulation" (Finger and Tamiotti 1999: 9). On the one hand, the move from traditional "command and control" style policy to the increased role of the private sector and non-state actors is leading to a privatization of (environmental) politics (see also Clapp 1998). On the other, there is an argument that a fundamental reorganization of international society is taking place, as seen in the growth of global governance (Finger and Tamiotti 1999).

A privatization of environmental governance is occurring, exemplified in the growing influence of private actors on decision-making, which in some cases is outweighing the influence of states. Evidence suggests that more and more private actors are initiating regimes which are later recognized by states and incorporated into their regulatory structures, one example being the ISO 14000 series, which specifies environmental management standards (Clapp 1998). In line with the mainstream belief that global environmental problems demand global solutions, the notion of global standards would seem an essential basis upon which to build harmonized global solutions. However, also in line with the mainstream, it ignores the unequal power structures within the global political economy. The membership of ISO, true to its hybrid nature, consists of a mixture of governments, mixed public–private actors, and private industry associations. The government members are made up predominantly of developed countries, while the private members' majority comes from within the OECD. Given that the decision-making process is heavily dominated by private interests, the voice of developing countries in the establishment of these global standards is marginalized (ibid.: 296–301).

The idea of establishing environmental standards within the remit of ISO was a response to *Agenda 21*'s recommendation for the role of industry in sustainable development (Clapp 1998: 302). The setting up of environmental *management* standards involved a change of direction from the ISO's traditional remit of *technical* standards (Finger and Tamiotti 1999: 12). As a result, the ISO does not address the key material recommendations of *Agenda 21* for industry, which are of particular importance to developing countries, namely the reduction of hazardous waste generation and the promotion of clean production and transfer of environmental technology (Clapp 1998: 305).

The shift toward global standards must further be seen in the context of trade liberalization and the WTO. The WTO's Agreement on Technical Barriers to Trade (TBT) encourages the use of international standards rather than national ones, which are seen as *technical* barriers to trade (Finger and Tamiotti 1999: 13; Clapp 1998: 305). In effect, the ISO environmental management standards, which were recognized by the WTO's predecessor, General Agreement on Tariffs and Trade, create a lowest common denominator and act as a mechanism for avoiding trade barriers. More importantly, it demonstrates the role of privately agreed voluntary standards in the re-regulation and public management of international trade.

With the latest global crisis in neoliberal capitalism and a seeming return to neo-Keynsian-style intervention, some green voices are proposing a "Green New Deal" as a solution to the interlinked crises of capital, energy, and climate. This would involve business and government as well as labor and environmental movements in bringing about a shift to green energy and green-collar jobs financed by re-regulating finance and taxation (GNDG 2008).

From the above we can see that transnational environmental movements and TNCs and their advocates and lobbyists are all clearly visible actors in global environmental politics. The question of the power of these diverse actors in global civil society is a complex one. For one, we have seen that this sphere involves a large variety of different types of actors – NGOs, transnational advocacy groups, TNCs, social movements. The liberal pluralist descriptions of this sphere do not analyze power relations within civil society. It seems questionable that business actors and NGOs are working on an equal footing. Business actors clearly have more "tacit power" over state actors on account of their close connection to economic growth creation (Newell 2000: 159). Further, among NGOs themselves there are differentiations that cannot be ignored. NGOs, like social movements, are not a homogeneous or necessarily a progressive force and are not immune to power relations of class, race, or gender or between North and South and are further differentiated on the basis of ideologies and strategies. Critical voices, on the other hand, embrace the diversity and complexity of the sphere, seeing it as a site of struggle for hegemony as well as counter-hegemony.

Conclusions

This chapter has provided an overview of transnational actors and their agency in global environmental politics. Over the last two decades we have seen a growing literature on the role of transnational actors in world politics. Few IR scholars would argue that they are completely irrelevant. Most would agree that transnational actors need to be part of the analysis in understanding the framework and processes of global politics. Transnational actors are of course a broad church, encompassing anything from transnational social movements to global business. They do not all operate on the same footing, nor do they employ the same tactics to achieve their goals. Different theoretical perspectives provide different analyses of how and why transnational actors matter to global environmental politics. Solving global environmental problems is clearly a political as well as an economic, cultural, and social struggle. States are not the only actors in this arena, and it is clear that transnational actors are an important part of the picture.

Note

1 I would like to thank Peter Doran, Jenneth Parker, Stephen Hurt, and Neil Stammers for feedback on this chapter.

Recommended reading

Betsill, M. M. (2006) "Transnational actors in international environmental politics," in M. M. Betsill, K. Hochstetler, and D. Stevis (eds), *Palgrave Advances in International Environmental Politics*, Basingstoke: Palgrave Macmillan.
Edwards, M., and Gaventa, J. (eds) (2001) *Global Citizen Action: Lessons and Challenges*, London: Earthscan.
Keck, M. E., and Sikkink, K. (1998) *Activists beyond Borders: Advocacy Networks in International Politics*, Ithaca, NY, and London: Cornell University Press.
Lipschutz, R. D., with Mayer, J. (1996) *Global Civil Society and Global Environmental Governance*, Albany: State University of New York Press.

References

Beder, S. (1997) *Global Spin: The Corporate Assault on Environmentalism*, Totnes: Green Books.
Betsill, M. M., Hochstetler, K., and Stevis, D. (eds) (2006) *Palgrave Advances in International Environmental Politics*, Basingstoke: Palgrave Macmillan.

Chatterjee, P., and Finger, M. (1994) *The Earth Brokers*, Routledge: London.

Clapp, J. (1998) "The privatisation of global environmental governance: ISO 14000 and the developing world," *Global Governance*, 4: 295–316.

—— (2005a) "Transnational corporations and global environmental governance," in P. Dauvergne (ed.), *Handbook of Global Environmental Politics*, Cheltenham: Edward Elgar.

—— (2005b) "Global environmental governance for corporate responsibility and accountability," *Global Environmental Politics*, 5(3): 23–34.

Cox, R. (1981) "Social forces, states and world order: beyond international relations theory," *Millennium: Journal of International Studies*, 10(2): 126–51.

—— (1993) "Gramsci, hegemony and international relations: an essay in method," in S. Gill (ed.), *Gramsci, Historical Materialism and International Relations*, Cambridge: Cambridge University Press.

Diani, M. (2000) "The concept of social movement," in K. Nash (ed.), *Readings in Contemporary Political Sociology*, Oxford: Blackwell.

Doran, P. (1993) "The Earth Summit (UNCED): ecology as spectacle," *Paradigms: The Kent Journal of International Relations*, 7(1): 55–65.

Douglas, I. (2000) "Globalization and the retreat of the state," in B. K. Gills (ed.), *Globalization and the Politics of Resistance*, Basingstoke: Macmillan.

Drainville, A. (2004) *Contesting Globalization: Space and Place in the World Economy*, London: Routledge.

Edwards, M., and Gaventa, J. (eds) (2001) *Global Citizen Action: Lessons and Challenges*, London: Earthscan.

Finger, M., and Tamiotti, L. (1999) "New global regulatory mechanisms and the environment: the emerging linkage between the WTO and the ISO," *IDS Bulletin*, 30(3): 8–15.

Ford, L. H. (2003) "Challenging global environmental governance: social movement agency and global civil society," *Global Environmental Politics*, 3(2): 120–34.

Gill, S. (2003) *Power and Resistance in the New World Order*, Basingstoke: Palgrave Macmillan.

GNDG (Green New Deal Group) (2008) *A Green New Deal: Joined up Policies to Solve the Triple Crunch of the Credit Crisis, Climate Change and High Oil Prices*, London: New Economics Foundation.

Grieco, J. M., and Ikenberry, G. J. (2003) *State Power and World Markets*, New York and London: W. W. Norton.

Griffiths, J. (2009) "The transition initiative: changing the scale of change," *Orion Magazine*, July/August. Available: www.orionmagazine.org/index.php/articles/article/4792 (accessed 29 June 2009).

Held, D., and McGrew, T. (eds) (2003) *The Global Transformations Reader*, Cambridge: Polity.

ICC (International Chamber of Commerce) (1991) *The Business Charter for Sustainable Development: Principles for Environmental Management*, Paris: ICC.

Kaldor, M. (2003) *Global Civil Society*, Cambridge: Polity.

Keck, M. E., and Sikkink, K. (1998) *Activists beyond Borders: Advocacy Networks in International Politics*, Ithaca, NY, and London: Cornell University Press.

Keohane, R., and Nye, J. (1977) *Power and Interdependence*, Boston: Little, Brown.

Lipschutz, R. D. (1992) "Reconstructing world politics: the emergence of global civil society," *Millennium: Journal of International Studies*, 3: 389–420.

Lipschutz, R. D., with Mayer, J. (1996) *Global Civil Society and Global Environmental Governance*, Albany: State University of New York Press.

Melucci, A. (1996) *Challenging Codes: Collective Action in the Information Age*, Cambridge: Cambridge University Press.

Mertes, T. (ed.) (2004) *A Movement of Movements: Is Another World Really Possible?*, London: Verso.

Murphy, D. F., and Bendell, J. (1997) *In the Company of Partners: Business, Environmental Groups and Sustainable Development Post-Rio*, Bristol: Policy Press.

Newell, P. (2000) *Climate for Change: Non-State Actors and the Global Politics of the Greenhouse*, Cambridge: Cambridge University Press.

Paterson, M. (1997) "Institutions of global environmental change: sovereignty," *Global Environmental Change*, 7(2): 175–7.

—— (2000) *Understanding Global Environmental Politics*, Basingstoke: Palgrave Macmillan.

Paterson, M., Humphreys, D., and Pettiford, L. (2003) "Conceptualising global environmental governance: from interstate regimes to counter-hegemonic struggles," *Global Environmental Politics*, 3(2):1–10.

Princen, T., and Finger, M. (1994) *Environmental NGOs in World Politics*, London: Routledge.

Schmidheiny, S. (1992) *Changing Course*, Cambridge, MA: MIT Press.

Shaw, M. (1994) "Civil society and global politics: beyond a social movements approach," *Millennium: Journal of International Studies*, 23(3): 647–67.

—— (2000) *Theory of the Global State: Globality as Unfinished Revolution*, Cambridge: Cambridge University Press.

Shiva, V. (1993) *Monocultures of the Mind*, London: Zed Books.

—— (2005) "From Doha to Hong Kong via Cancun". Available: www.zmag.org/znet/viewArticle/4835 (accessed 20 January 2009).

Smith, J., Pagnucco, R., and Chatfield, C. (1997) "Social movements and world politics: a theoretical framework," in J. Smith, C. Chatfield, and R. Pagnucco (eds), *Transnational Social Movements and Global Politics*, Syracuse, NY: Syracuse University Press.

Stammers, N, and Eschle, C. (2005) "Social movements and global activism," in W. de Jong, M. Shaw, and N. Stammers (eds), *Global Activism Global Media*, London: Pluto Press.

Tarrow, S. (1994) *Power in Movement: Social Movements, Collective Action and Politics*, Cambridge: Cambridge University Press.

Third World Network (n.d.) "WTO – Shrink or Sink". Available: www.twnside.org.sg/title/shrink.htm (accessed 12 December 2008).

Trisoglio, A., and ten Kate, K. (1991) *From WICEM to WICEM II: A Report to Assess Progress in the Implementation of the WICEM Recommendations*, Geneva: UNEP.

UNCGG (UN Commission on Global Governance) (1995) *Our Global Neighbourhood*, Oxford: Oxford University Press.

UNGC (UN Global Compact) (n.d.) "Overview of the UN Global Compact". Available: www. unglobalcompact.org/AboutTheGC/index.html (accessed 15 January 2009).

United Nations (1992) *Agenda 21: The United Nations Programme of Action from Rio*, Geneva: UN Department of Economic and Social Affairs.

Vogler, J. (2003) "Taking institutions seriously: how regime analysis can be relevant to multilevel environmental governance," *Global Environmental Politics*, 3(2): 25–39.

Walker, R. B. J. (1994) "Social movements/world politics," *Millennium: Journal of International Studies*, 23(3): 669–700.

Wapner, P. (1996) *Environmental Activism and World Civic Politics*, Albany: State University of New York Press.

Williams, M., and Ford, L. (1999) "The World Trade Organisation, social movements and global environmental management," in C. Rootes (ed.), *Environmental Movements: Local, National and Global*, London: Frank Cass.

Young, O. R. (ed.) (1997) *Global Governance: Drawing Insights from the Environmental Experience*, Cambridge, MA: MIT Press.

Young, Z. (1999) "NGOs and the Global Environmental Facility: friendly foes," in C. Rootes (ed.), *Environmental Movements: Local, National and Global*, London: Frank Cass.

3 Environment and global political economy

Jennifer Clapp

The past thirty years have seen a remarkable increase in the volume and value of global trade, investment, and finance. The intensification of economic globalization during this period has sparked a great deal of debate over the impact of global economic relationships on the natural environment (see Clapp and Dauvergne 2005). On the one hand, proponents of economic globalization stress the positive impacts that this process has on the environment and push for policies that promote further international economic integration as a means by which to promote global sustainable development. Critics of globalization, on the other hand, see mainly negative environmental impacts as a result of growing international economic relationships and push for environmental policies that rein in global economic transactions. Many see this debate as too polarized, and as a result a third view has begun to gain prominence. This "middle-ground" perspective sees strengths and weaknesses in both arguments. According to this view, while in some instances global economic linkages can lead to environmental harm, with proper management the global economy can be a force for environmental improvement.

There is a great deal of polarization between the "globalization is good for the environment" and the "globalization is bad for the environment" views, and this can paralyze efforts to address environmental problems. At the same time, however, opting for the "middle ground" also has its challenges. Following a brief overview of the broad debate over the impact of globalization on the environment, this chapter examines how this debate has played out more specifically with respect to three key areas of the global economy: trade, investment, and finance.

Globalization, economic growth, and the environment

Debate over the environmental impact of global economic integration emerged in full force in the early 1990s. At that time the North American Free Trade Agreement (NAFTA) was being negotiated, bringing with it heightened concern over the environmental implications of a more integrated global economy (Williams 2001). The UN Conference on Environment and Development, held in 1992, also brought international prominence to these debates.

Two basic schools of economic thought on the environment came forward in the debate over global economic integration and the environment. Mainstream environmental economists, drawing on neoclassical economic thinking, see economic growth as a potentially positive force for the environment. For environmental economists, markets are viewed as efficient tools for correcting environmental problems, especially where the correct incentives are put in place. Ecological economists, on the other hand, draw on theories of ecology and physics as much as on neoclassical economics. They differ from mainstream environmental economists in that they see economic growth as having on balance a negative impact on the environment. While they do not dismiss the power of markets, ecological economists argue that the environmental impact of the size of the overall economy cannot be corrected by markets alone.

The general thrust of the arguments put forward by proponents of economic globalization has largely followed environmental economic thinking that draws heavily on classical economic ideas about markets and trade. The concept of comparative advantage, dating back to the writings of David Ricardo in the early 1800s, is central to this viewpoint. The theory of comparative advantage posits that, when trading partners export goods for which they have the least opportunity cost (i.e. goods for which they have a domestic cost advantage in producing compared to other products, regardless of whether they have absolute cost advantages over other countries) and import goods for which they have a higher opportunity cost to produce, they will gain from international trade. The implication is that if all countries focus on producing what they are comparatively best at producing, and engage in international trade, the overall welfare of the trading partners will rise. In this sense, international trade is seen to be an important source of economic growth which in turn creates wealth for those who participate. Today comparative advantage is used to justify not only international trade but also participation in international investment and finance, each of which is seen to contribute to economic growth.

What does economic growth have to do with the environment? For proponents of globalization, it is a good force for the natural environment because economic growth and wealth created by it provide the financial resources necessary for environmental protection. This thinking is based upon environmental economics research from the early 1990s on what has come to be known as the Environmental Kuznets Curve (EKC). This research shows that in OECD countries there appears to be an inverted "U"-shaped relationship between income growth and environmental pollutants. In other words, as incomes rise in an economy, the concentration of pollutants tends at first to rise, but once an economy reaches a certain threshold of income the concentration of those pollutants tends to fall (World Bank 1992; Grossman and Krueger 1995).

The implication of this finding is that economic growth, while at first it may generate some environmental harm, in the long run brings about environmental improvements. This relationship is explained in the literature as a result of higher incomes leading to a greater demand by the population for a cleaner environment, a greater ability of governments to respond by enacting stricter environmental laws, and the capability of firms to develop and market "green" environmental products. In this way, economic growth and environmental protection are seen to reinforce one another, and can continue to do so indefinitely into the future. The liberalization of international trade, investment, and finance – which are seen to foster economic growth – are then considered to be key components in the pursuit of environmental protection. This policy prescription has been promoted especially in developing countries as a route to "sustainable development."

This version of the "globalization–economic growth–environment" linkage has not gone unchallenged. Critics have pointed out that the environmental impacts of economic growth are not so straightforward. And they have raised questions about the environmental impact of inequality, which is seen to be an additional consequence of economic globalization. In terms of the growth question, critical thinkers, including ecological economists and more radical environmental thinkers, have stressed that increased economic activity ultimately leads to environmental harm. Although the amount varies, there is a physical dimension to all economic activity: natural resources are drawn upon for inputs and both the production process and the act of consumption generate waste. Ecological economists call this physical dimension of economic growth "throughput." Drawing on the laws of thermodynamics, ecological economists argue that there are real environmental limits to economic growth because the Earth can sustain only so much throughput (Georgescu-Roegen 1971; Daly 1996). This is directly counter to the neoclassical economic view which assumes that natural resources and waste sinks are infinitely available to support economic growth. For ecological economists, however, economic growth has already surpassed what is seen to be a sustainable limit. Further promotion of growth via international economic integration is seen then only to contribute to the additional depletion of natural resources and increased amounts of waste.

Other critical thinkers have focused on the potential of economic globalization to exacerbate inequality. They point to the fact that, as the world economy has become more integrated over the past fifty years, inequality has also become more pronounced. Extremes of both wealth and poverty are seen to be contributing to environmental problems. Overconsumption in rich industrialized countries has led to greater use of resources and increased levels of waste. At the same time extreme poverty in the world's poorest countries has led to resource depletion and the overcultivation of marginal lands. In the words of Wolfgang Sachs, "in a closed space with finite resources the underconsumption of one party is the necessary condition for the overconsumption of the other party ... the rising tide, before lifting all boats, is likely to burst through the banks" (Sachs 1999: 168).

In a globalized world economy, a large part of the problem is that the environmental impact of both poverty and wealth tends to be concentrated in the world's poorest countries. For example, ecological shadows of the North's consumption are cast on those developing countries that produce goods for export markets. In these cases, poor countries experience the pollution from the production of those products, while those in rich countries enjoy the benefits (Dauvergne 2008). These ecological shadows become even more pronounced when the rich world's waste is exported to developing countries (Clapp 2002). At the same time, the very poorest in the developing world have little choice but to rely heavily on the environment around them as a means by which to make a living (Mabogunje 2002).

While these two extreme views of the impact of global economic integration on the environment have been present over the past few decades, a "middle-ground" position on the question has begun to emerge. It is increasingly recognized that in some instances global economic integration can lead directly to environmental harm – as is the case with the international trade in hazardous wastes, the trade in endangered species, and the international trade in unsustainable timber products (Clapp 2001; Dauvergne 2001). But those taking a middle-ground position see these cases, while important, to be somewhat isolated. In other areas, economic integration is seen to lead to direct benefits, especially where growth can reduce poverty and encourage cleaner production (Neumayer 2004). The way to address this situation, then, is to pursue targeted policy interventions which address specific cases of environmental harm arising from international trade and investment and finance, while at the same time encouraging the positive environmental benefits of economic growth. In other words, the idea from this viewpoint is not to shut down the global economy completely, but rather to address specific instances where it may cause environmental harm and to foster its positive impacts on the environment. More specific middle-ground arguments on both theory and policy have been put forward in recent years with respect to international trade, investment, and finance.

International trade

The international trade of goods across borders has grown remarkably over the past fifty years. World trade expanded from 25 per cent of global GDP in 1960 to 87 per cent in 2006.

Between 1948 and 2007 the annual value of world trade expanded from US$58 million to US$12 trillion, while the volume of trade also increased by a factor of 27 (WTO 2007).

The specific impact of international trade on the environment has been the subject of heated debate in the past decade. Those arguing that it has an overall positive impact on the environment have tended to fall within the neoclassical economic camp, as explained above. But that is not the only reason for the promotion of international trade. A further argument has been that it fosters more efficient allocation of resources, which should ultimately result in less depletion of those resources and fewer wastes to manage. In addition, trade barriers such as tariffs, quotas, and subsidies are seen to result in economic inefficiencies such as the underpricing of natural resources, which in turn leads to their overuse (Bhagwati 1993). For this reason neoclassical economists see trade restrictions as poor tools for promoting environmental protection and argue that improved environmental policy combined with free trade policies provide the best context for the promotion of sustainable development.

Critics of free trade argue that, while efficiency gains may occur as a result of free trade, the economic growth resulting from the process reverses those gains on account of increased throughput in the economy (Sachs 1999; Daly and Farley 2003). But this is not the only reason that they are skeptical of international trade. Critics are particularly concerned about the potential for a regulatory "race to the bottom," whereby countries may lower their environmental standards in a context of trade liberalization in order to enhance their trade competitiveness (Daly 1993; Porter 1999). At the same time, critics argue that increased international trade necessarily means more transportation of goods around the world and its associated environmental impacts (Conca 2000). Because of these particular problems associated with international trade, from this critical viewpoint it is perfectly legitimate to restrict trade on environmental grounds.

Those taking the middle-ground perspective see that both sides of this more polarized debate have some good points. Their core policy recommendation has been to restrict free trade in cases that are obviously harmful to the environment, such as the trade in toxic substances and dangerous chemicals. But they also advocate a promotion of trade liberalization where efficiency gains are most likely, such as in the case of cuts to export subsidies for natural resources (see Esty 2001; Neumayer 2001).

This broader theoretical debate over trade and environment is crucial for the more policy-focused debates dealing with international trade agreements. Historically, international trade agreements have paid little attention to the interactions between trade and the environment, following along with neoclassical economic thinking which has tended to see these processes as mutually beneficial, or at the very least neutral. The 1947 General Agreement on Tariffs and Trade (GATT), for example, included no specific reference to the environment. With the establishment in 1995 of the World Trade Organization (WTO), there has been increased recognition of the importance of understanding the relationship between trade and environment. But, while the preamble to the WTO agreement mentions "sustainable development," there are no specific regulations under the WTO that allow for a relaxation of trade rules in the name of environmental protection. What the original GATT agreement does suggest, however, is that countries are not allowed to discriminate in trade against products based on country of origin or the method by which they were produced. This requirement thus does not enable countries to discriminate against the trade in goods known to be produced in environmentally damaging ways (Esty 1994: 49–51).

One exception regarding production methods is Article XX of the GATT, which spells out circumstances under which states may be eligible to apply trade restrictions in order to protect the environment. These include measures to protect human, animal, or plant life or health, or to ensure the conservation of natural resources. But, to make use of these exceptions, countries must demonstrate that these measures are "necessary" in order to achieve the desired outcome. Measures taken to ensure conservation must be applied strictly to the depletion of natural resources and must be taken in conjunction with domestic measures to protect that particular resource. In addition, countries that take measures under this article must demonstrate that they have done so in a way that is not arbitrary or unjustified. Finally, these exemptions apply only to environmental issues within a country's borders and not to measures taken to protect the global commons (see Esty 1994; Charnovitz 2007).

With so many qualifications to Article XX, very few countries have successfully used it to restrict trade on environmental grounds. For example, in the tuna–dolphin disputes of 1991 and 1994, US environmental regulations that banned the import of tuna that did not meet dolphin protection standards were struck down by GATT dispute panels for not meeting all of its requirements (Esty 1994). In this and other cases, the GATT and subsequently the WTO dispute-panel rulings – regarding gasoline, shrimp, and asbestos – have indicated that the trade body has a preference for dealing with environmental issues through multilateral efforts such as international environmental agreements and other forms of international cooperation rather than via trade restrictions. Some have argued that the WTO itself is not necessarily anti-environment per se, but rather that the conditions for applying exemptions to the rules have not been met in the cases brought before a dispute panel (see DeSombre and Barkin 2002; Charnovitz 2007).

Further debate has also focused on the relationship between international trade rules under the WTO and multilateral environmental agreements (MEAs). There are over 200 MEAs in place, and approximately 10 per cent of those agreements incorporate trade provisions. Prominent examples of MEAs that include trade provisions as a means by which to address environmental problems are the Basel Convention (regulating trade in hazardous wastes), the Cartagena Protocol (setting rules for cross-border trade in genetically modified organisms), the Kyoto Protocol (incorporating measures to address climate change, among them international trade in carbon credits), the Montreal Protocol (mandating trade restrictions against non-parties), and the Rotterdam and Stockholm conventions (regulating the international production, use, and trade in pesticides and persistent organic pollutants respectively). The rules incorporated under each of these agreements aim to restrict trade in dangerous or hazardous products in particular. A number of other multilateral environmental agreements include control measures that have the potential to affect trade, such as provisions regarding prior informed consent and technology transfer (Stilwell and Tarasofsky 2001).

The debate over MEAs and trade relates mainly to the question of whether trade agreements or environmental agreements should take precedence. The GATT/WTO Committee on Trade and Environment (CTE) took up this issue in the mid-1990s, but little progress has been made in clarifying the answer to this question. At the launch of the Doha Round trade talks in 2001, WTO ministers agreed to undertake talks to clarify the relationship between trade rules and environmental rules. But, soon after the launch of the round, this issue has effectively been pushed to the back burner. Some have argued that, as a result, trade rules have by and large trumped environmental rules at the international level, and have called for a world environment organization (Biermann 2000), or similar institution at the international level, with powers to enforce environmental agreements. Others, however, have advocated caution on this front (Najam 2003; Young 2008).

Regional trade agreements and organizations have also been important in the governance of trade and environment. The North American Free Trade Agreement (NAFTA), for example, was negotiated in the early 1990s and differs from the GATT and the WTO in that it explicitly attempted to incorporate environmental concerns directly into its main text. It does this by mentioning specific international environmental treaties that should take precedence over trade rules incorporated into the agreement, provided they are carried out in the least trade-distorting manner (Soloway 2002). An environmental side agreement to the NAFTA, the North American Agreement on Environmental Cooperation (NAAEC), aims to ensure that states comply with and enforce their own national environmental laws and establishes a dispute-settlement mechanism. The NAAEC is overseen by a Commission on Environmental Cooperation (CEC) that allows citizen input into reporting on international environmental violations. While the NAFTA incorporates more explicit environmental language, assessments of its first ten years in operation have raised questions about its effectiveness in promoting environmental protection (Mumme 2007).

Transnational investment

In addition to international trade, cross-border and transnational investment is an important component of economic globalization. Today there are over 79,000 TNC parent firms globally, up from just 7,000 in 1970. In addition there are 790,000 foreign affiliate firms (corporations affiliated with a TNC). Together, these firms make up 11% of world GDP and one-third of world exports (UNCTAD 2008). Flows of foreign direct investment have also grown, from US$9.2 billion in 1970 to US$1.8 trillion in 2007 (UNCTAD 2008). This investment has important implications for the environment. Its volume alone represents an enormous amount of economic activity. Moreover, TNCs are key investors in some of the most environmentally damaging industries, such as resource extraction, chemical production, and electronics.

Theoretical debates on transnational investment and the environment have tended to focus on the question of whether firms relocate in order to take advantage of weaker environmental standards in other countries as well as on arguments over corporate voluntary greening and their effectiveness (Clapp 2002; Wheeler 2002). Critics of globalization have maintained that transnational corporations seek out jurisdictions where environmental regulations are weak. Firms may flee from countries with higher environmental standards, a phenomenon known as "industrial flight." Such firms may also be lured to relocate to what are known as "pollution havens," typically developing countries that have deliberately set environmental standards at a low level in order to attract foreign direct investment. This can lead to "double standards" where we might see different branches of the same corporation operating on different sets of environmental standards in different parts of the world (Clapp 2001). From this viewpoint, a liberalized transnational investment environment only exacerbates the race to the bottom problem under which states may lower their standards, not only to improve their trade competitiveness but also to attract foreign direct investment.

Proponents of globalization are not as concerned about transnational investment flows and corporate behavior with respect to the environment. For them, differing environmental standards in different countries form a normal part of a country's comparative advantage. Further, there is little statistical proof to show that pollution havens actually exist (Mani and Wheeler 1998). Because environmental costs form such a low percentage of the operating costs of large transnational corporations when compared to such costs as labor, environmental factors are not seen to be significant enough to be the main cause for firms relocating to developing countries. Instead of seeing them as contributing to environmental degradation, a number of studies from this perspective have argued that TNCs helped to improve environmental performance by bringing state-of-the-art environmental technology with them wherever they operate around the world, including developing countries (Wheeler 2002).

Although this debate has remained unresolved since the 1970s, most agree that the share of pollution intensity is rising in the developing world and that it is cause for concern. Recent literature on transnational investment and the environment has advocated a middle-ground position on the debate. Even in the absence of hard evidence that pollution havens exist or that industrial flight is occurring, some have noted that policy action could still be taken to discourage states from trying to enhance their competitiveness by weakening of environmental standards (Neumayer 2001).

In addition to debates over the environmental impact of transnational investment have been those emerging over the influence of transnational corporations on global environmental governance more broadly (see Utting 2005; Utting and Clapp 2008). Since the 1990s, TNCs have increased their participation in the shaping of global environmental governance. These actors have been much more visible and active as lobbyists at both the national and the international level, particularly with respect to the negotiation of international environmental agreements. Corporate lobby groups have also been active in global forums such as the Rio Earth Summit in 1992 and the World Summit on Sustainable Development (WSSD) in 2002. At Rio, for example, transnational corporate actors formed the World Business Council for Sustainable Development in order to provide a coherent and single voice from industry in global negotiations on sustainability issues. Similarly, at WSSD, the Business Action on Sustainable Development was formed to act as a single business lobby voice.

This trend of enhanced lobby power on the part of industry actors in global foruns has been seen in both positive and negative lights. Proponents of globalization have argued that it is important to foster transnational business participation in the international negotiation of treaties and in global environmental summits, because these actors are not just a source of problems but also an integral part of solutions (Holme and Watts 2000). Critics, however, have expressed concern that giving industry actors a strong voice at the table could lead to diluted agreements, because industry has an interest in ensuring that regulations on its own activities are not very stringent (Bruno 2002).

There are other ways beyond lobbying in which transnational corporate actors can influence global environmental governance, a point commonly raised by critical thinkers. Firms are seen by some to exert a form of discursive power, meaning that they have the power to shape the way in which terms are defined in the broader public discourse, which in turn affects the way they are governed. Critical thinkers have pointed out, for example, that transnational corporate actors have played a key role in defining what is meant by "sustainable development" (Sklair 2001; Fuchs 2005). Transnational corporations, by engaging in the formation of the discourse of sustainability, can shape it in ways that maintain their goals of economic globalization, openness to global investment, and the favoring of soft, voluntary approaches over hard, regulatory approaches to environmental policy. Others have pointed to the "structural power" of corporate actors in the global political economy. This power operates in ways that enable transnational corporate actors to set agendas simply by being powerful within the broader economy. In other words, states often pursue policy outcomes that would be acceptable to corporations in order to keep or attract investment to their country. The structural power of capital at both the national and the international level has been seen by some to be a key factor in explaining industry influence in global environmental negotiations (Levy and Newell 2005).

The past two decades have also seen the rise of private forms of governance, such as voluntary corporate initiatives and codes of conduct, to promote environmental sustainability

(Cashore 2002; Falkner 2003). These voluntary industry standards include initiatives such as ISO 14000 environmental management standards, corporate environmental reporting, and sector-based industry codes of conduct such as Responsible Care in the Chemicals Sector. Private standards have been promoted by pro-globalization advocates as demonstrating that firms are taking proactive measures to improve their performance and voluntarily adopting practices beyond regulatory requirements (Prakash and Potoski 2006). Critics argue that these voluntary corporate initiatives represent industry's attempt to exert both structural and discursive power over global environmental governance. Because they are voluntary and overseen by industry itself, such standards tend to be much weaker than state-based regulations would be, and as a result their impact on the environment is not significant (Utting 2005). Some have gone so far as to advocate a global treaty on corporate accountability that would impose binding requirements on TNCs with respect to environmental performance. While proposals were put forward for such a treaty by several environmental groups at the WSSD in 2002, they did not gain widespread support (Clapp 2005). A middle-ground position is starting to take shape on this debate, with the idea of "ratcheting up" voluntary codes to give them more teeth through more stringent monitoring and enforcement (Utting 2008).

International development finance

In addition to international trade and investment, the international flow of finance has environmental implications and has been subject to heated debate. Large sums of money are lent to developing countries by international lending agencies, and these transactions have gained increased attention in recent decades for their environmental impact. The World Bank, for example, is the world's largest development lending agency, providing loans in the order of US$27 billion per year to developing countries for both projects and balance of payments support (World Bank 2008). Rich industrialized countries also operate what are known as export credit agencies, which have provided funds to developing countries to enable them to purchase specific imports or to pursue particular projects tied to the exports of goods and services from lending countries. These forms of international development finance have drawn strong criticism from environmental groups, which have claimed that such lending has had negative environmental impacts in developing countries.

The bulk of World Bank lending has historically been for project loans, and today this accounts for around three-quarters of its loans to developing countries (World Bank 2008). Since the 1980s, World Bank project lending has been heavily criticized by environmental groups for not taking environmental concerns adequately into account. At the time the critiques began, the World Bank's project design and evaluation procedures devoted little attention to environmental issues. It was widely assumed within the World Bank that economic growth that was supposed to flow from these projects would provide environmental benefits along the lines of the pro-globalization perspective (Reed 1997). Critics, however, became increasingly concerned about the environmental side effects of the World Bank's typical large-scale projects, including infrastructure – roads, dams, and power projects – as well as industrial agriculture and migration schemes. These critics pointed out that, although the World Bank had some modest environmental policies in place in the 1980s, these were not adequately followed. The result was that the environmental side effects of large-scale projects continued (Wade 1997). Undertakings such as the Polonoreste road project in Brazil, linked to deforestation in the Amazon, and the Narmada dams scheme in India, which led to the resettlement of thousands of people, were targeted by environmental groups as being particularly destructive (Rich 1994).

In the face of strong pressure, even from the US government following lobbying by environmental groups, the World Bank made efforts in the late 1980s and early 1990s to step up its environmental policies. Specifically, it undertook a major restructuring that saw the creation of a new environment department and increased environment staff. Around this time the World Bank also began to require environmental impact assessments on all of its projects. These changes were seen by many to be insufficient. Although environmental project lending increased considerably, it was still only a minor proportion of overall World Bank lending. Environmental lending as a percent of the overall lending stagnated between 1995 and 2003, in some years even falling (IEG 2008). Between 2003 and 2008, however, loans directed specifically to improving the environment increased from 5 per cent to 11 per cent of overall lending (World Bank 2008). But the critique was also about process. Environmental groups were concerned that the World Bank still did not engage in adequate consultation with NGOs or with communities in which projects were taking place. A recent independent evaluation of the World Bank's environment lending has found its performance weak and has recommended further reform (IEG 2008).

As part of its efforts to green itself in the early 1990s, the World Bank also became the lead agency in the Global Environment Facility (GEF), a multilateral funding agency for developing countries created specifically to fund projects with global environmental benefits. The GEF provides grant funding to developing countries to cover the "incremental costs" of meeting obligations under international environmental agreements. These incremental costs refer to the additional costs incurred by developing countries to undertake projects with global benefits (Streck 2001). Projects that protect international waters, address climate change, and reduce ozone depletion, biodiversity loss, land degradation, and persistent organic pollutants are all eligible for GEF funding. In its early years the GEF was criticized by environmental groups for the same reasons they were dissatisfied with World Bank project lending in general (Fairman 1996).In the 1990s the GEF underwent restructuring which brought about more democratic decision-making procedures and more consultation with NGOs and affected communities, but critics remain skeptical of the organization (Horta *et al.* 2002).

Since the mid-1980s the World Bank has dramatically increased the amount it lends for general balance of payments support under programs of structural adjustment. These loans provide balance of payments financing in return for macro-economic policy change such as the liberalization of trade policies, the removal of subsidies, the opening up of investment policies, cuts to government expenditures, and currency devaluation. These measures are designed to help foster growth and improve the ability of developing countries to repay external debts. As it increased its lending for structural adjustment, the World Bank did not explicitly include environmental protection. The primary reason for this was because it was largely assumed that, since they were designed to promote economic growth, these policies would have an overall positive impact on the environment. But critics skeptical of economic globalization have made the argument that liberalization of developing country economies, combined with cuts to government spending, have contributed to a number of environmental problems. These include rising rates of deforestation associated with stepped-up efforts to increase timber exports in countries such as Brazil, Ghana, Cameroon, the Philippines, and Zambia (Toye 1991; George 1992). Liberalized investment policies have also led to more mining and the extraction of other natural resources, also seen to be responsible for growing environmental problems in a number of countries, such as the Philippines, Ecuador, and Guyana (FoE 1999).

Although the World Bank has been criticized for its adjustment policies and their impact on the environment, it has defended its record, indicating that in most cases the impact of this type of lending has been neutral and even positive (World Bank 1994). From the perspective of the pro-globalization camp, the removal of subsidies and other inefficiencies in the economy under programs of structural adjustment leads to more realistic prices for natural resources which better reflect their scarcity. Further, it is argued that economic liberalization has mainly encouraged production of export crops that have strong root systems – such as coffee, rubber, palm oil, and cocoa – which can help prevent soil erosion rather than contribute to land degradation.

While these debates have raged regarding the environmental impact of lending from multilateral development agencies such as the World Bank, other lending agencies have also had their environmental records questioned. In particular, export credit agencies (ECAs) provide developing countries with government-backed credit, investment guarantees, and insurance which are specifically tied to business contracts with companies based in the lending country (Rich 2000; Goldzimer 2003). Most industrialized countries have at least one export credit agency that they support – for example, the Ex-Im Bank and the US Overseas Private Investment Corporation in the United States, the Japan Bank for International Cooperation/International Financial Corporation in Japan, and Export Development Canada. Export credit agencies globally provide over US$400 billion in lending annually, with some US$55 billion of that going toward projects in developing countries (OECD 2007; FERN 2008). ECAs are extremely important global financial actors for developing countries, accounting for roughly a quarter of developing country debt owed to official creditors (FERN 2008).

ECAs have come under increased fire over the past decade for the environmental impact of their loans and the fact that they have few rules requiring environmental impact assessments and tend to operate in a somewhat secretive manner (Rich 2000). They have been particularly scrutinized because they are typically involved in risky ventures, among them the provision of financing and insurance for projects focused on the extraction of natural resources, including oil, gas, logging, and minerals as well as loans and contracts for large-scale dam, nuclear power, chemical plant, and road-building projects. The agencies based in the United States, because they have close links to the US Agency for International Development, are required to follow strict environmental standards. But those based in other countries do not have to follow such strict requirements. If an ECA from the US rejects a project on environmental grounds, that project can easily be taken up by another agency from another country. A classic case of this problem is the Three Gorges dam in China, which was funded by Canadian, German, Swedish, and Swiss ECAs after the US Ex-Im bank turned it down on environmental grounds (FoE *et al.* 1999). Following incidents such as this, environmental critics have stepped up their pressure on ECAs through the OECD to work toward a common set of environmental standards. In 1998 the OECD agreed to a statement regarding export credits and the environment, and in 2001 it adopted a voluntary framework for common approaches to environmental assessment and export credit finance. This framework was strengthened in 2003 and again in 2007 (OECD 2007).

Project financing provided to developing countries from private lending agencies has also been under increased scrutiny for its environmental implications (Wright and Rwabizambuga 2006). In this case, however, rather than reacting to specific high-profile campaigns organized by environmental groups, as dominated in the 1980s and 1990s, private banks adopted a voluntary code of conduct in keeping with a emerging trend of voluntary corporate initiatives as a means by which to promote sustainable development. Private banks in consultation with environmental groups and the International Finance Corporation, the private-sector lending arm of the World Bank, established the Equator Principles in 2003 to promote both environmental and social sustainability in developing country project finance. In the face of some critique from NGOs that they were too weak, the principles were revised and strengthened in 2006 (Equator Principles 2006). As of 2008, some fifty-nine private banking institutions had signed up to these principles, including some ECAs such as Export Development Canada (Cappon 2008).

Conclusion

Theoretical debates over the interactions between the global political economy and the environment continue and have not been resolved (Clapp and Dauvergne 2005). But, while proponents and critics of economic globalization maintain their differences on the forces underlying global economic relationships and their implications for environmental quality, in practice a "middle-ground" policy position has emerged on several fronts. On trade, many see the more explicit consideration of environmental issues in NAFTA, as well as the renewed interest in resolving potential conflicts between trade agreements and environmental agreements in the WTO, as evidence that, despite theoretical differences, practical policy solutions can be reached which address the concerns of both sides of the debate. Similarly, the ratcheting up of voluntary measures among firms and the self-greening of the World Bank and environmental codes of conduct for private banks and ECAs are seen to be acknowledgement that the environmental performance of these entities could stand to be improved. The fact that these newer measures have been designed in ways that can be monitored more easily than the practices of the past provides an opening to maintain pressure for continued improvement.

Recommended reading

Clapp, J., and Dauvergne, P. (2005) *Paths to a Green World: The Political Economy of the Global Environment*, Cambridge, MA: MIT Press.
Levy, D., and Newell, P. (eds) (2004) *The Business of Global Environmental Governance*, Cambridge, MA: MIT Press.
Neumayer, E. (2001) *Greening Trade and Investment: Environmental Protection without Protectionism*, London: Earthscan.
Sachs, W. (1999) *Planet Dialectics: Explorations in Environment and Development*, London: Zed Books.

References

Bhagwati, J. (1993) "The case for free trade," *Scientific American*, 269 (November): 42–9.
Biermann, F. (2000) "The case for a world environment organization," *Environment*, 42(9): 22–31.
Bruno, K. (2002) *Greenwash + 10: The UN's Global Compact, Corporate Accountability and the Johannesburg Earth Summit*, San Francisco: Corporate Watch. Available: www.corpwatch.org/article.php?id=1348 (accessed 22 December 2008).
Cappon, N. (2008) "Equator Principles: promoting greater responsibility in project financing," *Exportwise*, spring.
Cashore, B. (2002) "Legitimacy and the privatization of environmental governance: how non-state market-driven (NSMD) governance systems gain rule-making authority," *Governance*, 15(4): 503–29.
Charnovitz, S. (2007) "The WTO's environmental progress," *Journal of International Economic Law*, 10(3): 685–706.
Clapp, J. (2001) *Toxic Exports: The Transfer of Hazardous Wastes from Rich to Poor Countries*, Ithaca, NY: Cornell University Press.

—— (2002) "What the pollution havens debate overlooks," *Global Environmental Politics*, 2(2): 11–19.

—— (2005) "Global environmental governance for corporate responsibility and accountability," *Global Environmental Politics*, 5(3): 23–34.

Clapp, J., and Dauvergne, P. (2005) *Paths to a Green World: The Political Economy of the Global Environment*, Cambridge, MA: MIT Press.

Conca, K. (2000) "The WTO and the undermining of global environmental governance," *Review of International Political Economy*, 7(3): 484–94.

Daly, H. (1993) "The perils of free trade," *Scientific American*, 269 (November): 50–57.

—— (1996) *Beyond Growth: The Economics of Sustainable Development*, Boston: Beacon Press.

Daly, H. E., and Farley, J. (2003) *Ecological Economics: Principles and Applications*, Washington, DC: Island Press.

Dauvergne, P. (2001) *Loggers and Degradation in the Asia-Pacific: Corporations and Environmental Management*, Cambridge: Cambridge University Press.

—— (2008) *The Shadows of Consumption: Consequences for the Global Environment*, Cambridge, MA: MIT Press.

DeSombre, E. R., and Barkin, J. S. (2002) "Turtles and trade: the WTO's acceptance of environmental trade restrictions," *Global Environmental Politics*, 2(1): 12–18.

Equator Principles (2006) "The Equator Principles: a financial industry benchmark for determining, assessing and managing social & environmental risk in project financing". Available: www.equator-principles.com/documents/Equator_Principles.pdf (accessed 6 January 2009).

Esty, D. (1994) *Greening the GATT: Trade, Environment and the Future*, Washington, DC: Institute for International Economics.

—— (2001) "Bridging the trade–environment divide," *Journal of Economic Perspectives*, 15(3): 113–30.

Fairman, D. (1996) "The Global Environment Facility: haunted by the shadow of the future," in R. Keohane and M. Levy (eds), *Institutes for the Earth*, Cambridge, MA: MIT Press.

Falkner, R. (2003) "Private environmental governance and international governance: exploring the links," *Global Environmental Politics*, 3(2): 72–87.

FERN (2008) "Trade and investment – Export credit agencies: the need for binding guidelines". Available: www.fern.org/campaign_area_extension.html?clid=3&id=2783 (accessed 23 December 2008).

FoE (Friends of the Earth) (1999) *The IMF: Selling the Environment Short*. Available: www.foe.org/res/pubs/pdf/imf.pdf (accessed 6 January 2009).

FoE *et al.* (1999) *A Race to the Bottom: Creating Risk, Generating Debt, and Guaranteeing Environmental Destruction*. Available: www.eca-watch.org/eca/race_bottom.pdf (accessed 23 December 2008).

Fuchs, D. (2005) *Understanding Business Power in Global Governance*, Baden-Baden: Nomos.

George, S. (1992) *The Debt Boomerang*, London: Pluto Press.

Georgescu-Roegen, N. (1971) *The Entropy Law and the Economic Process*, Cambridge, MA: Havard University Press.

Goldzimer, A. (2003) "Worse than the World Bank? Export credit agencies – the secret engine of globalization," *Food First Backgrounder*, 9(1). Available: www.foodfirst.org/pubs/backgrdrs/2003/w03v9n1.pdf (accessed 23 December 2008).

Grossman, G., and Krueger, A. (1995) "Economic growth and the environment," *Quarterly Journal of Economics*, May: 353–77.

Holme, R., and Watts, P. (2000) *Corporate Social Responsibility: Making Good Business Sense*, Geneva: World Business Council for Sustainable Development.

Horta, K., Round, R., and Young, Z. (2002) *The Global Environmental Facility: The First Ten Years – Growing Pains or Inherent Flaws?* Washington, DC, and Ottawa: Environmental Defense and the Halifax Initiative.

IEG (Independent Evaluation Group of the World Bank) (2008) *Environmental Sustainability: An Evaluation of World Bank Group Support*, Washington, DC: World Bank.

Levy, D., and Newell, P. (eds) (2005) *The Business of Global Environmental Governance*, Cambridge, MA: MIT Press.

Mabogunje, A. (2002) "Poverty and environmental degradation: challenges within the global economy," *Environment*, 44(1): 9–18.

Mani, M., and Wheeler, D. (1998) "In search of pollution havens? Dirty industry in the world economy, 1960–93," *Journal of Environment and Development*, 7(3): 215–47.

Mumme, S. (2007) "Trade integration, neoliberal reform, and environmental protection in Mexico: lessons for the Americas," *Latin American Perspectives*, 34(3): 91–107.

Najam, A. (2003) "The case against a new international environment organization," *Global Governance*, 9: 367–84.

Neumayer, E. (2001) *Greening Trade and Investment: Environmental Protection without Protectionism*, London: Earthscan.

—— (2004) *Weak versus Strong Sustainability: Exploring the Limits of Two Opposing Paradigms*, 2nd ed., Cheltenham: Edward Elgar.

OECD (2007) *About Environment and Export Credits*, Paris: OECD. Available: www.oecd.org/document/26/0,3343,en_2649_34181_39960154_1_1_1_1,00.html (accessed 23 December 2008).

Porter, G. (1999) "Trade competition and pollution standards: 'race to the bottom' or 'Stuck at the Bottom'?," *Journal of Environment and Development*, 8(2): 133–51.

Prakash, A., and Potoski, M. (2006) *The Voluntary Environmentalists: Green Clubs, ISO 14001, and Voluntary Environmental Regulations*, Cambridge: Cambridge University Press.

Reed, D. (1997) "The environmental legacy of Bretton Woods: the World Bank," in O. R. Young (ed.), *Global Governance: Drawing Insights from the Environmental Experience*, Cambridge (MA): MIT Press.

Rich, B. (1994) *Mortgaging the Earth: The World Bank, Environmental Impoverishment, and the Crisis of Development*, London: Earthscan.

—— (2000) "Exporting destruction," *Environmental Forum*, September–October: 32–40.

Sachs, W. (1999) *Planet Dialectics: Explorations in Environment and Development*, London: Zed Books.

Sklair, L. (2001) *The Transnational Capitalist Class*, Oxford: Blackwell.

Soloway, J. (2002) "The North American Free Trade Agreement: alternative models of managing trade and the environment," in R. Steinberg (ed.), *The Greening of Trade Law: International Trade Organizations and Environmental Issues*, Lanham, MD: Rowman & Littlefield.

Stilwell, M., and Tarasofsky, R. (2001) *Towards Coherent Environmental and Economic Governance: Legal and Practical Approaches to MEA–WTO Linkages*, Gland and Conches, Switzerland: WWF and CIEL. Available: www.ciel.org/Publications/Coherent_EnvirEco_Governance.pdf.

Streck, C. (2001) "The Global Environment Facility: a role model for international governance?," *Global Environmental Politics*, 1(2): 71–94.

Toye, J. (1991) "Ghana," in P. Mosley, J. Harrigan, and J. Toye (eds), *Aid and Power*, Volume 2, London: Routledge.

UNCTAD (2008) *World Investment Report 2008: Transnational Corporations and Export Competitiveness*. New York: United Nations.

Utting, P. (2005) *Rethinking Business Regulation: From Self-Regulation to Social Control*, UNRISD Paper, No. 15. Available: www.unrisd.org.

—— (2008) "Social and environmental liabilities of transnational corporations: new directions, opportunities and constraints," in P. Utting and J. Clapp (eds), *Corporate Accountability and Sustainable Development*, Delhi: Oxford University Press.

Utting, P., and Clapp, J. (2008) "Corporate responsibility, accountability and law: an introduction," in P. Utting and J. Clapp (eds), *Corporate Accountability and Sustainable Development*, Delhi: Oxford University Press.

Wade, R. (1997) "Greening the bank: the struggle over the environment, 1970–95," in J. Lewis and R. Webb (eds), *The World Bank: Its First Half Century*, Volume 2, Washington DC: Brookings Institution.

Wheeler, D. (2002) "Beyond pollution havens," *Global Environmental Politics*, 2(20): 1–10.

Williams, M. (2001) "In search of global standards: the political economy of trade and the environment," in D. Stevis and V. Assetto (eds), *The International Political Economy of the Environment: Critical Perspectives*, Boulder, CO: Lynne Rienner.

World Bank (1992) *World Development Report 1992*. New York: Oxford University Press.

—— (1994) *Adjustment in Africa: Reforms, Results and the Road Ahead*, Oxford: Oxford University Press.

—— (2008) *The World Bank Annual Report 2008: Year in Review*, Oxford: Oxford University Press. Available: http://siteresources.worldbank.org/EXTANNREP2K8/Resources/YR00_Year_in_Review_English.pdf (accessed 22 December 2008).

Wright, C., and Rwabizambuga, A. (2006) "Institutional pressures, corporate reputation and voluntary codes of conduct: an examination of the equator principles," *Business and Society Review*, 111(1): 89–117.

WTO (World Trade Organization) (2007) *International Trade Statistics 2007*, Geneva: WTO.

Young, O. (2008) "The architecture of global environmental governance: bringing science to bear on policy," *Global Environmental Politics*, 8(1): 14–32.

4   Environmental security

Shlomi Dinar

Of the various topical issues often associated with the non-traditional security school (i.e. disease, immigration, poverty, etc.), the environment has received the most scrutiny. Pundits, policy-makers, and academics have all reflected on the so-called environmental security subfield. Lester Brown's (1977) Worldwatch piece is probably most recognized for bringing this issue to the fore. But writings have generally taken two opposing sides in discussing the relationship between security and the environment.

Generally, proponents of linking the terms "environment" and "security" point to the roots of resource scarcity and environmental degradation in promoting intrastate and interstate violent conflict and wars. Both theoretical and empirical studies have considered this relationship, particularly in the developing world (Homer-Dixon 1999; Hauge and Ellingsen 1998). The link between the environment and human security has likewise been touted (Najam 2003). To that extent, these non-traditionalist thinkers believe that the traditional definition of security, restricted to the polemics of state sovereignty, military affairs between states, and the threat of interstate war as a function of threats to territorial integrity, should be expanded to include other issues, such as the environment (Mathews 1989). These analysts have also regarded the linkage itself important in elevating environmental issues to the forefront of national security affairs, creating the political urgency to resolve environmental problems (Ullman 1983).

Critics of the linkage between the concepts of environment and security generally dismiss the relationship on several grounds. First and foremost, these analysts (regarded as traditionalist thinkers) believe that expanding the definition of security, as it is traditionally regarded, threatens the viability and parsimoniousness of the concept (Walt 1991). Others criticize the link, claiming that the environment is antithetical to everything society often regards as security, and for that reason connecting the two concepts will prevent us from thinking critically about dealing with environmental problems (Deudney 1999).

Another important, yet often forgotten, element of discussion is the cooperative side of the environment and security coin (Diehl and Gleditsch 2001: 4). In other words, security is likewise advanced if successful cooperation resolves a particular environmental dispute which may contribute to instability or reduces the well-being of countries (Esty 1999; Brock 1992).

If cooperation (like conflict) is to become an important analytical concept in the subfield of environmental security, then we must better understand how and when scarcity and degradation affect interstate coordination and how environmental negotiations succeed or fail (Ostrom *et al.* 1999; Young 1989, 1994; Barrett 2003). Since international environmental negotiations often take place among asymmetric and unequal parties, understanding how such country differences may challenge environmental cooperation is also paramount. Consequently, including such elements of bargaining and treaty design in the study of cooperation allows for a more comprehensive consideration of the concept of environmental security and likewise highlights its important place in the larger field of global environmental politics.

Environment and security in context

The subfield of environmental security emanated from a flurry of interest in environmental issues and related writings that appeared in the late 1960s and early 1970s. Writings by Paul Ehrlich (1968) and Garrett Hardin (1968) underscored the magnitude of the environmental crisis related to such issues as exponential population growth and the "tragedy of the commons." At the same time, the 1972 United Nations Conference on the Environment held in Stockholm – and the related Stockholm Declaration (UNEP 1972) – placed environmental issues on the global agenda, setting the stage for such important international institutions as the United Nations Environmental Programme (Matthew 1999: 4). This important institutional development later ushered in another global meeting, the 1992 Conference on Environment and Development in Rio de Janeiro – and the related Rio Declaration (UNEP 1992) – which also elaborated on the concept of sustainable development (Matthew 1999: 5).

According to Dabelko (2004: 3), however, interest in environment and security issues truly solidified in the mid-1990s. For one, the findings of Thomas Homer-Dixon's investigation into the links between environmental scarcity and acute conflict were published in the influential scholarly journal *International Security* (Homer-Dixon 1991, 1994). In 1994, the *Atlantic Monthly* featured Robert Kaplan's provocative article "The coming anarchy" (Kaplan 1994), which also brought the topic of environmental security to the wider public and policy circles by considering how environmental change was leading to intrastate and interstate conflicts.

That same year the term "human security" was touted by the United Nations Development Programme, through its *Human Development Report*, emphasizing the security of the individual with linkages to the environment. Perhaps most striking in the more recent history of environmental security, however, was the establishment of the Environmental Change and Security Program (ECSP) at the Woodrow Wilson International Center for Scholars in 1994. To this day, ECSP has been transcending both the academic and policy worlds in an effort to bring attention and focus to the security aspects of environmental change, conflict, and cooperation (Dabelko 2004: 3).

Interestingly, throughout the evolution of the concept of environmental security, and its interconnected issue areas, a lively debate has been taking place in the background. In particular, scholars and policy-makers have been deliberating the utility and ramifications of linking the terms "environment" and "security." This debate has been couched in a more general discussion between so-called traditionalists and non-traditionalists of security studies.

Debating environment and security: traditionalists, non-traditionalists, critics, and proponents

The debate between traditional security thinkers and non-traditional security thinkers stems largely from the various assumptions each side makes about international politics and the importance each side places on particular actors and phenomena in the international system. Yet the academic debate has also had its share of influence on policy. Rothschild (1995: 57–9) identifies four such impacts: providing direction and guidance to policies of government officials; guiding public opinion about policy; contesting existing principles; and influencing directly the distribution of money and power. These four principles have likewise undergirded the debate between scholars who support linking "environment" and "security" and those who oppose it.

Traditionalists and non-traditionalists

Traditionalists argue in favor of the primacy of military security as a goal of nation-states (Morgenthau 1948: 121). Accordingly, security is the study of the threat, use, and control of military force. The field of security studies, according to traditionalists, explores the conditions that make the use of force more likely and the policies that states adopt in order to prepare for, prevent, or engage in war (Walt 1991: 212). Given the anarchic international system, military security and survival are paramount and should supersede other non-military issues (Waltz 1979: 126). Based on a realist world view, the traditionalist argument holds that the nation-state is the ultimate unit of analysis, defending itself in a self-help system.

Non-traditionalists expand the definition of security to encompass a variety of threats faced by nations, individuals, and the international system. Wolfers, for example, is quick to point out that the security concerns of traditionalists, while legitimate, should not crowd out other issues of import. In fact, despite the realist and neo-realist contentions that a state's "survival" is paramount, not all states are faced with the same degree of danger and consequently do not act uniformly (Wolfers 1952: 486). In other words, states face different dangers and concerns that in turn affect their individual security.

As a challenge to the military-centric and state-centric view of traditionalists, non-traditionalists support the essence of complex interdependence, essentially arguing that there is no hierarchy of issues and that military security should not consistently dominate the agenda (Keohane and Nye 1989: 24–5). Buzan *et al.* (1998), for example, maintain that the field of security studies should be reconceptualized beyond the limits placed on it by traditional scholars. Security involves perceived threats to the survival of some highly valued referent object. Such objects may involve state and non-state actors, abstract principles, and nature itself. The authors also submit that threats may come from various sources, including other states or natural phenomena and trends such as the environment (ibid.: 23). In another attempt to define security more broadly, Ullman (1983) has suggested that a danger to national security is that which: a) threatens drastically and over a brief span of time to degrade the quality of life for the inhabitants of a state, and b) threatens significantly to narrow the range of policy choices available to the government and different groups within the state. The definition of security has also been expanded to account for the individual and the community, rather than just the nation-state (UNDP 1994; Suhrke 1999; Najam 2003).

Non-traditionalists are steadfast in their claim that the traditional school of security studies seems poorly equipped to deal with the realities of the post-Cold War world, maintaining a narrow military conception of national security that excludes other public policy goals. Its sole preoccupation with military statecraft and sovereignty limits its ability to address the many foreign and domestic problems that either are not amenable to military solutions or that underlie interstate or intra-state problems and lead to conflict, military or otherwise (Baldwin 1997: 16; Ullman 1983: 133–5). Haftendorn (1991) concurs, arguing that the traditionalist definition of security doesn't describe current security affairs. What is needed, she asserts, is a new paradigm of security that can explain changes in various regions and is not limited to a single issue area or level of analysis (ibid.: 12–13).

Traditionalists, on the other hand, claim that, while issues unrelated to war (such as disease, poverty, and the environment) are important, they should not be regarded as part of the definition of security as they "destroy its intellectual coherence and make it more difficult to devise solutions to any of these important problems" (Walt 1991: 213). Paris (2001: 88), criticizing the concept of human security, claims that the definition tends to be too expansive and vague, encompassing a multitude of physical and psychological aspects. In turn, this impreciseness leaves policy-makers with little guidance in the prioritization of competing policy goals and academics with little sense of what needs to be studied.

The environmental component of security studies has been couched largely in the context of the non-traditional school. Yet debate has raged here as well, with regard to linking these two concepts. Interestingly, circles of the environmentally concerned have voiced the most reservations (Soroos 1994: 319).

Environmental security: proponents and critics

PROPONENTS

Environmental security issues have generally transcended the individual, national, and international levels. On the individual level, scholars have argued that environmental change may undermine human security by reducing access to, and the quality of, natural resources that are important to sustain livelihoods (Renner 1996; Barnett et al. 2008; Barnett and Adger 2007). On the national or intrastate level, scholars have considered the manner by which resource scarcity and environmental degradation have their social effects and in turn could lead to violent conflicts within states, either among differing ethnic groups or among certain classes of society vying for scarce resources (Homer-Dixon 1999).[1] Accordingly, environmental change could have alarming repercussions, particularly when these threaten political outcomes affecting the viability of state boundaries, state institutions, or governing elites, or when they weaken the capacity of states and regimes to act effectively (Mathews 1989: 175; Myers 1993: 24–5; Ullman 1983: 141–3). While it is more likely that environmental degradation tends to affect human security or instigate violent intrastate conflict in the developing world, indirect effects could very well be felt in the developed world. Scholars have suggested that the consequence of environmental degradation and violent conflict (such as migration waves, impacts on trade, and regime instability) could affect the developed world, both politically and economically, and its policies toward the developing world (de Serbinin 1995; Esty 1999; Allenby 2000; Ferraro 2003; Rice et al. 2006).

On the international level, studies have claimed that resource scarcity and degradation could likewise lead to violent conflict between states and, at the very worst, wars (Westing 1986; Mandel 1988; Bächler and Spillman 1996; Bächler 1998; Klare 2001). Other studies have taken a more nuanced approach to the study of interstate conflict over resource scarcity and environmental degradation, considering the political and non-violent disputes that take place and their relationship to security (Goldstone 2001; Lipschutz and Holdren 1990). The effects of climate change, transboundary air pollution, and biodiversity depletion have been analyzed largely in this context (Benedick 1998; NICGC 2000; McNeely 2005; IPCC 2007; Jopp and Kaestner 2008).[2]

Beyond theoretical and case-study approaches that have contributed to the study of environmental security, empirical works have also provided great insight – further attesting to the security aspects of environmental issues across a large spectrum of observations. The majority of these empirical studies consider the intrastate nature of violence as a consequence of resource scarcity and environmental degradation, while the majority of the studies that consider the relationship in an interstate context investigate conflict over freshwater and international rivers.

Hauge and Ellingsen (1998) provide perhaps one of the first large quantitative examinations of the environment–conflict contention. While their work pertains to the intrastate level, the authors find a positive correlation between such variables as water scarcity, deforestation, and civil conflict. More recently, Levy *et al.* (2005) consider the effects of climate change on civil wars. The authors find that decreased rainfall has a positive effect on intrastate conflicts. Finding somewhat weaker results for the effects of climate change on civil conflict, Raleigh and Urdal (2007) reveal that such variables as population growth, population density, water scarcity, and land degradation have, nonetheless, a very moderate effect on the risk of civil conflict.

Building on Choucri and North's (1975) lateral pressure theory, Tir and Diehl (1998) find a modest relationship between population pressures (which accelerate resource depletion and decrease economic growth) and the likelihood of interstate conflict. Focusing on shared rivers, Toset *et al.* (2000: 992–3) find that, while water scarcity is not necessarily the only, or the main, issue in explaining armed conflict, "low availability of water in both countries of the dyad is significantly related to disputes." Although Gleditsch *et al.* (2006: 376) find some ambiguity pertaining to this relationship, their findings suggest that countries experiencing low average rainfall have a higher risk of interstate conflict. Specifically, focusing on competing claims over cross-border rivers, Hensel *et al.* (2006: 390) also conclude that interstate militarized disputes are more likely to take place in regions where water is more scarce. The authors contend that resource-poor areas are environments where the creation of institutions to manage conflict will be lacking and/or ineffective (ibid.: 385, 388, 408–9). Specifically, between the years 1900 and 2001 the authors find seventeen occasions where water disputes turned violent.

True for most all of the above-mentioned studies are the associated political and economic factors that are likewise important for understanding conflict. This does not deny the importance of environmental factors in explaining conflict or instability but does suggest that economic and political variables often exacerbate (or mitigate) conflict. Therefore, the extent to which resource sovereignty is ill-defined, the governing regime does not employ farsighted decisions vis-à-vis environmental stewardship, the country suffers from relative underdevelopment, existing institutions are weak or debilitated by political turmoil, and that environmental change outpaces the capacity of existing institutions to deal with that change, will affect the extent and severity of conflict (Gleditsch 1998; Giordano *et al.* 2005).

CRITICS

Scholars that criticize the environment and security link often adopt the traditional definition of security. Consequently, they claim that, if all the forces that threaten life, property, and well-being are considered as threats to national security, the term itself will be drained of any meaning (Deudney 1991: 23–4). Deudney (1999), for example, suggests that it is analytically misleading to think of environmental degradation as a national security threat because the traditional focus of national security has little in common with environmental problems or solutions. Furthermore, by depicting the environment as a legitimate security concern, scholars may help justify military action on environmental grounds (Brock 1992: 95). Since traditional security is likewise associated with nationalism and sovereignty, attempts to harness global action, which environmental problems demand, are undermined. In other words, environmental problems and solutions are global in nature and are therefore the antithesis of the nation-state just as much as the nation-state is the antithesis of the emerging global environmental agenda (Stern 1999: 138).

Finally, such scholars also claim that environmental degradation is not likely to cause interstate wars (Deudney 1999; Barnett 2000). Rather, human ingenuity mitigates against conflict in the face of scarcity (Simon 1981). Other rejectionists of the connection between environment and security also tend to dismiss any direct causal link between environmental problems and security. They cite the (above-mentioned) political, economic, and institutional components of a state or society as more important in understanding how violent conflicts may take place. Despite acknowledgement by proponents that political and economic factors indeed play an important role in explaining the likelihood of conflict (Homer-Dixon and Levy 1995–6), critics still claim that it is often very difficult to isolate those environmental components or that environmental degradation merely serves as a side effect. To the extent that environmental change is causative rather than associative, the tangled chains of causation may prove to be intractable for analysis or turn out to be highly situation-dependent (Critchley and Terriff 1993: 337).

Critics also claim that those who link environmental issues with security studies are engaged in a rhetorical ploy simply to depict environmental issues in a new manner. They view this effort as an attempt to hijack the security issue in order to capture the attention of politicians and the public, both of whom, they believe, may pay deference to it (Levy 1995: 45).

Another criticism considers the Northern biases of the term "environmental security." In other words, globalization, modernity, industrialization, and the diffusion of global capital have had serious economic, political, and environmental effects on the global South or developing world. To that extent, by using the concept of environmental security the industrialized world is essentially maintaining the status quo rather than acknowledging the essential changes that need to be undertaken to alleviate environmental problems. In addition, the focus should be on the global North – to a large degree the main producer of such environmental problems (Barnett 2000; Dalby 2002; Watts 2004).

Finally, it is also claimed that, because environmental degradation may actually lead to cooperation and joint efforts by countries to deal with that degradation, the environment simply cannot be associated with a concept such as security (Thorsell 1990; Deudney 1999; Barnett 2000). In other words, environmental issues engender global action, interdependence, and international cooperation while the concept of security engenders such ideas as sovereignty and nationalism.

Concluding thoughts on the debate

Clearly, the concept of environmental security has invited much debate. Yet critics of the term seem to focus principally on realist influences pertaining to the security field. This may be unwarranted. First, the concept of security has always been characterized by a relatively ambiguous definition (Wolfers 1952; Goldstone 1996). In fact, considering the history of the concept of security reveals its multifaceted and multilevel dimensions, which included the individual and the state (Rothschild 1995: 62–3, 66–7; Brauch 2008: 75–6). Second, the concept of security does not necessitate a sole focus on the state. The lens is also open to non-state actors and domestic forces. Indeed, environmental issues require the participation of a multitude of actors so as to achieve effective implementation of environmental governance (see, for example, Conca 2006). Still, this does not deny the important role of the state in international environmental stewardship, especially given the transboundary nature of many environmental problems and the need for coordinated state action. Third, perhaps one of the most important contributions of the concept of environmental security has been to elevate environmental issues to the realm of high politics and the public interest (Græger

1996: 111). Presently, climate change is high on the agenda, as evidenced, for example, in the recent National Intelligence Assessment (House of Representatives 2008). While the Assessment finds that few direct effects of climate change will be felt in the United States before 2030, the most significant impact will be in the form of climate-driven events on other countries, which will affect these states' economic development levels, agricultural productivity, and lead to out-migration. This will in turn have security ramifications for the United States. (Whether the securitization of climate change has had the desired effects on policy-making, however, is yet to be seen.)

Finally, and as is the focus of the following section, it is precisely because environmental degradation and resource scarcity necessitate and motivate cooperation, and cooperation in turn may reduce instability, that the concepts of environment and security are not in opposition to one another. Environmental collective prevention and environmental collective defense (Soroos 1994: 323–4) are at the heart of international cooperation and in turn are at the core of environmental security. As Pirages and DeGeest (2004) contend, ecological change and increasing environmental vulnerability are progressively shaping the future of an emerging global system. These environmental phenomena necessitate an eco-revolutionary perspective that requires foresight and anticipatory thinking to "avoid the harsh consequences of failing to recognize emerging problems and issues that could generate tragedies in the long run" (ibid.: 5–6). These consequences are linked to globalization, famine, development strategies, and the gap between North and South. At the same time, promoting ecological security requires a type of global governance inclusive of non-governmental organizations and international institutions. Simultaneously, a coherent governance is likewise necessary in forging agreements that deal with the many issues related to ecological security (ibid.: 226).

Cooperation, security, and the environment

Telling for this general debate between traditional and non-traditional security scholars and opponents and proponents of the environmental security term are Benjamin Miller's thoughts on the definition of security. Miller, a realist, seems to depart from the traditional perspective of security studies, suggesting that realists make two errors by minimizing the concept. First, they de-emphasize peace as an important component of the security field and, second, they diminish non-military causes or means affecting national as well as regional and international security (Miller 2001: 14). In line with the above discussion on environmental security, Miller claims that "environmental degradation should be part of the security field only to the extent that environmental factors affect the likelihood of armed conflict, namely war and peace" (ibid.).

Indeed, Miller departs from the main traditionalist qualms relevant to expanding the concept of security by emphasizing peace and non-military causes of international (in)stability. To that extent he seems to be in agreement with some of the above scholars who consider how natural resources or resource scarcity may lead to interstate and intrastate violent conflict. However, since Miller considers only the occurrence (or absence) of war and violence as the dependent variable to depict the nature of security, he dismisses other important elements. Ignored are circumstances or environmental issues that transcend simple violent conflict, such as conflicts of interest or political disputes (Goldstone 2001). In addition, while Miller discusses the value of the peace side of the security coin, he effectively ignores another important component of that same side – cooperation. In other words, other elements associated with peace and stability more generally, such as interstate cooperation on other common fronts such as the environment, are sidelined (Conca and Dabelko 2002;

Brauch 2008: 71–4). Since environmental issues may cause conflict or instability, resolving them is equally important. Given that countries are interdependent by the sheer environmental resources that they share, diplomacy, cooperation, and regulatory regimes are necessary to manage these resources and coordinate state actions (Mathews 1989: 174–7).

While some evidence exists as to the relationship between environmental change, resource scarcity, and interstate conflict, there seems to be more support for the argument that (formal) violent conflict over scarce resources is a relative anomaly in the international (interstate) arena. Interestingly, this claim is also in line with the ideas of those critics of the concept of environmental security (Deudney 1999; Barnett 2000; Dalby 2002). This assessment is most clear in the context of freshwater, as academia has largely rejected the popular "water wars" theory (Wolf and Hamner 2000). In particular, Wolf and Hamner have claimed that "the more valuable lesson of international water is as a source whose characteristics tend to induce cooperation and incite violence only in the exception" (ibid.: 66).

Yet just because physical violence on the interstate level is not likely to be a result of resource scarcity or environmental degradation does not mean security is uncompromised. This type of non-violent conflict, a consequence of environmental degradation and resource scarcity, is likewise relevant for the concept of security as it may create regional and international tensions or perhaps exacerbate other existing tensions unrelated to the environment. Depending on the environmental issue or the respective resource under discussion, such political tensions are especially likely to escalate further in regions with less institutional capacity or a less salient history of cooperation among the protagonists. It is perhaps of little surprise that the great majority of escalated interstate tensions over freshwater, for example, have taken place in the Middle East, North Africa, and Central Asia (Horsman 2001; Hensel *et al.* 2006). As mentioned above, other environmental goods and resources, which are more likely to instigate political dispute between states, or have various consequences for security, include climate change, ozone depletion, transboundary air pollution, and biodiversity. Cooperation, in turn, may work to reduce those non-violent (or violent) tensions and consequently advance regional and international stability and security.

Recall that various critics of the environmental security concept made exactly this claim in an effort to discount the relationship between the concepts of environment and security. Daniel Deudney (1999: 203) asserts that "analysts of environmental conflict do not systematically consider ways in which environmental scarcity or change can stimulate cooperation." Barnett (2000: 274) agrees, claiming that the majority of studies in this area have given the ontological priority to conflict over cooperation.

As enumerated above, however, critics overlook such aspects of environmental cooperation as relevant for the concept of security. In fact, it is precisely because regional and international stability may be advanced – if successful cooperation and regime creation resolve a particular environmental dispute – that a strong case may exist for linking environment and security (Brock 1992; Esty 1999). By some accounts such cooperation also advances trust among states, establishes cooperative habits, creates shared regional identities around shared resources, and establishes mutually recognized rights and expectations (Conca *et al.* 2005).

In conclusion, it is possible that, the more pressing environmental issues become, the less likely they are to be resolved. In line with Malthusian and realist thinking, such environmental issues may encourage some type of interstate conflict (Haas 1990: 38). Such conflict is also a function of the interdependence ascribed to states, given the sheer environmental resources they share, as they attempt to reduce their dependence on each other (Waltz 1979: 106, 154–5). However, it is just as plausible that the interdependence of states vis-à-vis a given environmental resource, combined with an urgency to act, motivates cooperation.

Whether it be harnessing a transboundary resource more efficiently or resolving a trans-boundary pollution problem, environmental interdependence creates a relationship in which neither riparian may act without some type of coordination with the other party.

Interstate coordination, as a result of scarcity and degradation, may in turn necessitate the establishment of international institutions and regimes so as to facilitate environmental cooperation. Analyzing institutionalized cooperation, in turn, necessitates an understanding of how such regimes evolve, including the factors that may inhibit or facilitate such coordination. In fact, it is in this context of regime formation, with the goal of environmental protection or resource allocation in mind, that a connection between the subfield of environmental security and the more general field of global environmental politics is highlighted.

Scarcity, cooperation, and international bargaining

If cooperation is to be considered an essential and equal counterpart to the conflict side of the environmental security coin, then several dimensions must be accounted for. First and foremost, further systematic investigation is needed into the conditions and levels/degrees of scarcity and degradation that may facilitate cooperation across various environmental resources (Dinar 2010). In reference to transboundary water issues, for example, such a research agenda has begun to take shape, with both theoretical (Wolf and Hamner 2000; Dinar 2009) and empirical works (Hamner 2009; Brochman and Hensel 2009; Tir and Ackerman 2009) exploring the effects of scarcity on interstate cooperation.

While scarcity and degradation may work to encourage interstate coordination, understanding the evolution of institutionalized cooperation also requires consideration of the development of regime formation. Although Chapter 1 of this book has gone into great detail discussing regime theory and global governance, several elements important for understanding environmental regime formation are highlighted here. In fact, one major factor that often complicates cooperation in the case of transboundary environmental resources is the asymmetric context in which states interact (Susskind 1994: 18–19). Understanding how these asymmetries, or differences among the parties, are overcome, either through bargaining strategy or treaty design (Young 1994: 128, 132–3; Raustiala and Victor 1998: 696), is thus likewise paramount for a more comprehensive understanding of environmental security. Two important asymmetries are mentioned below.

The first type of country asymmetry is the economic differences among the parties. Such differences likewise have ramifications for the way in which states consider the effects of pollution or environmental degradation, with poorer countries often prioritizing more pressing issues over environmental protection (Barkin and Shambaugh 1999a: 13; 1999b: 178). Environmental protection is also expensive to institute, and poorer countries do not necessarily have all the means to engage in, say, pollution abatement. To that extent, a regional or global regime that would potentially be devised for the sake of environmental stewardship may be affected, as one party may sense more urgency to deal with an environmental problem compared with another.

The case of ozone depletion, and the 1987 Montreal Protocol, is very instructive when considering economic asymmetries and cooperation. From a security perspective, the consequences of ozone depletion could be potentially grave and life threatening. A depleted ozone layer would essentially mean that more ultra-violet radiation would enter the Earth, resulting in more skin cancer cases, lower yields in agriculture, and an increase in smog. When the ozone regime was first conceived, richer and developed countries were relatively more eager and ready to conclude a regime over the abatement of chlorofluorocarbons (CFCs) – the main chemical agents found to be depleting the ozone layer. Major developing countries, on the other hand, played a very minor role in the initial negotiations, largely because they did not see the benefits in cooperation relative to the costs of abatement they would have to incur (Barrett 2003: 346). Over time, however, it was becoming increasingly clear that, without the participation of large developing countries (and CFC producers and consumers) such as India and China, efforts by the developed world to reduce the effects of CFCs on the ozone layer would be inadequate in the long run. The bargaining strength of the developing world was thus affected. In 1990 the original protocol was amended to include a compensation clause incentivizing participation by developing countries. In this particular case, side payments (and technical assistance in the form of technology transfers) to developing countries offset the economic asymmetries that in turn challenged cooperation.

A second type of asymmetry pertains to the geographical location of the respective countries along the resource commons (Giordano 2003: 371–2). In the case of transboundary water or transboundary air pollution, this is quite apparent. Upstream or upwind states are often able to pollute, or simply to control the source (in the case of river water), while assuming fewer of the pollution costs, which are more often felt by downstream or downwind countries. If a poorer country is likewise located upstream, this could further exacerbate the problem, since the richer downstream or downwind state has a much lower tolerance for pollution.

The case of transboundary rivers, and specifically the Syr Darya and Amu Darya rivers in Central Asia, provides a very instructive lesson when assessing geographical asymmetry. From an environmental security standpoint, the Aral Sea Basin (in which the Syr Darya and Amu Darya are situated) not only supports 75 percent of Central Asia's population but contributes to the region's irrigated agriculture, particularly cotton production – the leading source of income for a number of those countries downstream, including Uzbekistan, Kazakhstan, and Turkmenistan. Hydropower, or the use of water for electricity production, provides another mode of economic development for upstream states such as Kyrgyzstan and Tajikistan. In general, the issue of water allocation and utilization has produced great political tensions in the region, which have escalated frequently into bellicose rhetoric and occasionally to military threats (Horsman 2001: 71–7). When these five republics gained independence from the Soviet Union in 1992, the problem of conflicting uses of water (cotton production versus hydropower generation) from the two rivers immediately surfaced and cooperation was inhibited. Given the underlying geographical and usage differences among the parties, a strategy that can best be described as 'issue linkage' was eventually sought as a means to offset the asymmetry. Thus, in return for timely releases of water in the spring and summer (the cotton-growing season), Kyrgyzstan would receive coal and natural gas in compensation for not being able to release these waters in the winter so as to generate hydroelectricity for its own energy needs. While this strategy of issue linkage in the context of the Aral Sea Basin is noteworthy (Weinthal 2002: 114; McKinney 2004: 199, 218), it is imperative to note that problems among the countries pertaining to conflicting uses of the two rivers have continued. Interestingly, some analysts have argued that the barter arrangements in place should be replaced with financial compensation or side payments from downstream states to upstream states to foster more efficient and stable cooperation (Mamatkanov 2008).

Conclusion

This chapter considered the history of the concept of environmental security and in that context provided some of the key arguments of the traditional and non-traditional schools of security studies. In this framework, the debate between proponents and critics of the concept of environmental security was also highlighted. While this latter debate is entrenched in various philosophical differences and policy consequences of associating the terms "environment" and "security," the two camps of the debate seem to agree on the importance of cooperation in the context of environmental degradation and resource scarcity. In short, while one side considers the interstate violent conflict that can erupt over scarce resources and environmental change, it also reflects on the importance of international treaties and interstate coordination in resolving the property rights disputes that are the catalyst for such conflicts. The other side of the debate, on the other hand, criticizes the relationship between violent conflict and resource scarcity, pointing instead to the cooperative-inducing characteristics of scarcity and degradation. While some empirical studies have demonstrated that resource scarcity and environmental degradation are correlated in some fashion with interstate militarized affairs, more support exists for the claim that violent conflict between states over resource scarcity is the exception rather than the rule. Of course, this is not the case for conflicts of interest between states, which proliferate across a multitude of environmental issues. Yet, even in such non-violent cases, conflict often leads to cooperation, and interstate coordination may work to increase trust among countries and increase regional and international stability, broadly defined. In other words, resource scarcity and environmental change, and the consequent interdependencies such conditions magnify, motivate cooperation between states so as to deal with the respective environmental problem.

As this chapter further attests, cooperation as a result of resource scarcity and environmental degradation is an important part of the environmental security paradigm. However, with very few exceptions, this area of research has been largely understudied. As previous scholars have reiterated, cooperation is an important side of the environment and security coin, yet it is often overshadowed by studies on conflict and the environment. It is also important to recognize how additional factors play a role in motivating (or inhibiting) cooperation. In particular, understanding how country differences affect negotiations, and in turn influence cooperation, is further related to the study of environmental security. Moreover, examining which mechanisms can be employed (i.e. side payments, issue linkage, and other types of treaty design components) to encourage cooperation (in light of these asymmetries) is likewise relevant for a comprehensive discussion of environment and security.

Indeed, acknowledging and emphasizing the peace and cooperation side of the security coin (in addition to the conflict side) is crucial for a more comprehensive understanding and use of the concept of environmental security. Consequently, bringing the cooperative element to the fore may bridge the gap between those proponents of the environmental security concept and its critics. Perhaps most importantly, by considering the cooperation side of the resource scarcity and environmental degradation equation, we note how the subfield of environmental security is associated with the larger field of international environmental politics. Issues of environmental governance and regime formation are thereby intrinsic to the study of environmental security.

Notes

1   Another area of study not mentioned above is related to the analysis of intra-state warfare as a function of resource abundance (primary commodities) or the struggle to control resource rents (Collier 2000; de Soysa 2000).
2   The above three arenas to which I relegated the topic of environmental security can be considered as the more conventional issues. Other questions related to the concept of environmental security are greening the military, using military and intelligence assets to support environmental initiatives, and providing disaster and humanitarian assistance (Matthew 2000, 112–15).

Recommended reading

Diehl, P., and Gleditsch, N. P. (eds) (2001) *Environmental Conflict*, Boulder, CO: Westview Press.

Dinar, S. (ed.) (2010) *Beyond Resource Wars: Scarcity, Environmental Degradation, and International Cooperation*, Cambridge, MA: MIT Press.

Homer-Dixon, T. (1999) *Environment, Scarcity, and Violence*, Princeton, NJ: Princeton University Press.

Pirages, D., and DeGeest, T. (2004) *Ecological Security: An Evolutionary Perspective on Globalization*, Lanham, MD: Rowman & Littlefield.

References

Allenby, B. (2000) "Environmental security: concept and implementation," *International Political Science Review*, 21(1): 5–21.

Bächler, G. (1998) "Why environmental transformation causes violence: a synthesis," *Environmental Change and Security Project Report*, 4: 24–44.

Bächler, G., and Spillman, K. (1996) *Environmental Degradation as a Cause of War*, Zurich: Rüegger.

Baldwin, D. (1997) "The concept of security," *Review of International Studies*, 23(1): 5–26.

Barkin, S., and Shambaugh, G. (1999a) "Hypotheses on the international politics of common pool resources," in S. Barkin and G. Shambaugh (eds), *Anarchy and the Environment: The International Relations of Common Pool Resources*, Albany: State University of New York Press.

—— (1999b) "Conclusions: common pool resources and international environmental negotiation," in S. Barkin and G. Shambaugh (eds), *Anarchy and the Environment: The International Relations of Common Pool Resources*, Albany: State University of New York Press.

Barnett, J. (2000) "Destabilizing the environment–conflict thesis," *Review of International Studies*, 26(2): 271–88.

Barnett, J., and Adger, N. (2007) "Climate change, human security and violent conflict," *Political Geography*, 26: 639–55.

Barnett, J., Matthew, R., and O'Brien, K. (2008) "Global environmental change and human security," in H. G. Brauch, U. O. Spring, C. Mesjasz, J. Grin, P. Dunay, N. C. Behera, B. Chourou, P. Kameri-Mbote, and P. Liotta (eds), *Globalization and Environmental Challenges: Reconceptualizing Security in the 21st Century*, Berlin: Springer.

Barrett, S. (2003) *Environment and Statecraft: The Strategy of Environmental Treaty Making*, Oxford: Oxford University Press.

Benedick, R. (1998) *Ozone Diplomacy: New Directions in Safeguarding the Planet*, Cambridge, MA: Harvard University Press.

Brauch, H.G. (2008) "Conceptual quartet: security and its linkages with peace, development, and environment," in H. G. Brauch, U. O. Spring, C. Mesjasz, J. Grin, P. Dunay, N. C. Behera, B. Chourou, P. Kameri-Mbote, and P. Liotta (eds), *Globalization and Environmental Challenges: Reconceptualizing Security in the 21st Century*, Berlin: Springer.

Brochmann, M., and Hensel, P. (2009) "Peaceful management of international river claims," *International Negotiation*, 14(2): 393–418.

Brock, L. (1992) "Security through defending the environment: an illusion?," in E. Boulding (ed.), *New Agendas for Peace Research: Conflict and Security Reexamined*, Boulder, CO: Lynne Rienner, pp. 79–102.

Brown, L. (1977) "Redefining national security," *Worldwatch Paper* 14, Washington, DC: Worldwatch Institute, pp. 5–46.

Buzan, B., Wæver, O., and de Wilde, J. (1998) *Security: A New Framework for Analysis*, Boulder, CO: Lynne Rienner.

Choucri, N., and North, R. (1975) *Nations in Conflict: National Growth and International Violence*, San Francisco: W. H. Freeman.

Collier, P. (2000) "Doing well out of war: an economic perspective," in M. Berdal and D. Malone (eds), *Greed and Grievance: Economic Agendas in Civil Wars*, Boulder, CO: Lynne Rienner.

Conca, K. (2006) *Governing Water: Contentious Transnational Politics and Global Institution Building*, Cambridge, MA: MIT Press.

Conca, K., and Dabelko, G. (2002) *Environmental Peacemaking*, Washington, DC, and Baltimore: Woodrow Wilson Center Press and Johns Hopkins University Press.

Conca, K., Alexander, C., and Dabelko, G. (2005) "Building peace through environmental cooperation," in *State of the World 2005: Redefining Global Security*, Washington, DC: Worldwatch Institute.

Critchley, H., and Terriff, T. (1993) "Environment and security," in R. Schultz and R. Godson (eds), *Security Studies for the 1990s*, Washington, DC: Brassey's.

Dabelko, G. (2004) "The next step for environment, security, and population," *Environmental Change and Security Program Report*, 10: 3–6.

Dalby, S. (2002) *Environmental Security*, Minneapolis: University of Minnesota Press.

de Serbinin, A. (1995) "World population growth and US security," *Environmental Change and Security Project Report*, 1: 24–39.

de Soysa, I. (2000) "The resource course: are civil wars driven by rapacity or paucity?," in M. Berdal and D. Malone (eds), *Greed and Grievance: Economic Agendas in Civil Wars*, Boulder, CO: Lynne Rienner.

Deudney, D. (1991) "Environment and security: muddled thinking," *Bulletin of the Atomic Scientists*, 47(3): 22–8.

—— (1999) "Environmental security: a critique," in D. Deudney and R. Matthew (eds), *Contested Grounds: Security and Conflict in the New Environmental Politics*, Albany: State University of New York Press.

Diehl, P., and Gleditsch, N. P. (eds) (2001) *Environmental Conflict*, Boulder, CO: Westview Press.

Dinar, S. (2009) "Scarcity and cooperation along international rivers," *Global Environmental Politics* 9(1): 107–33.

—— (ed.) (2010) *Beyond Resource Wars: Scarcity, Environmental Degradation, and International Cooperation*, Cambridge, MA: MIT Press.

Ehrlich, P. (1968) *The Population Bomb*, New York: Ballantine Books.

Esty, D. (1999) "Pivotal states and the environment," in R. Chase, E. Hill, and P. Kennedy (eds), *The Pivotal States: A New Framework for US Policy in the Developing World*, New York: W. W. Norton.

Ferraro, V. (2003) "Globalizing weakness: is global poverty a threat to the interests of states?," in V. Ferraro *et al.*, *Should Global Poverty be Considered a US National Security Issue*, Environmental Change and Security Program, Commentaries, Washington DC: Woodrow Wilson International Center for Scholars.

Giordano, M. (2003) "The geography of the commons: the role of scale and space," *Annals of the Association of American Geographers*, 93(2): 366–75.

Giordano, M., Giordano, M., and Wolf, A. (2005) "International resource conflict and mitigation," *Journal of Peace Research*, 42(1): 47–65.

Gleditsch, N. P. (1998) "Armed conflict and the environment: a critique of the literature," *Journal of Peace Research*, 35(3): 381–400.

Gleditsch, N. P., Furlong, K., Hegre, H., Lacina, B., and Owen, T. (2006) "Conflict over shared rivers: resource scarcity or fuzzy boundaries," *Political Geography*, 25(4): 361–82.

Goldstone, J. (1996) "Debate," *Environmental Change and Security Program Report*, 2: 66–71.

—— (2001) "Demography, environment, and security," in P. Diehl and N. P. Gleditsch (eds), *Environmental Conflict*, Boulder, CO: Westview Press.

Græger, N. (1996) "Environmental security?," *Journal of Peace Research*, 33(1): 109–16.

Haas, P. (1990) *Saving the Mediterranean: The Politics of International Environmental Cooperation*, New York: Columbia University Press.

Haftendorn, H. (1991) "The security puzzle: theory-building and discipline building in international security," *International Studies Quarterly*, 35(1): 3–17.

Hamner, J. (2009) "Drought and the likelihood of water treaty formation," paper presented at the 2009 International Studies Association Convention, New York, 15–18 February.

Hardin, G. (1968) "The tragedy of the commons," *Science*, 162: 1243–8.

Hauge, W., and Ellingsen, T. (1998) **"Beyond environmental scarcity: causal pathways to conflict,"** *Journal of Peace Research*, 35(3): 299–317.

Hensel, P., Mitchell, S. M., and Sowers, T. (2006) "Conflict management of riparian disputes," *Political Geography*, 25(4): 383–411.

Homer-Dixon, T. (1991) "On the threshold: environmental changes as causes of acute conflict," *International Security*, 16(2): 76–116.

—— (1994) "Environmental scarcities and violent conflict," *International Security*, 19(1): 5–40.

—— (1999) *Environment, Scarcity, and Violence*, Princeton, NJ: Princeton University Press.

Homer-Dixon, T., and Levy, M. (1995–6) "Correspondence: environment and security," *International Security*, 20(3): 189–98.

Horsman, S. (2001) "Water in Central Asia: regional cooperation or conflict," in R. Allison and L. Jonson (eds), *Central Asian Security: The New International Context*, London and Washington, DC: Royal Institute of International Affairs and Brookings Institution.

House of Representatives, Permanent Select Committee on Intelligence and Select Committee on Energy Independence and Global Warming (2008) *National Intelligence Assessment on the National Security Implications of Global Climate Change to 2030*, available: www.dni.gov/testimonies/20080625_testimony.pdf.

IPCC (Intergovernmental Panel on Climate Change) (2007) *Synthesis Report*. Geneva: IPCC.

Jopp, H. D., and Kaestner, R. (2008) "Climate change and security in the 21st century," in H. G. Brauch, U. O. Spring, C. Mesjasz, J. Grin, P. Dunay, N. C. Behera, B. Chourou, P. Kameri-Mbote, and P. Liotta (eds), *Globalization and Environmental Challenges: Reconceptualizing Security in the 21st Century*, Berlin: Springer.

Kaplan, R. (1994) "The coming anarchy," *Atlantic Monthly*, 273(2).

Keohane, R., and Nye, J. (1989) *Power and Interdependence*, New York: HarperCollins.

Klare, M. (2001) *Resource Wars: The New Landscape of Global Conflict*, New York: Metropolitan Books.

Levy, M. (1995) "Is the environment a national security issue," *International Security*, 20(2): 35–62.

Levy, M., Sorkelson, C., Vörösmarty, C., Douglas, E., and Humphreys, M. (2005) "Freshwater availability anomalies and outbreak of internal war: results from a global spatial time series analysis," paper presented at the Human Security and Climate Change International Workshop, Asker, Norway, 21–3 June.

Lipschutz, R., and Holdren, K. (1990) "Crossing borders: resource flows, the global environment, and international security," *Bulletin of Peace Proposals*, 21(2): 121–33.

McKinney, D. (2004) 'Cooperative management of transboundary water resources in Central Asia', in D. Burghart and T. Sabonis-Helf (eds), *In the Tracks of Tamerlane: Central Asia's Path to the 21st Century*, Washington, DC: National Defense University, Center for Technology and National Security Policy.

McNeely, J. (2005) "Biodiversity and security," in F. Dodds and T. Pippard (eds), *Human and Environmental Security: An Agenda for Change*, London: Earthscan.

Mamatkanov, D. (2008) 'Mechanisms for improvement of transboundary water resources management in Central Asia', in J. Moerlins, M. Khankhasayev, and E. Makhmudov (eds), *Transboundary Water Resources: A Foundation for Regional Stability in Central Asia*, Dordrecht: Springer.

Mandel, R. (1988) *Conflict over the World's Resources: Background, Trends, Case Studies, and Considerations for the Future*, New York: Greenwood Press.

Mathews, J. (1989) "Redefining security," *Foreign Affairs*, 68(2): 162–77.

Matthew, R. (1999) "Introduction: mapping contested grounds," in D. Deudney and R. Matthew (eds), *Contested Grounds: Security and Conflict in the New Environmental Politics*, Albany: State University of New York Press.

—— (2000) "The environment as a national security issue," *Journal of Policy History*, 12(1): 101–22.

Miller, B. (2001) "The concept of security: should it be redefined?," *Journal of Strategic Studies*, 24(2): 13–42.

Morgenthau, H. (1948) *Politics among Nations: The Struggle for Power and Peace*, New York: Knopf.

Myers, N. (1993) *Ultimate Security: The Environment as the Basis of Political Stability*, New York: W. W. Norton.

Najam, A. (ed.) (2003) *Environment, Development, and Human Security: Perspectives from South Asia*, Lanham, MD: University Press of America.

NICGC (Nautilus Institute and Center for Global Communications) (2000) Energy, Environment and Security in Northeast Asia: Defining a US–Japan Partnership for Regional Comprehensive Security, Berkeley, CA: Nautilus Institute and Center for Global Communications.

Ostrom, E., Burger, J., Field, C., Norgaard, R. and Policansky, D. (1999) "Revisiting the commons: local lessons, global challenges," *Science*, 284: 278–82.

Paris, R. (2001) "Human security: paradigm shift or hot Air?," *International Security*, 26(2): 87–102.

Pirages, D., and DeGeest, T. (2004) *Ecological Security: An Evolutionary Perspective on Globalization*, Lanham, MD: Rowman & Littlefield.

Raleigh, C., and Urdal, H. (2007) "Climate change, environmental degradation, and armed conflict," *Political Geography*, 26: 674–94.

Raustiala, K., and Victor, D. (1998) "Conclusions," in D. Victor, K. Raustiala, and E. Skolnikoff (eds), *The Implementation and Effectiveness of International Environmental Commitments: Theory and Practice*, Cambridge, MA: MIT Press.

Renner, M. (1996) *Fighting for Survival: Environmental Decline, Social Conflict, and the New Age of Insecurity*, Washington, DC: Worldwatch Institute.

Rice, S. E., Graff, C., and Lewis, J. (2006) *Poverty and Civil War: What Policymakers Need to Know*, Global Economy and Development Working Paper, Washington, DC: Brookings Institution.

Rothschild, E. (1995) "What is security?," *Daedalus*, 24(3): 53–98.

Simon, J. (1981) *The Ultimate Resource*, Oxford: Martin Robertson.

Soroos, M. (1994) "Environmental security and the prisoner's dilemma," *Journal of Peace Research*, 31(3): 317–32.

Stern, E. (1999) "The case for comprehensive security," in D. Deudney and R. Matthew (eds), *Contested Grounds: Security and Conflict in the New Environmental Politics*, Albany: State University of New York Press.

Suhrke, A. (1999) "Human security and the interests of states," *Security Dialogue*, 30(3): 265–76.

Susskind, L. (1994) *Environmental Diplomacy: Negotiating More effective Environmental Regimes*, Oxford: Oxford University Press.

Thorsell, J. (1990) "Through hot and cold wars, parks endure," *Natural History*, 99(6): 56–8.

Tir, J., and Ackerman, J. (2009) "Politics of formalized river cooperation," *Journal of Peace Research*, 46(5): 623–40.

Tir, J., and Diehl, P. (1998) "Demographic pressure and interstate conflict: linking population growth and density to militarized disputes and wars," *Journal of Peace Research*, 35(3): 319–39.

Toset, H. P. W., Gleditsch, N. P., and Hegre, H. (2000) "Shared rivers and interstate conflict," *Political Geography*, 19(8): 971–96.

Ullman, R. (1983) "Redefining security," *International Security*, 8(1): 129–53.

UNDP (United Nations Development Programme) (1994) *Human Development Report*, New York: Oxford University Press.

UNEP (United Nations Environment Programme) (1972) *Stockholm Declaration on the Human Environment*, 16 June, available: www.unep.org/Documents/?DocumentID=97&ArticleID=1503.

—— (1992) Rio Declaration on Environment and Development, 3–4 June, available: www.unep.org/Documents.Multilingual/Default.asp?DocumentID=78&ArticleID=1163.

Walt, S. (1991) "The renaissance of security studies," *International Studies Quarterly*, 35: 211–39.

Waltz, K. (1979) *Theory of International Politics*, Reading, MA: Addison-Wesley.

Watts, M. (2004) "Antinomies of community: some thoughts on geography, resources and empire," *Transactions of the Institute of British Geographers*, 29(2): 195–216.

Weinthal, E. (2002) 'The promises and pitfalls of environmental peacemaking in the Aral Sea Basin', in K. Conca and G. Dabelko (eds), *Environmental Peacemaking*, Washington, DC, and Baltimore: Woodrow Wilson Press and Johns Hopkins University Press.

Westing, A. (1986) "Global resources and international conflict," in A. Westing (ed.), *Global Resources and International Conflict*, Oxford: Oxford University Press.

Wolf, A., and Hamner, J. (2000) "Trends in transboundary water disputes and dispute resolution," in *Water for Peace in the Middle East and Southern Africa*, Geneva: Green Cross International.

Wolfers, A. (1952) "National security as an ambiguous symbol," *Political Science Quarterly*, 67(4): 481–502.

Young, O. (1989) 'The politics of international regime formation: managing natural resources and the environment', *International Organization*, 43(3): 349–75.

—— (1994) *International Governance: Protecting the Environment in a Stateless Society*, Ithaca, NY: Cornell University Press.

5 Sustainable consumption

Doris Fuchs and Frederike Boll

Introduction

The notion of sustainable consumption approaches environmental problems through the lens of consumption decisions. Thereby, it aims to highlight the underlying and most fundamental causes of environmental problems and to attribute responsibility where it is due. Specifically, a large share of the environmental degradation arising from production processes in developing countries then has to be linked to consumption decisions made in industrialized countries. At the same time, sustainable consumption pinpoints the question of social justice in the use of the world's ecological resources and highlights the enormous asymmetries existing there.

Consumption patterns and levels can therefore no longer be seen as an individual or national problem; they have become a global political issue. Additional links to global politics arise because various aspects of the global political economy, such as the politics of trade and finance, impact consumption patterns and levels and their environmental (and social) implications (Fuchs and Lorek 2002). Not surprisingly, sustainable consumption has been explicitly present on the global political agenda, in the form of *Agenda 21*, since the Earth Summit in Rio in 1992 (UN 1992).

This chapter explores the concept of sustainable consumption and delineates the task faced by sustainable consumption governance. It then identifies relevant political actors in global sustainable consumption governance, traces current affairs, discusses obstacles to progress in this field, and explores policy implications. Finally, it briefly introduces current lines of enquiry and research fields in the area of sustainable consumption.

What is consumption and why study it?

The *International Encyclopedia of the Social Sciences* (Eglitis 2008: 105) defines consumption as "the personal expenditure of individuals and families that involves the selection, usage, and disposal or reuse of goods and services." In other words, consumption entails all phases of our dealing with goods (and services to some extent): purchase, use, and disposal. As sociologists and psychologists will tell us, such consumption can take place for a variety of purposes. Food and water as well as the need for shelter and some way to stay warm are all requisites for survival. In today's developed societies, however, the purpose of consumption goes beyond this necessary fulfillment of fundamental needs. We consume to entertain ourselves, to increase our happiness (even though we sometimes achieve the opposite), to define our identity, and/or to express status.

But why is consumption a topic in environmental politics and policy? The answer to this question becomes highly obvious if we consider the resource use associated with our consumption.

Western society spends huge amounts of resources and creates huge amounts of pollution with its consumption patterns and levels. In fact, this consumer society may be identified as the main villain when identifying causes of the absence of sustainability in development.

It is more convenient to attribute responsibility for environmental degradation to production methods and processes, of course. After all, one can argue that the consumer has little information or influence on the environmental degradation caused at that stage. Moreover, the number of companies involved may still be large, but it is certainly smaller than the number of consumers and thus easier to reach and regulate. Likewise, environmental degradation caused by a production plant is much more visible and concentrated, and can be targeted more directly. Finally, and perhaps most fundamentally, it is politically much more acceptable to regulate production than to constrain consumption, as long as we view consumer choice as part of our freedom in the pursuit of happiness and as long as economic growth, which in turn is supposed to depend on consumption, remains the primary and unassailable political goal.

Yet, a focus on production is insufficient for a range of reasons. For example, it does not include the environmental degradation caused during the use and final disposal of a product. Most importantly, a focus that is limited to production hides the ultimate driving forces behind environmental degradation. Thereby, it fails to attribute responsibility where it is due. Simultaneously, it obscures a substantial share of potential strategies for intervention and change.

The question of responsibility is also one of the starting points of the focus on sustainable consumption in the scientific and political community. It originally arose in the context of debates on the main causes of environmental problems in the world today. At international conferences, developed countries tended to be concerned about population growth in developing countries, while developing countries pointed out the environmental degradation caused by consumption levels and patterns in developed countries. Thus, consumption also has a moral and an ethical side. Indeed, the sustainable consumption debate gained considerable momentum when environmental activists and scholars started to highlight that in his or her lifetime a single American will consume the same amount of environmental resources as a large number of Indians (Durning 1992). Even in today's political debates, we run into these questions of justice again and again. The Chinese can not only easily challenge demands to reduce their greenhouse gas emissions by juxtaposing their per capita emissions with those of the developed countries; they can also challenge such demands on the basis that a large share of the emissions is caused by production for Western consumers.

The concept of sustainable consumption

Without sustainable consumption, sustainable development is impossible. As pointed out above, unsustainable consumption patterns and levels, especially in industrialized countries, are currently driving a large share of environmental degradation in the world (Haake and Jolivet 2001). But what is sustainable consumption? The Oslo Roundtable defined it as

> the use of services and related products which respond to basic needs and bring a better quality of life while minimizing the use of natural resources and toxic materials as well as the emissions of waste and pollutants over the life cycle of the service or product so as not to jeopardize the needs of further generations.
>
> (Ministry of the Environment Norway 1994)

It is important, however, to differentiate between strong and weak sustainable consumption. Weak sustainable consumption can result from increases in the efficiency of production and consumption, which are typically reached via technological improvements. In this case, improvements in the sustainability of consumption result from a reduction in resource consumption per consumption unit due to improvements in production processes or, for example, an efficiency-friendly design. Many times, such improvements are win–win scenarios.

Weak sustainable consumption can be seen as the necessary condition to achieve sustainable development. However, existing limits to the Earth's resources and to its capacity to serve as a sink for pollutants mean that improvements in the efficiency of consumption will not suffice for achieving sustainable development. As research on the so-called rebound effect has documented, achievements based on efficiency alone are almost always overcompensated by a growth in consumption volumes (Greening *et al.* 2000).

In consequence, changes in patterns and reductions in levels in industrialized countries – i.e. strong sustainable consumption – need to be pursued if we want to achieve sustainability. Strong sustainable consumption can then be defined as a sufficient condition for sustainable development. It requires changes in infrastructures and choices as well as a questioning of the levels and drivers of consumption. The necessary steps for achieving strong sustainable consumption are of course, politically speaking, highly controversial. Yet there are those issues that take center stage when approaching sustainable development from the perspective of sustainable consumption rather than sustainable production.

Not surprisingly, the concepts of strong and weak sustainable consumption were introduced into the scientific debate in the context of analyses of the promises and pitfalls of sustainable consumption governance (Fuchs and Lorek 2005). These analyses started from the observation that a considerable amount of activity was taking place under the heading of sustainable consumption in global governance, while little substantial progress was being achieved. In consequence, scholars delineated the specific objectives of the various activities and demonstrated the narrowness of their focus on efficiency questions. They subsequently explained the almost complete absence of strong sustainable consumption governance by assessing the interests and relative influence of the various state and non-state actors involved in this policy field (see below). Thus, the distinction between strong and weak sustainable consumption serves as a useful analytical tool for differentiating between the pursuit of marginal improvements and substantial (and thus politically costly) changes in the sustainability of consumption as derived from changes in patterns and levels.

Beyond the fundamental distinction between strong and weak sustainable consumption governance, a number of alternative or supplementary conceptual distinctions for sustainable consumption exist in the literature (Charkiewicz *et al.* 2001; Cohen and Murphy 2001; Princen *et al.* 2002). Philosophical and sociological approaches, for instance, emphasize differentiations between motivations, allowing for an enhanced understanding of the meaning of consumption today. Princen (1999), for instance, develops categories such as *misconsumption* and *overconsumption* to pinpoint the problematic aspects of the consumption behavior of today's consumer class. A similar perspective shows up in the four consumption categories identified by UNEP. The *Consumption Opportunities* report (UNEP 2001) differentiates between efficient consumption, different consumption, conscious consumption, and appropriate consumption, associating the first with dematerialization and the latter three with the optimization of consumption.

The task

In order to pursue sustainable consumption, one needs first to understand the causes and drivers of consumption decisions and the consumption areas causing a particular burden for the environment and society. In industrialized countries, consumption generally goes far beyond attempts to satisfy people's needs for food and shelter. Rather, decisions are influenced by aspects such as convenience, identity setting, signaling of status, distraction, participation, and/or creativeness. Political measures to improve the sustainability of consumption need to take these aspects into account if they want to be successful.

Moreover, consumers make their decisions in specific socio-economic, political, and cultural contexts. They act rarely as fully autonomous individuals, but rather within constraints set by their professional and social environment (Georg 1999; Schor 1999). These constraints include factors such as time and money, but also expectations or traditions. In fact, the individualization of the responsibility for sustainable consumption frequently advocated by politicians and business has to be viewed very critically (Princen *et al.* 2002). In consequence, political steps to improve the sustainability of consumption should take not just (and maybe not even primarily) the individual consumer into account but also the consumption environment.

Furthermore, such political strategies need to target the consumption clusters associated with the largest environmental and social burdens. Research has identified food, mobility, and housing as three major areas of concern here (Lorek and Spangenberg 2001). First, the increasing quantity of meat consumption, greenhouse production, and pesticide use, the introduction of genetically modified organisms (GMOs), and the dominance of long-distance transport are known for the detriment they cause to sustainability. Second, distances travelled by car (as well as urban planning practices that lead to a growing need to use cars), the fuel efficiency of the car fleet, and, most importantly, the dramatic rise in miles travelled by air transport are all areas of primary concern. Third, the growing size of homes and associated heating and cooling needs, as well as the destruction of open space, cause major challenges to sustainable development.

Finally, a particular challenge to sustainable consumption politics and policy arises from the context of globalization (Fuchs and Lorek 2002; Haake and Jolivet 2001). Consumption patterns and levels are a moving target and are influenced by transnational interactions in trade, finance, information, and technology. The extent and breadth of the influence of globalization means that it has the potential to undermine any sustainable consumption policy which ignores this context. Given the further existence of a significant free-rider problem, sustainable consumption cannot be pursued at the national level alone but has to be an objective of global governance.

The global politics of sustainable consumption[1]

Sustainable consumption explicitly appeared on the global governance agenda when the United Nations Conference on Environment and Development (UNCED) called for the adoption of sustainable consumption patterns in *Agenda 21* (UN 1992: Chapter 4). Since then, various actors, notably international governmental organizations (IGOs), have addressed the issue of sustainable consumption. Their goals have lacked ambition, however, and any progress has yet to be achieved. In particular, the politically controversial issue of strong sustainable consumption vanished from the agenda. Global sustainable consumption governance has to date concentrated almost exclusively on questions of efficiency (and even here we find more rhetoric than action). The earliest "global" meetings on sustainable consumption, in particular the Oslo meeting in 1994, adopted a much broader approach. It explicitly noted that a focus on eco-efficiency would not provide a sufficiently comprehensive framework for identifying, understanding, and changing unsustainable consumption patterns. In the following years, however, IGOs systematically reduced the focus and ambitions of sustainable consumption governance, and this more comprehensive understanding disappeared from the political agendas.

Actors in global sustainable consumption governance

The Commission on Sustainable Development and the Division on Sustainable Development

The Commission on Sustainable Development (CSD) has been among the most active participants in the sustainable consumption arena. Its work has drawn on the technical and organizational resources of the Division for Sustainable Development (DSD), which, in turn, is part of the United Nations Department for Economic and Social Affairs (UNDESA). The CSD adopted an International Work Program on Changing Consumption and Production Patterns in 1995 and conducted and commissioned work on a range of aspects, such as consumption trends and impacts and relevant policy measures (UNDESA 1995). It fostered especially the development of sustainable consumption indicators and the revision of the UN *Guidelines on Consumer Protection* (UNDESA 2003).

In parallel, the DSD decided to make changing consumption and production patterns part of its multiyear program, collaborating, for instance, with the International Institute for Sustainable Development (IISD). Based on this cooperation, the IISD developed and maintained a website from 1997 to 2000 covering definitions and concepts of sustainable consumption, key resources on the topic, and a compendium of policy instruments for changing consumption and production patterns.

The work of the CSD and DSD on sustainable consumption trends, indicators, and policy measures was important. It provided sustainable consumption with increased visibility on the global governance agenda. Yet both institutions failed in broadly fostering the implementation of Chapter 4 of *Agenda 21*, as they did not manage to move beyond the debate and indicator stage. Moreover, they neglected strong sustainable consumption as a governance goal. Questions regarding fundamental changes in consumption patterns and reductions in consumption levels were raised only in the context of discussions at the CSD of "common but differentiated responsibilities" and did not find their way into official reports and documents.

UNEP

UNEP's Sustainable Consumption Program is housed in the Production and Consumption Unit of the Division of Technology, Industry, and Economics (DTIE). The program started in 1998 with the intention of developing demand-side-oriented activities to complement the DTIE's supply-side-oriented ones. Its stated goal has been to understand the forces driving global consumption patterns, to develop appropriate activities for business and other stakeholders, and to look for potential advances for business, governments, and NGOs. In addition, the DTIE has conducted a "global consumer survey" to gain a better understanding of consumer wants. Finally, it has investigated consumption trends and indicators in a variety of fields. Overall, then, UNEP has addressed a substantial range of topics related to sustainable consumption. Yet its work up to 2001 focused almost exclusively on increasing the eco-efficiency of consumption, with a particular interest in innovations for business.

Interestingly, UNEP's report *Consumption Opportunities* (UNEP 2001) explicitly addressed the politically sensitive topic of overconsumption. However, UNEP did not pursue the ambitious goals of the report further, but instead initiated a Sustainable Consumption Opportunities for Europe (SCOPE) process, with a regional emphasis on Central and Eastern Europe (thus avoiding the most critical overconsuming countries), and little attention has been paid to these politically sensitive questions.

Finally, in 2002, UNEP issued a *Global Status Report* (UNEP 2002), identifying six strategic areas in which it perceives the greatest need for further work on sustainable consumption, such as clarifying the various meanings of the term "consumption," developing better feedback indicators to measure consumption pressures and quality of life, and supporting and enhancing localized campaigns to transform trends in the consumption of certain resources or goods and services. In addition, UNEP quickly picked up the idea of a 10-Year Framework of Programmes following the World Summit on Sustainable Development (WSSD) in Johannesburg in 2002 (see below), an idea that had originally been promoted by the European Union. Thus at that stage UNEP's plans and activities again appeared broad and promising. However, it has yet to demonstrate its willingness and ability to move beyond its former intentional and explicit exclusion of the strong sustainable consumption perspective.

The Organization for Economic Cooperation and Development

The OECD is another important actor that has worked substantially on sustainable consumption. Acknowledging that the OECD countries are home to 19 per cent of the world's population but consume 80 per cent of the world's resources, the organization started to address the subject in 1995 with an integrated work program, Environmental Impacts of Production and Consumption. Its focus has been on resource efficiency and the link between technological change and the environment, through which the program aimed to explore mutually supportive relationships between environmental improvements and economic growth. The core activities were similar to those of the CSD and included the development of a conceptual framework and indicators as well as analyses of trends in and policy options for OECD countries.

The OECD explicitly concentrated on important sectors and consumption clusters, specifically tourism, food, energy and water consumption, and waste generation (OECD 2002). In addition, it conducted and commissioned reports on policy instruments, information and consumer decision-making, and participatory decision-making with respect to sustainable consumption. Yet, the framework for its consumption work was clearly set in line with the OECD's traditional focus on economic growth. Thus, in the end it failed to go beyond the aim of improving eco-efficiency and the mutual pursuit of economic growth and environmental quality.

In 2008, the OECD started to approach (sustainable) consumption from a different angle by analyzing the distributional effects of environmental policies. The jury is still out on whether this shift in perspective will allow it to play a more noteworthy role in sustainable consumption governance.

The European Union

In 2001, the European Council adopted a Sustainable Development Strategy (EU SDS), revised in 2006, which made sustainable consumption and production one of the key objectives and priorities at the European level. In response to the WSSD in Johannesburg, the European Council strengthened its position in 2003 by stressing again its leading role in promoting and supporting sustainable consumption and production. Several European

stakeholder meetings took place involving representatives of governments, the private sector, civil society, and NGOs. However, these meetings turned out to be "discussion platforms" rather than "working platforms."

The *Monitoring Report* of the EU SDS (Eurostat 2007), besides stressing the importance of weak sustainable consumption in the form of eco-efficiency, mentioned that sustainable development can only be achieved by changing patterns of consumption and production, which is part of strong sustainable consumption governance. Additionally, the report underscores the importance of decoupling environmental degradation and economic growth as well as of successful national initiatives which are part of the sustainable development strategy. The impression arises that the European Union is trying to put real effort into fulfilling its goal of having a leading role in shaping policies for sustainable global consumption.

In 2008, the Sustainable Consumption and Production and Sustainable Industrial Policy Action Plan was presented by the EU and defined concrete actions such as eco-design requirements for more products, reinforced energy, and environmental labeling, and supported resource efficiency, eco-innovation, and enhancing the environmental potential of industry. However, the action plan, in comparison with the monitoring report, again focuses solely on weak sustainable consumption and mentions only eco-efficiency and innovations as the major driving forces to achieve sustainable consumption and production. Thereby, it strengthens these aspects in the work of the European Environmental Agency but does not allow it to go further. In addition, mandatory commitments are still very rare. For example, EU labeling of environmentally friendly products is still voluntary.

Thus, the EU in some respects has taken a number of initiatives and actions to meet its leading role in promoting sustainable consumption and production by starting to stimulate and foster these processes. However, it has yet to address consistently and support strong sustainable consumption and the associated, necessary mandatory commitments.

National governments

National governments and NGOs, as well as researchers and research networks, have also been active in the area of sustainable consumption. Except for perhaps national governments, these actors clearly are not in the same privileged position as IGOs when it comes to the forging of global agreements. Nevertheless, efforts by individual governments to promote national sustainable consumption dialogues and measures can prepare the ground for global sustainable consumption governance. Particularly noteworthy have been the efforts of the Norwegian and Danish governments, which have not only sponsored a substantial amount of research on the topic of sustainable consumption but also pursued specific initiatives to foster global and national sustainable consumption governance. The Norwegian government has been particularly active with respect to the global agenda. It hosted sustainable consumption workshops in 1994 and 1995 and pushed for a broad understanding of requirements and potentials for sustainable consumption governance. It has also collaborated with Norwegian research centers in promoting sustainable consumption ideas at the national level. The Danish government took the lead in the preparation of the WSSD and initiated the development of the 10-Year Framework of Programmes under its EU presidency. However, these efforts have to date failed to address and endorse policy measures for fostering strong sustainable consumption systematically.

Only a few countries accepted the challenge to develop an explicit sustainable consumption and production (SCP) action plan, and they did so with very different approaches and different levels of ambition. For example, while the SCP program of the UK emphasizes the role of business in advancing its agenda, Sweden counts on the involvement of consumers and Finland on R&D and stakeholders. In any case, the popularity of weak instruments (i.e. informational tools) is evident throughout. All SCP programs give very scarce attention to the possibilities of governmental regulation in the context of sustainable consumption and production. The political difficulties involved with this topic were most evident in Sweden, where a change in government led the program to be canceled immediately.

NGOs

NGOs have played a strong and active role in the global campaign to promote sustainable production and consumption. Throughout the many program cycles of the CSD, NGOs working on production and consumption patterns regularly coordinated their advocacy and education efforts, and eventually organized themselves into the International Coalition for Sustainable Production and Consumption (ICSPAC).

Many of these NGOs ask politically sensitive questions regarding consumption patterns and levels. Moreover, they contribute to the development of strong sustainable consumption governance by promoting the diffusion of alternative lifestyles and values. A mapping of the North American civil society movement revealed how many NGOs and other civil society groups are contributing their share to make sustainable consumption possible, or at least to address the structural unsustainability of current consumption patterns. Voluntary simplicity and "right to know" groups, local money and social investment groups, eco-labeling, and fair trade initiatives all are trying to make a difference – but have so far failed to develop a larger potential via collaborative action. After the Marrakech Process (see below) was launched, NGOs created an online discussion forum to evaluate current developments of the international governmental community and to help promote their ideas of principles, practices, and policies concerning sustainable production and consumption. While NGOs clearly aim to increase their strength via transnational coalitions and coordination activities, their influence at the global level has thus far proven to be limited.

Academia

Scholars have also contributed much to the understanding of sustainable consumption. Importantly, current research addresses a whole range of sustainable consumption issues, including controversial questions of overconsumption and the need for changes in levels and patterns. Most notably in Europe, assessments of the willingness and ability of people to reduce their consumption have been the focus of numerous research efforts and collaborations. Unfortunately, few of the critical ideas raised by this research reach the official global sustainable consumption discourse. Some national and international agencies have assumed the role of a "translator" between politics and science in this respect; however, the results of such efforts have to date been rather poor. To improve this situation, the Sustainable Consumption Research Exchange (SCORE) network was established, which has tried to contribute knowledge and momentum to the 10-Year Framework of Programmes on the basis of a collaborative effort of scientists and NGO activists. Its success remains to be seen.

Business

The International Chamber of Commerce and the World Business Council for Sustainable Development issued a report dealing with the topic of sustainable consumption (WBCSD

2002). The report gave consumers the key role in shaping markets, thus placing responsibility firmly on the demand side rather than on the supply side. It identified increasing eco-efficiency as business's contribution to sustainable consumption, but clearly avoided any discussion of the role of business in driving and reducing overconsumption. The only additional responsibility the report attributed to business was to inform consumers about the social and environmental effects of their choices and to offer them appropriate options. A later report again analyzed sustainable consumption facts and trends from a business perspective and identified roles for consumers, businesses, NGOs, and governments (WBCSD 2008). Not surprisingly, according to this report, little responsibility for fundamental change rests with the business community.

The state of affairs

The central outcome of the last global summit on sustainable development, the WSSD in 2002, was the call for governments to "*encourage* and *promote* the development of a 10-year framework of programmes in support of regional and national initiatives to accelerate the shift towards sustainable consumption and production" (UN/WSSD 2002; emphasis added). This specification is vague and does not mention aspects of strong sustainable consumption. However, even this outcome has to be seen as a positive result in some respects. It was achieved only after long and controversial discussions about the inclusion of the issue of sustainable consumption in the plan of implementation (Barber 2003). Moreover, here the aspect of life-cycle analysis has been included in an approved UN document for the first time.

In 2003, the first major conference after Johannesburg, held in Marrakech, Morocco, launched the "Marrakech Process." This process is meant to support the elaboration and implementation of the 10-Year Framework of Programmes (10YFP). The goals of the Marrakech Process are divided into four areas: providing assistance to countries to develop sustainability; strengthening them to "green" their economies; developing sustainable business models; and encouraging consumers to make more sustainable consumption choices. A range of activities is taking place in the context of the Marrakech Process. UNEP and UNDESA are the leading agencies, and they decided that sustainable production and consumption would continue to appear as a cross-cutting issue in the CSD's 2004–17 Multi-Year Program of Work and that the 2010–11 cycle would additionally highlight the 10YFP as a thematic cluster. Several international and regional meetings have been held around the world since 2003 to foster the Marrakech Process. Nevertheless, these meetings have so far failed to provide substantial changes and served merely as platforms for the exchange of knowledge.

The Marrakech Process has shown major weaknesses already. There was much controversy over the architecture of an institution which could lead it, so it took five years to create an advisory committee, which was supposed to initiate and to develop the first official draft of the 10YFP. The framework draft considered as global objectives decoupling economic growth from environmental degradation, promoting more sustainable lifestyles, cities, and societies, and supporting regional and national sustainable consumption and production initiatives.

Could this be the beginning of a shift toward strong consumption governance? In the draft, the initiatives to promote sustainable consumption are voluntary rather than prescriptive. Every country can decide whether it will support the strategy of strong or weak sustainable consumption. Yet, in respect to the emerging world, especially to China and India, one can see that the increasing hunger for resources and energy should encourage the international community to find mandatory global (including the industrialized, developing, and emerging world) regulations to stop environmental degradation.

The framework draft will be continually enhanced until the year 2011 and will finally be discussed at the nineteenth session of the UN Commission on Sustainable Development. There is still a chance of a conceptual shift toward strong sustainable consumption, a starting point for real change. However, an evaluation of the progress that the Marrakech Process has made in the last five years does not inspire confidence. Unfortunately, past experience makes it difficult to believe in a successful transition to (strong) global sustainable consumption governance.

From the beginning, NGOs criticized the fact that the 10YFP was developed as part of the Johannesburg Plan of Implementation. Implementation was already requested in 2002, and the weak wording of the documents did not indicate any substantial progress. If such progress is to be achieved, the 10YFP has to forward a binding commitment to develop national policy frameworks on sustainable production and consumption. It also has to enable the development of legal frameworks and multilateral agreements to ensure that the actions taken indeed lead to sustainability in practice.

Obstacles to progress

In sum, weak sustainable consumption has received some attention, while strong sustainable consumption is almost entirely absent from global governance (Fuchs and Lorek 2005). Strong sustainable consumption exists only in marginal sectors of society and research or as a symbolic reminder in official documents. The activities of IGOs, in particular, have avoided strong sustainable consumption issues. How can this development be explained if strong sustainable consumption is after all a fundamental precondition for sustainable development? The answer to this question lies in the "weakness" of IGOs and the alignment of consumer and business interests against strong measures.

IGOs initially took on the issue of sustainable consumption as such but started to restrict their focus during the early phases of issue definition on account of its political sensitivity. They shied away from a more ambitious approach because strong measures would be highly unpopular with consumers in industrialized countries, with business, and, as a consequence, with governments. Contrary to frequent claims of the increasing environmental activism of consumers and the growth of corporate citizenship – which the more optimistic sustainable consumption literature cites as a source of much hope – the prospects for support for such strategies from consumers and business are rather weak.

As consumers are also voters, their opposition would reduce the inclination of governments to agree to appropriate international policy measures. Some scholars and practitioners proclaim a new awareness and interest among people in the environmental and social effects of consumption. Similarly, surveys tend to report a high ratio of consumers concerned about the impacts of their behavior. Yet environmental, social, or sustainability values are competing with a multitude of criteria in their influence on consumption decisions in real life (Jackson 2004; Røpke 1999). In the sum of global communications, "sustainability" messages are overpowered by opposing ones (Fuchs and Lorek 2002). In fact, there is ample evidence that sustainability criteria often rank low compared withcompeting aims. This is the case even when the question is just one of consuming a different product. When it comes to consuming less, the hurdle is even higher (Jackson 2005). In other words, while there is some indication of a willingness to move toward green consumption, there is little evidence of a fundamental change toward reducing consumption for sustainability objectives. Rather, consumption is proclaimed more than ever to be an individual right, allowing the expression of self, the pursuit of one's legitimate professional and social goals, and the opportunity to exercise freedom of choice.

Similar opposition to (strong) sustainable consumption governance exists in the business community. Most business actors tend to reject the notion that they carry any responsibility with respect to consumption levels. According to representatives of the business sector, the latter's role is to promote eco-efficiency. Some optimistic scholars and activists point out that business opposition to strong sustainable consumption governance does not necessarily have to be the case. They argue that business may earn its profits through, for instance, the selling of fewer but more expensive products with a higher profit margin. However, the ability of products to achieve distinction on the basis of quality irrespective of price is limited, as only a share of products can be marketed accordingly. Moreover, the globalized economy is characterized to a large extent by a high level of competition in mass markets and cheap products and correspondingly high pressures for externalization of social and environmental costs. Likewise, corporate social responsibility and related measures often proclaimed to signal the ethical turn in business conduct tend to perform badly when it comes to actual improvements. More importantly, these measures are unlikely to contribute to improvements in strong sustainable consumption. The only area in which business may be interested in fostering strong sustainable consumption is in the area of eco-efficient services – i.e. the purchase of a service instead of the ownership of a good – which actually involve a reduction in consumption levels (Michaelis 2003). However, eco-efficient services only provide an option in certain areas and are frequently not accepted by consumers.

Given this lack of consumer and business support for strong sustainable consumption governance, then, one should not expect too much activity in this respect on the part of governments or of IGOs, who in turn depend on their member governments. In addition, governments and IGOs themselves are still attached to the growth discourse and tend to want to foster consumption in order to encourage growth. Accordingly, they may sign up to continued efforts to increase eco-efficiency, but will not agree to or pass policies that seriously transform consumption patterns or reduce consumption levels.

Policy implications

What will the future of global sustainable consumption governance look like? Our analysis of developments to date has shown that some efforts to improve the efficiency of consumption exist. Thus, we can expect, for instance, policy proposals promoting efficient technologies for consumer products. However, a rather significant number of scholars argue that sustainable consumption can only be achieved if consumers in industrialized countries shift patterns and reduce levels. As our analysis has shown, hardly any progress has been made on these issues as a result of constraints imposed by the global political and economic setting. Moreover, the potential for future strong sustainable consumption efforts is limited. The alignment of consumer and business interests against such measures means that both IGOs and national governments (of industrialized countries) will continue to frame sustainability in terms of improvements in efficiency. In consequence, we should expect few policy proposals addressing consumption levels.

In this situation, political rather than policy recommendations are needed. The question is not how to design policies allowing further or maybe faster progress in sustainable consumption governance. The question has to be how a new area of governance can be opened up. For this, one of two developments would have to take place. First, the strengthening of relevant IGOs would potentially provide them with sufficient leeway to address strong sustainable consumption issues, even if they are controversial with consumers, business, and therefore governments. Such a strengthening could take place in the form of a change in institutional structure and competencies. The expansion of UNEP to a global environmental organization with broad expertise, sanctioning, and enforcement capacities similar to the WTO, which has repeatedly been discussed, would be one possibility in this context.

The strength of IGOs, however, is not just a function of their institutional structures and formal sanctioning and enforcement capacities; it is also a function of the willingness and ability of the individuals in the organization to provide leadership. While global governance scholars are correct in questioning exaggerated accounts of a general acquisition of "new" political capacities by IGOs, even those without such capacities can play important political roles. History has shown IGOs and/or the individuals leading them as effective agenda-setters and farsighted promoters of crucial policy initiatives. In fact, IGOs sometimes seek to justify their existence precisely by forcefully pursuing new societal visions and goals. The current lack of activities by IGOs on strong sustainable consumption governance, then, is not just a function of their lack of formal competencies, but also a question of ideational leadership. Therefore, a smaller but related institutional change, for example, could be the relocating of UNEP's sustainable consumption work away from the DTIE, with its traditional focus on industry, and its location higher up in the organizational hierarchy.

The second development that could potentially foster strong sustainable consumption governance is the adoption of new political strategies by relevant NGOs. Given the current alignment of interests against strong sustainable consumption, improved coalition-building of NGOs with academia and developing countries would be needed to provide some basis for political effectiveness. Moreover, such coalitions should make the question of organizational venues in IGOs (the relevance of which the above discussion demonstrated) part of their strategy. Clearly, coalitions between NGOs, academia, and developing countries would still face the problem of limited capacities. The strong sustainable consumption message would still have to compete with extensive advertising and consumption-inducing communication through the mass media. Moreover, NGOs and, increasingly, academic research do depend on public and financial support. Therefore, even some environmental NGOs and scholars convinced of the need to reduce consumption levels shy away from such a discussion. Despite all of these obstacles, however, such coalitions are likely to remain the only potentially significant driving force for strong sustainable consumption governance.

Current research developments

The research field of sustainable consumption and production has gained increasing attention over recent decades. It took some time to establish a firm link between consumption and sustainable development. But since the early 1990s sustainable consumption issues have acquired visibility and acceptance in environmental research. Concerns about unsustainable production processes were broadened to include those pertaining to misconsumption and overconsumption as well as the long-distance effects of what had been seen as local activities of societies.

One reason the field of sustainable consumption research is so vibrant and interesting at this point is the truly interdisciplinary nature of the topic. Such research receives contributions from a wide variety of disciplines, including political science, economics, sociology, anthropology, psychology, philosophy, and cultural studies, and focuses on a broad range of topics.

Thus scholars are still trying to gain a better understanding of the determinants of consumer behavior. To this end, they try to identify different types of consumers and lifestyles in order to develop targeted strategies to reduce and change their patterns of consumption.

A second focus today is on the gap between knowledge/values on the one hand and action on the other (Lebel *et al.* 2006). Surveys show that most people believe that they can change environmental degradation by consuming less or in a different way. Moreover, they tend to report that their consumption decisions are influenced significantly by environmental criteria. However, there is a wide gap between this reported environmental consciousness and action as expressed in actual consumption decisions.

In addition, it is not only the consumer who is in charge of sustainable development. Put differently, consumption decisions are made under socio-economic, political, and temporal constraints (Røpke 1999). The structural contexts of the consumer environment strongly influence the characteristics of the available options for such decisions (Fuchs and Lorek 2002). In order to not overestimate the individual's responsibility and ability for change, sustainable consumption research has to take an integrated perspective and link consumer decisions to their societal environment as well as develop a joint production–consumption strategy.

Furthermore, sustainable consumption research is taking up the long-neglected question of the social dimension of sustainability. Retail food standards, for example, have the potential to improve environmental conditions as well as food safety in industrialized countries while threatening rural incomes in developing countries (Fuchs and Kalfagianni 2010). In consequence, research also has to pursue an integrated perspective.

Finally, of course, the question of how to improve the sustainability of consumption remains. Scholars thus continue to try to derive strategies against the background of the size of the task faced. After all, the objective is to change consumption levels and patterns of entire societies in the structural context of a system in which more tends to be viewed as better. Accordingly, scholars explore the potential of alliances between different political and societal actors as well as the availability of alternative models and lighthouse projects and their diffusion.

Conclusion

Sixteen years after the World Summit in Rio, progression toward the political pursuit of sustainable consumption is far from satisfactory. This chapter has highlighted more political weaknesses and obstacles than progress, and the future of sustainable consumption governance is still bleak. Meanwhile the pressure to achieve sustainable development through sustainable consumption and production is mounting because of climate change, environmental degradation, and continuing worldwide poverty.

Many reports, meetings, and/or frameworks were initiated and many actors are involved in the process, so there is hope that a change in sustainable consumption and production policy can be achieved. As mentioned above, IGOs could play a leading role in this context. They would have to push a global solution by overcoming national interests and by strengthening their power in global politics to achieve improvements. This, in turn, requires leadership.

As it applies to nearly every policy field, it is important that the approach of sustainable consumption governance is a global and integrated one, which is linked not only to environmental policy but also to economic and/or social policy. Moreover, it has to be an approach that makes strong sustainable consumption governance a central focus. Weak sustainable consumption governance found its way onto the international and national political agendas, but strong sustainable consumption governance is still neglected by most political actors. Without this, however, the international community will not be able to fulfill its responsibility for sustainable development.

Note

1 For a detailed discussion of the role of the various actors, see Fuchs and Lorek (2005).

Recommended reading

Dauvergne, P. (2008) *The Shadows of Consumption: Consequences for the Global Environment*, Cambridge, MA: MIT Press.
Jackson, T. (2006) *The Earthscan Reader in Sustainable Consumption*, London: Earthscan.
Princen, T. (2005) *The Logic of Sufficiency*, Cambridge, MA: MIT Press.
Worldwatch (2004) *State of the world 2004: Special Focus: The Consumer Society*, Washington, DC: Worldwatch Institute.

References

Barber, J. (2003) "Production, consumption and the World Summit on Sustainable Development," *Environment, Development and Sustainability*, 5: 63–93.
Charkiewicz, E., Bennekom, S., and Young, A. (2001) *Transitions to Sustainable Production and Consumption: Concepts, Policies, and Actions*, The Hague: Tools for Transition.
Cohen, M. J., and Murphy, J. (2001) *Exploring Sustainable Consumption: Environmental Policy and the Social Sciences*, Oxford: Pergamon Press.
Durning, A. (1992) *How Much is Enough?* Washington, DC: Worldwatch Institute.
Eglitis, D. S. (2008) "Consumption," in *International Encyclopedia of the Social Sciences*, 2nd ed., Detroit: Thomson Gale.
Eurostat (2007) *Measuring Progress towards a More Sustainable Europe: Monitoring Report of the EU Sustainable Development Strategy,* Luxembourg: European Commission.
Fuchs, D., and Lorek, S. (2002) "Sustainable consumption governance in a globalizing world," *Global Environmental Politics*, 2(1): 19–45.
—— (2005) "Sustainable consumption governance: a history of promises and failures," *Journal of Consumer Policy*, 28(3): 261–88.
Fuchs, D., and Kalfagianni, A. (2010) "Private food governance and implications for social sustainability and democratic legitimacy," in P. Utting and J. C. Marques (eds), *Business, Social Policy and Corporate Political Influence in Developing Countries*, New York: Palgrave Macmillan, pp. 225–47.
Georg, S. (1999) "The social shaping of household consumption," *Ecological Economics*, 28: 455–6.
Greening, L. A., Green, D. L., and Difiglio, C. (2000) "Energy efficiency and consumption – the rebound effect: a survey," *Energy Policy*, 28: 389–401.
Haake, J., and Jolivet, P. (2001) "The link between production and consumption for sustainable development," *International Journal of Sustainable Development*, 4(1) [special issue].
Jackson, T. (2004) *Motivating Sustainable Consumption: A Review of Evidence on Consumer Behaviour and Behavioural Change*, Guildford: University of Surrey, Centre for Environmental Strategy.
—— (2005) "Live better by consuming less? Is there a 'double dividend' in sustainable consumption?," *Journal of Industrial Ecology*, 9(1): 19–36.
Lebel, L., Fuchs, D., Garden, P., Giap, D., *et al.* (2006) *Linking Knowledge and Action for Sustainable Production and Consumption Systems*, USER Working Paper WP-2006-09, Chiang Mai: Unit for Social and Environmental Research.

Lorek, S., and Spangenberg, J. H. (2001) "Indicators for environmentally sustainable household consumption," *International Journal of Sustainable Development*, 4: 101–20.

Michaelis, L. (2003) "The role of business in sustainable consumption," *Journal of Cleaner Production*, 11(8): 915–21.

Ministry of the Environment Norway (1995) *Report of the Oslo Ministerial Roundtable*, Oslo: Ministry of the Environment Norway.

OECD (2002) *Towards Sustainable Household Consumption? Trends and Policies in OECD Countries*, Paris: Organization for Economic Cooperation and Development.

Princen, T. (1999) "Consumption and environment: some conceptual issues," *Ecological Economics*, 31: 347–63.

Princen, T., Maniates, M., and Conca, K. (eds) (2002) *Confronting Consumption*, Cambridge, MA: MIT Press.

Røpke, I. (1999) "The dynamics of willingness to consume," *Ecological Economics*, 28: 399–420.

Schor, J. (1999) *The Overspent American: Why We Want What We Don't Need*, New York: Harper.

UN (1992) *Earth Summit: Agenda 21: The United Nations Programme of Action from Rio*, New York: United Nations.

UNDESA (1995) *International Work Programme on Changing Consumption and Production Patterns*, New York: United Nations.

—— (2003) *United Nations Guidelines for Consumer Protection (as Expanded in 1999)*, New York: United Nations.

UNEP (2001) *Consumption Opportunities: Strategies for Change*, Paris: United Nations.

—— (2002) *A Global Status Report*, Paris: United Nations Environmental Programme.

UN/WSSD (2002) *Plan of Implementation*, New York: United Nations.

WBCSD (2002) *Sustainable Production and Consumption: A Business Perspective*, Geneva: World Business Council for Sustainable Development.

—— (2008) *Sustainable Consumption Facts and Trends from a Business Perspective*, Geneva: World Business Council for Sustainable Development.

6 International environmental and ecological justice

Timothy Ehresman and Dimitris Stevis

Models of climate change show that the developing world – already pressed by needs to feed and support growing populations – will likely be impacted the worst by global warming. Yet it is the rich countries of the North that are among the highest greenhouse gas emitters. Consider another scenario: financial assistance packages from the International Monetary Fund (IMF) to countries in the South have required borrower compliance with lending conditions that will produce particular and sometimes drastic effects upon their populations and environmental resources. These conditions largely reflect the economic and political policy prescriptions of the wealthy countries in the North, which collectively control the voting on matters of policy within the IMF. Do these situations warrant concern?

Scholars in the field of international relations have for some time raised concerns regarding the fairness and moral urgency of these and other problems in global environmental politics. And, as scholarly work on global environmental issues, initiatives, and institutions has advanced over time, the concept of justice has become central to the broader environmental policy debates. Motivated by this growing significance of justice and equity for global environmental politics, this chapter offers a historical and analytical overview of international environmental justice (IEJ). We start with a brief clarification of the concept of IEJ, followed by a historical outline of the treatment of IEJ by international relations scholars. The main part of the chapter then presents an overview of IEJ based on an analytical scheme that we have found useful.

In any consideration of the contours and potential of international environmental justice as a body of scholarship and source of advocacy, the threshold question that must be asked is "Why justice?" That is, isn't it enough that we have already identified specific moral values and obligations with respect to the environment that render particular states of affairs and specific dimensions of human activity as arguably good or bad?

As a general matter, justice is not usually applied to identify an action or inaction as right or wrong per se. For example, while we would hold rape and murder to be culpable, such atrocities would typically be characterized as wrong, hateful, or even insane, but not necessarily "unjust." This is because justice involves circumstances imbued with some preexisting relationship, debt, or entitlement between or among two or more persons or entities, the violation of which triggers a sense that the violation was in some fashion also "unfair" to the aggrieved party or parties. It is this sort of appeal to the additional dimension of fundamental fairness with respect to environmental impacts and resource and decision-making access that has come to be considered in terms of international justice.

Once we have agreed and determined that the notion of justice is an important and applicable concept in global environmental politics, we need to understand the specific implications of such a move. First, where justice is held to pertain, the weight and depth of obligation on the part of those in a position to extend or withhold it is measurably intensified (e.g. Baxter 2000). For instance, when national leaders fail to engage pressing issues of environmental degradation within their borders, they can be criticized on the grounds that they "should" pay more attention to them. But where their inaction is held to be unjust, they can be criticized for not doing what they "must" do and, as a result, be accused of failing both a moral *and* a quasi-legal obligation.

This leads to the second and perhaps most important ramification of applying a justice standard to a particular problem setting. That is, whenever we argue that someone has an obligation to act in accordance with justice, we necessarily thereby invest the proffered recipients of that obligation with a specific right and a defensible expectation that the obligation must be respected. This is so even if the recipients cannot themselves defend that right or secure its application by political or legal force. A commonly offered example is that we accord the human infant and infirm full human rights, even though they themselves are not able to exercise or defend the full panoply of those rights. Thus applying a standard of IEJ highlights and strengthens the accountability and responsibility of states, transnational corporations, and other environmental actors in ways that positing only a moral obligation does not.

We use here the terms "environmental justice" and "environmental equity" interchangeably. Some scholars differ over who is best served by using one term or the other. We note that in most of the literature surveyed for this chapter, and in the conduct of global environmental politics, they are used interchangeably, and thus we have elected to bypass this debate.

Historical overview of international environmental justice

The history of IEJ is best understood as progressing both as part of the global environmental politics literature and as part of the practice of global environmental politics itself. Moreover, while this chapter focuses mostly on international relations scholarship, there are also important contributors to the development of and debates about IEJ from other disciplines such as economics, sociology, philosophy, and geography.

In 1972, the United Nations convened a landmark conference on the environment: the UN Conference on the Human Environment, held in Stockholm, Sweden. Observers disagree as to the extent to which Stockholm effectively addressed issues of North–South equity, but it is indisputably the case that the South viewed the proceedings through the lens of justice in identifying the industry and lifestyles of the affluent North as a primary source of environmental degradation in the South.

Scholarly and even popular sentiment regarding a pending global environmental crisis was further propelled at this time by the scarcity discourse, seminally presented in the Club of Rome's *The Limits to Growth* (Meadows *et al.* 1972). This report raised the specter of an overpopulated and resource-spent earth no longer capable of sustaining a healthy and satisfactory human existence. The global environmental politics literature and community during this period was not, however, focused explicitly on issues of equity, although as early scholars such as Richard Falk (1971) began raising concern within academic circles regarding the inequality and unsustainability of then prevailing global environmental practices and proposals. Falk was also instrumental in 1967 in founding the World Order Models Project, which in its periodic meetings, conferences, and associated publications since that time has contended for global justice, and specifically justice between the North and South. Others who raised questions of environmental equity include R. I. Sikora and Brian Barry (1978), Kenneth Dahlberg (1979), and David Orr and Marvin Soroos (1979).

By way of seeking to focus and advance the global environmental debate, the UN in 1982 formed the World Commission on Environment and Development, which was tasked with conducting a broad analysis of the relationship between economic growth, environmental limits, and equity issues such as global poverty. Their work culminated in the publication of *Our Common Future* (WCED 1987), which remains the widely accepted foundational authority on sustainable development – a notion thereby firmly established as the umbrella concept for the relationship between the environment and economic development. The report identifies inequality as a fundamental global environmental problem and asserts that we must address the underlying conditions of world poverty and inequality if we are to make real progress on urgent environmental problems and issues. Most importantly for our purposes, environmental issues and impacts were now placed squarely within the realm of debates over global equity and fairness.

As noted by Bradley Parks and Timmons Roberts (2006), at this juncture developments on the ground in the United States also came to have a significant impact on work in IEJ. In 1982 the state of North Carolina proposed to construct in its Warren County a PCB disposal site, a move ultimately approved by the US Environmental Protection Agency (EPA). Warren County was primarily poor and African American, and a sense of unfairness mushroomed as local residents took to the streets in protest. Many were imprisoned. Warren County ultimately did get the PCB dump, but the move to expose this sort of environmental "injustice" was on.

As the issue received increasing attention in the US, it became evident that indeed effluent industries and waste contractors often chose to site their operations in areas where land and labor were cheap. As these locales were typically high in minority and poor populations, arguments were and are still being made that this works an injustice on the poor and on people of color. Robert Bullard's large-scale study of environmental racism through the siting of hazardous waste facilities in the US South, *Dumping in Dixie* (Bullard 1990) – the first of its kind – was followed by extensive work on environmental justice issues by scholars such as Evan Ringquist (1998). Since that time the concept of environmental justice has been formally recognized in the US by the formation of a specialized environmental justice office within the EPA, and in an executive order in 1994 requiring agencies of the federal government to ensure that their operations do not result in environmental injustice.

Parallel to these political and social developments, a number of political philosophers began to open up notional space for the concept of IEJ. These include David Miller (1976) and his book on social justice, Brian Barry's work on theories of justice (Barry 1989, 1995), and Peter Wenz's (1988) treatise on environmental justice. Also of note was the extension by many of the egalitarian approach of John Rawls ([1971] 1999) to the international sphere as a matter of global justice generally (e.g. Barry *supra*). Indeed, the impact of Rawls's work on subsequent developments concerning justice in the international sphere is hard to overstate. These authors continue to be cited as sources of authority and conceptual clarity in formulating the philosophical basis for IEJ (e.g. Dobson 1998; Hurrell 2002). It was not until the late 1980s, however, that international relations scholars addressed IEJ as an important component of global environmental politics, for example an edited work by Steven Luper-Foy (1988) and a book by Edith Brown Weiss (1989). Weiss's work can be considered an important turning point, but it focused on obligations to future generations as distinct from questions of intra-generational justice. (As to intra-generational justice, see e.g. Agarwal and Narain 1991.) During that same period the newly founded journal *Capitalism, Nature, Socialism* provided a forum for addressing issues of environmental equity from a historical materialist point of view. Finally, various environmental ethicists argued that we should move beyond considerations of human rights to consider also the rights of nature, thus providing the foundations for what has been termed "ecological justice" (e.g. Rollin 1988).

Perhaps the most extensive treatment and formal adoption of the concept of IEJ took place at the 1992 UN Conference on Environment and Development, held in Rio de Janeiro, Brazil. Nearly all of the products of the conference, for example the Convention on Biological Diversity, the UN Framework Convention on Climate Change, the Rio Declaration on Environment and Development, and Rio's sustainable development global action plan – *Agenda 21* – expressly included formal provisions concerning international environmental equity. Though the end result of Rio was a determined attempt to accommodate economic development and environmental protection, the politics associated with it catalyzed a sustained concern for IEJ among academics and practitioners. Following Rio, a flurry of attention to the issue ensued (e.g. Henry Shue 1992, Maria Mies and Vandana Shiva 1993; Ted Benton 1993; Fen Osler Hampson and Judith Reppy 1996; David Harvey 1996; Paul Wapner 1997; Andrew Dobson 1998; Nicholas Low and Brendan Gleeson 1998; Nigel Dower 1998; Robin Attfield 1999; Dimitris Stevis 2000; John Barkdull 2000; and Avner de-Shalit 2000).

The third UN conference on development and the environment – the World Summit on Sustainable Development (WSSD) – was held in Johannesburg, South Africa, in 2002. While some commentators laud its results, principally for its advances in public–private partnerships for the environment, others note that by this time the demands for development were coming to eclipse environmental concerns, blunting somewhat the clarity of vision present at the Rio conference. Prospects for significant new multilateral environmental initiatives were also diminished by the global setting in 2002. As Ken Conca and Geoffrey Dabelko (2004) point out, levels of energy consumption and waste generation in the North had continued to increase unabated since the 1972 Stockholm conference. And much of the 1992 optimism had faded in the face of persistent international political, economic, and cultural conflict.

Following the WSSD, however, there has been a flourishing of works explicitly dealing with IEJ as a core concept within the global environmental politics literature, including books by Ruchi Anand (2004), John Byrne, Leigh Glover, and Cecilia Martinez (2002), Paul Harris (2001, 2003), Joan Martinez-Alier (2002), Chukwumerije Okereke (2008), Jouni Paavola and Ian Lowe (2005), Edward Page (2006), David Pellow and Robert Brulle (2005), David Schlosberg (2007), Kristin Shrader-Frechette (2002), and Laura Westra (2008).

It is worth noting that work on IEJ is expanding rapidly not only in the international relations literature, but also in other fields such as public health (e.g. Lambert Colomeda 1999) and environmental sociology (e.g. Pellow 2007). Neo-Marxist sociologists such as Ted Benton (mentioned above) and James O'Connor (1998) have left their mark, as have the more recent works of sociologists James Rice (2007) and Andrew Jorganson (2006). While the terminology may be different, such as the use within sociology of the term "ecological unequal exchange" to refer to breaches of IEJ in North–South relations, the focus is the same.

The literature on IEJ

We turn now to a consideration of the theoretical basis and content of the present state of scholarship, thought, and debate in the field of international environmental justice. In what follows we employ a heuristic typology that reflects the diversity of the origins and concerns of the scholarship and allows us to present the growing literature in a systematic way. The categorizations in the typology reflect differences among scholars in political and environmental world views, varying foci with respect to the scale and scope of IEJ and also the impact of differing fundamental ontologies as regards international relations theory.

In terms of its scope the IEJ literature can be categorized as intra-generational and inter-generational. Because of the centrality of North–South relations we have further divided intra-generational work into that which looks at IEJ in global terms and that which focuses more explicitly on the North–South dimension. It is not sufficient, however, to stop here, because over the years there has emerged significant work that looks at intra-generational and intergenerational justice issues from different theoretical perspectives. We capture this diversity by employing the categories of "narrow environmental justice," "broad environmental justice," and "ecological justice" (see Table 6.1).

Views in the narrow environmental justice category advance arguments that are founded on deliberative processes that privilege human needs, wants, and ingenuity in the process of securing environmental protection. In this category environmental concerns are formulated more narrowly – that is, they generally reflect the acceptance of existing national and global institutions and regimes to deal with environmental issues and justice. While not the only conceivable demarcation, our conception of the narrow category centrally includes views that are concerned with distributive IEJ.

The broad environmental justice column seeks to capture those points of view which contend that appropriate and necessary environmental protection will not ensue absent attendant concerns for broader social and economic issues. In this approach, effectively addressing environmental concerns must go beyond distributive matters, must implicate issues of social welfare and capacity, and may also be directed to address structural impediments to these social goods.

Finally, in the ecological justice view, nature must be valued in its own right. The importance of human needs must be counterbalanced by the equally important needs of non-human nature. Guarding non-human nature may acceptably result in some cases in deleterious impacts on justice among humans.

Plainly, work on IEJ does not always fit so neatly into only one of our nine categories and many scholars and issues indeed cross our gridlines in their work. Nonetheless the categorizations do trace the broad outlines of the different approaches to IEJ. The discussions which follow are not intended to be exhaustive with respect to the literature in each category, but rather provide key examples of the views represented therein.

Narrow environmental justice

The most characteristic approach within this category is the classical liberal (though, as discussed below, not necessarily neoliberal) approach to IEJ (cf. Richardson 2001). The focus is on distributive justice, as highlighted in Table 6.1, and the elemental unit of concern is the individual and his or her political and economic rights and liberties. At a system level, this form of liberalism seeks environmental solutions that are in general consistent with support for democratic political structures, free markets, and largely autonomous global economic relations. Much of the literature surveyed for this chapter supports to some degree liberalism so construed (e.g. Beckerman 1999; Achterberg 2001; Lal 2002; Wissenburg 2006; and Morvaridi 2008). This is owing both to principle – the widespread acceptance of the liberal political and economic model – and to practicality – the advocacy of liberal approaches even by those who call for more radical solutions globally, resigned in the belief that deep changes to the global capitalist system will not likely be forthcoming any time soon.

Table 6.1 The IEJ literature

Categories of justice	Views of justice		
	Narrow environmental justice	Broad environmental justice	Ecological justice
Environmental injustice	The maldistribution of environmental burdens and benefits and decision-making authority	Systemic barriers, distortions, and power disparities which impact environmental effects and access and which cannot be addressed by distribution alone	Privileging human needs and wants with no or insufficient regard for the needs of non-human nature
1 Intra-generational justice: a) Global dimension	Environmental policy Economic growth	Systemic reform	Nature has inherent value
2 Intra-generational justice: b) North–South dimension	Environmental burdens and transfers	Focus on structural injustice	Natural limits
3 Intergenerational justice	Weak sustainability	Broad sustainability	Strong sustainability

Intra-generational justice, global dimension

The liberal view raises the focus on individual and distributive rights to a global level and retains a commitment to seek to address both the burdens and the benefits of environmental resources and externalities. Justice enters the picture directly when these burdens and benefits are allocated disproportionately among domestic populations or nation-states. And, as is true in some form of most approaches to IEJ, the liberal approach also retains a concern with unfair patterns of participation in environmental decision-making.

Liberal scholars call for such solutions as a broader public discourse and a moral consensus on environmental justice – a stronger procedural justice; an attendant increased role for and decision-making access by civil society; strengthened international institutions; stronger domestic and international law on the environment, including international treaties and agreements to protect humans and the environment; and domestic and international constitutional measures and provisions that will enshrine the rights of humans to a clean and safe environment. In this approach, what is needed is not a rejection of the current global system, but the infusing of current discourse and practice with environmental sensitivities which will drive changes in policies, institutional mandates, and operations and increase stakeholder participation.

One particular form of liberalism takes a highly optimistic approach to global environmental issues, arguing for example that the Earth's resources will likely be sufficient to meet present and future human needs, and that the carrying capacity limits argued for in reports such as *The Limits to Growth* (Meadows *et al.* 1972) are overstated. This is what is termed the "Promethean" or "cornucopian" view of the human–nature relationship. We focus on it here, along with the neoliberal economics it propounds, because of the global dominance of these views over the past two decades (see e.g. discussion in Byrne and Glover 2002).

Where scarcity may impinge on human development, our ever advancing technological capacities will in this view certainly provide answers and tools which permit us to abate harmful environmental effects and extend or replace limited resources. Among early advocates of this view were Julian Simon (1984) and Gregg Easterbrook (1995). Bjørn Lomborg (2001), the author of *The Skeptical Environmentalist*, is perhaps the best-known contemporary advocate. He is the head of the Copenhagen Consensus, a think tank of well-known economists (including a majority of Nobel Laureates) who meet periodically to assign priorities to global initiatives, including environmental concerns. Most controversially, these scholars determine issue priority on the basis of a cost–benefit analysis of the measurable impact of a particular initiative.

As to justice, the growth ethos of the Promethean view matches well with neoliberal economic and political policies to minimize government intervention in the operations of private markets and to accord individuals the maximum economic liberty and latitude possible. Here the work of Freidrich Hayek (1976) and Milton Friedman (1962) is central in founding the arguments that social justice and well-being will be best served not by the intervention of governing authorities, but rather by free market economic development (e.g. Bhagwati 2004; see also discussion in Chasek *et al.* 2006).

As to environmental justice, this approach draws on concepts such as the Environmental "Kuznets Curve." Applied first to income inequality, this principle is extended by neoliberals and cornucopians to environmental degradation, which is the argument that, while early industrialization will inevitably create harmful environmental externalities, as industrial society advances and matures, the will and resources to address negative environmental effects will strengthen and come to prevail (Desai 1998; see also discussion in Clapp 2006).

Intra-generational justice, North–South dimension

In this arena, liberals and in particular neoliberals would make the same argument for North–South economic and political relations, contending that the best way to obtain social and environmental justice for the global poor is to open up local markets, permit currencies to float, privatize government functions, and allow the greatest latitude for foreign capital, investment, and trade. This view has been so predominant within the IMF and World Bank, at the urging of the US, that it is referred to by many as the "Washington Consensus."

The liberal approach extends into North–South relations the distributive dimension of the environmental justice movement in the US described above. More specifically, much of this literature is concerned with the maldistribution of environmental burdens upon the global poor and economically vulnerable communities (e.g. Shue 1999). Some who echo these concerns would also raise caution, however, with respect to neoliberal economic growth, pointing to the possibility of an environmental "race to the bottom" where highly effluent industries seek foreign havens of low environmental regulation and enforcement (e.g. Grossman 2002; Bryner 2004; Meyer 2005). Another relevant issue would be the state of affairs with respect to the transboundary shipment of waste, in particular hazardous waste, from North to South (e.g. Shrader-Frechette 2002; and Pellow 2007).

Inter-generational justice

The narrow environmental justice approach to justice for future generations takes the form of "weak sustainability." "Sustainability" refers to the extent to which the natural environment is conserved, preserved, and guarded. Weak sustainability allows that present generations have only a low-level obligation to future generations. This implicitly accepts the view that a high degree of substitutability is allowed – the possibility that the exhaustion of a particular natural resource can be compensated for by the substitution of reproducible goods, human capital, alternative resources, or some combination thereof. This is demonstrated in economic terms in the work of Robert Solow (1974), who has provided inspiration for contemporary advocates of this view (see e.g. discussion in Dobson 1998).

We note here the lively debate regarding whether or not future generations can be fairly accorded the rights with which they would be infused if the substantive claims of intergenerational justice are held to apply. Wilfred Beckerman and Joanna Pasek (2001) are well-known contemporary advocates of the view that persons who do not exist cannot have rights. Some scholars contend that a weak sustainability response to these arguments can take procedural justice as a fallback position. That is, what is important is not so much the theoretical debates over what intergenerational justice includes, but rather that, in contemporary decision- and policy-making, we explicitly empower and require a consideration of the rights, interests, and concerns of future persons (e.g. Holland 1999; Agius 2006).

Broad environmental justice

In the broad IEJ approach, we cannot settle for distributive justice alone, but must also address the very structure of the contemporary global economic and political system. Social rights and impacts become important as we move away from the more narrow neoliberal preoccupation with economic rights and effects. However, in the discussion which follows we caution that there is an important risk here, namely that, in the pursuit of social improvements, the environment may be forgotten.

Intra-generational justice: global dimension

The question here is whether we need to challenge and transform the global system itself, or whether we might find sufficient ground in seeking reform within the system. Thus this section will discuss the debates over whether justice is attainable under the current system of international politics and economics (principally a classical liberal, but not necessarily neoliberal, model), or whether deeper change is necessary (e.g. Levy and Newell 2005).

SOCIAL JUSTICE AS LIBERAL REFORM

Not all liberals are fully enamored with the extent to and means by which economic neoliberalism and the Washington Consensus has operated over the past twenty years (e.g. discussion in Kymlicka 1996; Agarwal *et al.* 2002; and Morvaridi 2008). It is the case that classical liberalism reflected a strong moral commitment to the weaker members of society and those who were victims of modernity and progress (Low and Gleeson 2002). Indeed, in its initial formulation liberalism held private property not to be inviolate, but to be defended and upheld only where enough was left in common for others.

Foundational to liberal reform in IEJ, recent scholars such as Amartya Sen, Martha Nussbaum, and Joseph Stiglitz contend for understandings of justice which, while situated in a liberal political and economic structures, shift focus onto elements of existence and flourishing that extend beyond an abbreviated concern with the health of private markets. In the case of Sen, a Nobel Laureate, and Nussbaum, what matters is that the individual has the freedom and liberty to pursue an array of publicly deliberated (Sen 1999) or specified

(Nussbaum 2000) basic capabilities which encompass not only obtaining sustenance needs such as food and shelter, but also higher order capabilities such as being able to earn a sufficient income and having the capacity to participate meaningfully in the life of the community. This approach goes beyond concern with the distribution of material goods, for, as both Sen and Nussbaum argue, income and economic wealth are not always the best indicators of overall well-being. Income distribution is still important, but it is the possession of and freedom to exercise capabilities to make meaningful use of income as well as other resources that should be distributed by government first and foremost.

While it is not above challenge (e.g. Page 2006), the capabilities approach is applied directly to issues of IEJ by environmental scholars such as David Schlosberg (2007), who argues for liberal reform in the context of human capabilities. In so doing he maintains that in many cases the environmental impact of the neoliberal global economy directly and unjustly limits the exercise of a full range of not only economic but also social and cultural capabilities by the global poor. In this regard, distributive justice alone – even the redistribution of environmental goods and bads – will not suffice because there may be underlying and thereby unaddressed systemic reasons for the maldistribution in the first place.

Stiglitz (2006) is critical of neoliberals who appealed to market forces, privatization, and deregulation to address poverty in the South. His proposed "post-Washington Consensus" retains liberal governance but adds the importance of the role of the state and international consortia in regulating global markets, reforming key international institutions such as the IMF, and remedying what he calls the global "democratic deficit" by developing a broader, more focused, and more inclusive discursive arena both within and outside international organizations and sovereign states. These and other measures are essential if we are to transform globalization effectively, which among other benefits realized will in Stiglitz's view facilitate managing and preserving global environmental resources and commons.

Environmental reform scholars such as Paul Wapner (1997) and Steven Bernstein (2001) have argued in that vein that liberalism may be fruitfully held true to its aspirational affirmations, thereby rendering global environmental politics more just and more reflective of the values and perspectives which are, as a conceptual matter, fundamental to liberalism. Such scholars also seek to address systemic social barriers to the full recognition and environmental decision-making participation of individuals and communities, and the extension of considerations of equity to the environmental impacts humans have on one another.

Liberal environmental reform movements have also highlighted two other potential approaches to change. First, "ecological economics," led by the economist Herman Daly (1996), argued that economic prescriptions for continued global economic growth – indeed, for sustainable development – were untenable. The objective in this view is what is termed "steady state" economics, where industry and growth are restrained and where population and resource limits are observed (Costanza 1989; Byrne and Glover 2002). Second, while not challenging the importance of free markets and trade at a fundamental level, the "ecological modernization" approach argues nonetheless that reform of political and economic institutions and relations and sparing use of regulatory restraints on trade and commercial activity are necessary to address environmental degradation (e.g. Mol 2002; Payne 2005).

SOCIAL JUSTICE AS SYSTEMIC CHANGE

Some environmental scholars of a more critical view argue, for example, that, if IEJ is to be meaningfully realized, nothing short of a new world order and government will suffice. Others contend that, at a minimum, the drivers of global injustice inherent in the very structure of the global economy must be addressed if we are to impose the burdens of environmental mitigation on those most responsible for environmental degradation (e.g. Martinez-Alier 2002). Critical environmental scholars also commonly envision and argue for a more inclusive and democratic global arena and community of discourse and consensus regarding global environmental issues, with a particular emphasis on including the global weak and poor (e.g. Hampson *et al.* 1996; Harvey 1996; Reus-Smit 1996).

Critical approaches may also take on a less systematic approach. Scholars such as Avner de-Shalit (2000) contend instead for the democratic accession to a socialist egalitarianism. Capitalist society is in this view incapable of dealing with the disparate ecological distribution of benefits and burdens in a manner that moves us toward effective environmental management. Solutions of a more socialist orientation are argued to be the answer because, first, egalitarian policies will release the altruism latent in everyone; second, where profits are distributed more evenly, workers can afford to relocate to venues with less environmental damage; and, third, these measures can accommodate and establish a minimum level of environmental well-being. In this view, to move these ideas toward reality, we need broader community and deeper participative, deliberative democracy.

In these views neoliberalism is wholly inadequate to address the rapidly expanding universe of global environmental concerns and issues regarding environmental fairness and equity (e.g. Harvey 1996; Stevis 2005; Parks and Roberts 2006). The environmental Kuznets Curve is challenged in that increased industrial production will inevitably produce increased emissions (e.g. Kütting 2004). And in the liberal model it is possible to solve the issue of human injustice without addressing related environmental issues (Stevis 2000). Indeed, what is needed is not more production, but greater social and environmental justice; global environmental issues and problems are both environmental *and* social (e.g. Taylor and Buttel 1992; Benton 1999; Newell 2007).

Intra-generational justice: North–South dimension

While the preceding debates between arguments for reform within the system and reform of the system are also relevant in North–South relations, we consider North–South justice separately because of the unique historical and political dynamics which have come to prevail. In this view IEJ will never be attained until we satisfy concerns for episodic and systematic relations of power disparity, bargaining strength differences, economic burdens on the poor for the benefit of the wealthy, and deleterious impacts of Northern consumption patterns. These scholars argue that there can be no environmental justice while poor communities are suffering the effects of social and economic injustice (e.g. Byrne, Martinez, and Glover 2002).

Some scholars, in arguing for environmental equity in North–South relations, go further and identify recognition and political participation, especially of the poor, as the primary practical elements and tests of IEJ (e.g. de-Shalit 2000; Amanor 2007). This is because, as noted earlier, merely ensuring a fair distribution of benefits and harm does not necessarily remedy the underlying causes of the maldistribution itself (e.g. Kütting 2003). In this view, procedural justice ensures recognition and participation in the face of sometimes intractable disagreement over the precise content of IEJ (e.g. Paavola 2005).

Finally, some authors in this strand provide explicit accountings of the sorts of values and concepts that IEJ requires. These commonly include the employment of precepts such as "common but differentiated responsibility" as between North and South, state rights to determine their own environmental conditions, among them control over their own natural resources, a minimum level of economic, political, and social development, the right to be compensated for environmental damage caused by another state, the precautionary principle, and the polluter pays principle (e.g. Anand 2004).

Inter-generational justice

Here the concern is not only with the environment but also with health, education, and social welfare – in short, human capabilities (e.g. Jacobs 1999; Boyce *et al.* 2007). In this more broad approach it is not merely a basic level of human welfare that must be preserved, but the opportunity for a comparable or improved quality of life. That is, what is to be passed on to future generations is the freedom and opportunity to exercise and enjoy the same set of broad and basic capabilities enjoyed by the current generation. In arguing that global justice requires global equality of opportunity, this approach is seen to go beyond fundamental rights which, though honored, may permit the perpetuation of vastly unequal lives.

Ecological justice

The ecological justice approach argues that what is at stake is not the impact of negative environmental effects upon humans, but rather the negative environmental impacts of humans upon nature. This view contends directly with what it sees as the anthropocentric tendencies of even a more socially progressive environmental discourse, program, and politics. We note that, for heuristic purposes, the range of views referred to throughout the following discussion renders the ecological justice approach amenable to division along "narrow" and "broad" lines, in similar fashion to our treatment of environmental IEJ.

The term "ecological justice" is commonly attributed to a work by Nicholas Low and Brendan Gleeson (1998), but as early as 1948 Aldo Leopold published *A Sand County Almanac* (Leopold [1948] 1968), in which he laid the foundation for the ecological justice movement by arguing that we must expand our moral community to take in the natural world. And the Norwegian philosopher Arne Naess (1973) gave formal voice and standing to the contemporary case for ecological justice, advanced in his essay as what he termed "deep ecology" – an approach ascribing moral status not only to sentient nature but also to the non-sentient.

The questioning of existing structures and hierarchies in this arena of discourse may have the same intellectual roots as the more critical views previously considered, and the following analysis centers on these views. We do note, however, that some liberal scholars, such as Derek Bell (2006), argue that liberal thought can also advocate for an ecological justice understanding. The difference here for both liberals and critical theorists is that what is sought is not primarily justice for humans, but justice for nature.

As in the previous arenas we have considered, issues such as according rights to other than present humans are problematic for some observers (see e.g. discussion in Baxter 2005). For our purposes here, however, we include points of view which contend that there are defensible rational reasons for extending moral standing to non-human nature. We note the importance of the literature on eco-feminism, which posits a connection between the domination of women and the deleterious dominance of nature, but as to which space limitations preclude detailed consideration.

Intra-generational ecological justice: global dimension

Nature is not only instrumentally, but inherently and objectively valuable. However, while those who advocate more extreme forms of ecological justice argue that there is absolute moral equivalence between animals and humans, others contend for principles to mediate conflicting claims, for example the conflicting interests of a small sleeping child on the one hand and those of a rattlesnake coiled under the child's bed on the other. These less stringent views allow for a continuum of the strength of moral claims as among human and non-human nature (e.g. Low and Gleeson 1998; and discussion in Baxter 2000). Nonetheless, the vision here is that non-human nature will be subject to contemporaneous flourishing in the acceptance of its overall moral significance (e.g. Byrne, Glover, and Martinez 2002; Roberts 2003). One can even extend the human capabilities approach to non-human nature, contending that animals, for example, retain a range of entitlements to life and the enjoyment of sentience (e.g. Schlosberg 2007).

Intra-generational ecological justice: North–South dimension

In this approach, the specific activities of global trade and investment are seen by many as principal barriers to ecological justice in the South. Indeed, in the view of such advocates, sustainable development is merely a tool of the North, which uses the concept to perpetuate the hegemony of its corporate interests and markets. Thus, for these scholars, the concerns of ecological justice cannot be addressed in the current capitalist global system (e.g. Faber and McCarthy 2003; Diefenbacher 2006).

In addition, multinational corporations (MNCs) are seen by many to occupy the most influential positions within discussions of sustainable development. Sustainable development and globalization are seen to have benefited mostly MNCs, which persistently and pervasively seek greater profits from global trade and investment (e.g. Glover 2002; Parks and Roberts 2006). Indeed, as seen in coercive approaches to granting industrial activity priority to indigenous lands, community efforts to accommodate ecological views of nature are seen as often disrespected by the neoliberal global economic and political mainstream.

Inter-generational ecological justice

We have seen in the narrow view calls for only a weak sustainability – a minimal regard for nature. And in broad sustainability advocates push for greater levels of human development and capabilities. In the ecological justice arena, it is strong sustainability that is argued for. That is, nature is seen to take on equivalence with, or, in the most extreme forms such as the work of David Foreman (2005), superiority over, some contemporary human life and interests. This approach contends for low or no substitutability, meaning that replacements of particular natural resources with reproducible human or natural capital goods or alternative resources are both seen as scenarios of deep and abiding loss. This is so even in the case of a pristine forest, for example, in that the harvesting of the forest is viewed as a loss despite the fact that it can be reseeded and grow back over time. This is the "physical stock" approach to what must be passed on to future generations – namely a largely intact set of natural resources. In this view, nature must at times be defended against human activity (see e.g. discussion in Dobson 1998).

Conclusion: for further study

We hope it is evident in the foregoing analysis that international environmental and ecological justice have risen to quite high levels of sophistication, conceptual clarity, and visibility among those who would seek to apply the tools and concepts of global environmental politics to particular environmental and ecological problems, issues, and policies. Yet there is much room for new contributions by scholars and advocates in each of the issue and literature fields we have covered, perhaps most usefully across the various issues we have surveyed.

For those interested in such an undertaking, the number of avenues into the substance and applicability of IEJ are many. While various aspects of the field are evident in and woven throughout this chapter, it may be helpful to highlight some of the specific routes by which IEJ scholars choose to organize and direct their work. For example, some find the greatest traction in taking up the issue of the identity and actual or potential impact of specific actors. These might be states, intergovernmental organizations, non-governmental organizations, multinational corporations, labor unions, or activist groups and associations based on gender, religion, or ethnicity (e.g. Humphreys 2001; Sachs 2002; Bryner 2004). Also, the important issues between North and South, and in our responsibilities to future generations, may be usefully combined into the concept of scale and the articulation of dimensions of IEJ in both time and geographical space (e.g. Agius 2006; Chasek *et al.* 2006).

As is evident in this chapter, there are also valuable questions to be asked and openings for study with respect to the difference between IEJ in process and outcomes – between procedural and substantive justice, respectively. That is, one may decide upon reflection to contend significantly for IEJ in decision-making procedures – in the recognition and participation of groups and individuals impacted by an environmental practice or policy (e.g. Shrader-Frechette 2002; Schlosberg 2007). Or one could focus on outcomes, for example, contending explicitly or implicitly that the results of procedural mechanisms may need to be augmented in the interests of ensuring desired results in environmental practice (e.g. Shue 1996; Rees and Westra 2003; Clapp 2005). And some scholars choose to emphasize both procedural and substantive IEJ (e.g. Low and Gleeson 2001; Anand 2004; Paavola 2005).

These issues implicate another potential focus: one's theoretical approach to work on IEJ and the articulation of the latter's philosophical basis. We have listed several excellent sources in this field for further reference.

Finally, one may choose to enter the IEJ debate by emphasizing a particular issue. Examples are a focus on the global trade in toxics (e.g. Clapp 2001; Shrader-Frechette 2002; Pellow 2007), on international trade and investment (e.g. Grossman 2002; Clapp 2005), on bio-diversity and natural resources (e.g. Conroy 2007; Amanor 2007), and on climate change (e.g. Harris 2003; Dow *et al.* 2006; Paavola 2008; Vanderheiden 2008).

In sum, we will consider this chapter to have succeeded best if it serves as the beginning of an ongoing engagement by the reader with the potential of the concept of justice to define and refine our understanding of and relating to the human and non-human global "others." To that end we include below a suggested reading list, some in addition to the works mentioned in text.

Recommended reading

Agyeman, J., Bullard, R. D., and Evans, B. (eds) (2003) *Just Sustainabilities: Development in an Unequal World*, Cambridge, MA: MIT Press.

Dobson, A. (1998) *Justice and the Environment*, Oxford: Oxford University Press.

Okereke, C. (2008) *Global Justice and Neoliberal Environmental Governance: Ethics, Sustainable Development and International Co-operation*, New York: Routledge.

Woods, K. (2006) "What does the language of human rights bring to campaigns for environmental justice?," *Environmental Politics*, 15: 572–91.

References

Achterberg, W. (2001) "Environmental justice and global democracy," in B. Gleeson and N. Low (eds), *Governing for the Environment: Global Problems, Ethics and Democracy*, Basingstoke: Palgrave.

Agarwal, A., and Narain, S. (1991) *Global Warming in an Unequal World: A Case of Environmental Colonialism*, New Delhi: Centre for Science and Environment.

Agarwal, A., Sunita, N., and Sharma, A. (2002) "The global commons and environmental justice – climate change," in J. Byrne, L. Glover, and C. Martinez (eds), *Environmental Justice: Discourses in International Political Economy, Energy and Environmental Policy*, New Brunswick, NJ: Transaction.

Agius, E. (2006) "Environmental ethics: towards an intergenerational perspective," in H. A. M. J. ten Have (ed.), *Environmental Ethics and International Policy*, Paris: UNESCO.

Amanor, K. S. (2007) "Natural assets and participatory forest management in West Africa," in J. K. Boyce, S. Narain, and E. A. Stanton (eds), *Reclaiming Nature: Environmental Justice and Ecological Restoration*, London: Anthem Press.

Anand, R. (2004) *International Environmental Justice: A North–South Dimension*, Aldershot: Ashgate.

Attfield, R. (1999) *The Ethics of the Global Environment*, West Lafayette, IN: Purdue University Press.

Barkdull, J. (2000) "Why environmental ethics matters to international relations," *Current History*, 99: 361–6.

Barry, B. (1989) *Theories of Justice*, Berkeley: University of California Press.

—— (1995) *Justice as Impartiality*, Oxford: Clarendon Press.

Baxter, B. H. (2000) "Ecological justice and justice as impartiality," *Environmental Politics*, 9(9): 43–64.

—— (2005) *A Theory of Ecological Justice*, London: Routledge.

Beckerman, W. (1999) "Sustainable development and our obligations to future generations," in A. Dobson (ed.), *Fairness and Futurity: Essays on Environmental Sustainability and Social Justice*, Oxford: Oxford University Press.

Beckerman, W., and Pasek, J. (2001) *Justice, Posterity and the Environment*, Oxford: Oxford University Press.

Bell, D. R. (2006) "Political liberalism and ecological justice," *Analyse & Kritik*, 28(2): 206–22.

Benton, T. (1993) *Natural Relations*, London: Verso.

—— (1999) "Sustainable development and the accumulation of capital: reconciling the irreconcilable?," in A. Dobson (ed.), *Fairness and Futurity: Essays on Environmental Sustainability and Social Justice*, Oxford: Oxford University Press.

Bernstein, S. (2001) *The Compromise of Liberal Environmentalism*, New York: Columbia University Press.

Bhagwati, J. (2004) *In Defense of Globalization*, New York and Oxford: Oxford University Press.

Boyce, J. K., Narain, S., and Stanton, E. A. (2007) "Introduction," in J. K. Boyce, S. Narain, and E. A. Stanton (eds), *Reclaiming Nature: Environmental Justice and Ecological Restoration*, London: Anthem Press.

Bryner, G. C. (2004) "Global interdependence," in R. F. Durant, D. J. Fiorino, and R. O'Leary (eds), *Environmental Governance Reconsidered: Challenges, Choices, and Opportunities*, Cambridge, MA: MIT Press, pp. 69–104.

Bullard, R. D. (1990) *Dumping in Dixie: Race, Class, and Environmental Quality*, Boulder, CO: Westview Press.

Byrne, J., and Glover, L. (2002) "A common future, or towards a future commons: globalization and sustainable development since UNCED," *International Review for Environmental Strategies*, 3(1): 5–25.

Byrne, J., Glover, L., and Martinez, C. (2002) "The production of unequal nature," in J. Byrne, L. Glover, and C. Martinez (eds), *Environmental Justice: International Discourses in Political Economy, Energy and Environmental Policy*, New Brunswick, NJ: Transaction.

Byrne, J., Martinez, C., and Glover, L. (2002) "A brief on environmental justice," in J. Byrne, L. Glover, and C. Martinez (eds), *Environmental Justice: International Discourses in Political Economy, Energy, and Environmental Policy*, New Brunswick, NJ: Transaction.

Chasek, P. S., Downie, D. L., and Brown, J. W. (2006) *Global Environmental Politics*, Boulder, CO: Westview Press.

Clapp, J. (2001) *Toxic Exports: The Transfer of Hazardous Wastes from Rich to Poor Countries*, Ithaca, NY: Cornell University Press.

—— (2005) "Global environmental governance for corporate responsibility and accountability," *Global Environmental Politics*, 5(3): 23–34.

—— (2006) "International political economy and the environment," in M. M. Betsill, K. Hochstetler, and D. Stevis (eds), *International Environmental Politics*, New York: Palgrave Macmillan.

Conca, K., and Dabelko, G. D. (2004) "Introduction: three decades of global environmental politics," in K. Conca and G. D. Dabelko (eds), *Green Planet Blues: Environmental Politics from Stockholm to Johannesburg*, Boulder, CO: Westview Press.

Conroy, M. E. (2007) "Certification systems as tools for natural asset building," in J. K. Boyce, S. Narain, and E. A. Stanton (eds), *Reclaiming Nature: Environmental Justice and Ecological Restoration*, London: Anthem Press.

Costanza, R. (1989) "What is ecological economics?," *Ecological Economics*, 1: 1–7.

Dahlberg, K. A. (1979) *Beyond the Green Revolution: The Ecology and Politics of Global Agricultural Development*, New York: Plenum Press.

Daly, H. E. (1996) *Beyond Growth: The Economics of Sustainable Development*, Boston: Beacon Press.

de-Shalit, A. (2000) *The Environment: Between Theory and Practice*, Oxford: Oxford University Press.

Desai, U. (1998) "Environment, economic growth, and government in developing countries," in U. Desai (ed.), *Ecological Policy and Politics in Developing Countries: Economic Growth, Democracy, and Environment*, Albany: State University of New York Press, pp. 1–17, 39–45.

Diefenbacher, H. (2006) "Environmental justice: some starting points for discussion from a perspective of ecological economics," *Ecotheology*, 11(3): 282–93.

Dobson, A. (1998) *Justice and the Environment*, Oxford: Oxford University Press.

Dow, K., Kasperson, R. E., and Bohn, M. (2006) "Exploring the social justice implications of adaptation and vulnerability," in N. W. Adger, J. Paavola, S. Huq, and M. J. Mace (eds), *Fairness in Adaptation to Climate Change*, Cambridge, MA: MIT Press.

Dower, N. (1998) *World Ethics: The New Agenda*, Edinburgh: Edinburgh University Press.

Easterbrook, G. (1995) *A Moment on the Earth: The Coming Age of Environmental Optimism*, New York: Viking.

Faber, D. R., and McCarthy, D. (2003) "Neo-liberalism, globalization and the struggle for ecological democracy: linking sustainability and environmental justice," in J. Agyeman, R. D. Bullard, and B. Evans (eds), *Just Sustainabilities: Development in an Unequal World*, Cambridg, MA: MIT Press.

Falk, R.A. (1971) *This Endangered Planet*, New York: Random House.

Foreman, D. (2005) "Putting the Earth first," in J. Dryzek and D. Schlosberg (eds), *Debating the Earth: The Environmental Politics Reader*, Oxford: Oxford University Press.

Friedman, M. (1962) *Capitalism and Freedom*, Chicago: University of Chicago Press.

Glover, L. (2002) "Globalization.com vs. ecologicaljustice.org: contesting the end of history," in J. Byrne, L. Glover, and C. Martinez (eds), *Environmental Justice: International Discourses in Political Economy, Energy and Environmental Policy*, New Brunswick, NJ: Transaction.

Grossman, P. (2002) "The effects of free trade on development, democracy, and environmental protection," *Sociological Inquiry*, 72(1): 131–50.

Hampson, F. O., and Reppy, J. (eds) (1996) *Earthly Goods: Environmental Change and Social Justice*, Ithaca, NY: Cornell University Press.

Hampson, F. O., Laberge, P., and Reppy, J. (1996) "Introduction: framing the debate," in F. O. Hampson and J. Reppy (eds), *Earthly Goods: Environmental Change and Social Justice*, Ithaca, NY: Cornell University Press.

Harris, P. G. (2001) *International Equity and Global Environmental Politics: Power and Principles in US Foreign Policy*, Aldershot: Ashgate.

—— (2003) "Climate change priorities for East Asia: socio-economic impacts and international justice," in P. G. Harris (ed.), *Global Warming and East Asia: The Domestic and International Politics of Climate Change*, London: Routledge.

Harvey, D. (1996) *Justice, Nature & the Geography of Difference*, Oxford: Blackwell.

Hayek, F. (1976) *Law, Legislation and Liberty: The Mirage of Social Justice*, Chicago: University of Chicago Press.

Holland, A. (1999) "Sustainability: should we start from here?," in A. Dobson (ed.), *Fairness and Futurity: Essays on Environmental Sustainability and Social Justice*, Oxford: Oxford University Press.

Humphreys, D. (2001) "Environmental accountability and transnational corporations," in B. Gleeson and N. Low (eds), *Governing for the Environment: Global Problems, Ethics and Democracy*, Basingstoke: Palgrave.

Hurrell, A. (2002) "Norms and ethics in international relations," in W. Carlsnaes, T. Risse, and B. A. Simmons (eds), *Handbook of International Relations*, London: Sage.

Jacobs, M. (1999) "Sustainable development as a contested concept," in A. Dobson (ed.), *Fairness and Futurity: Essays on Environmental Sustainability and Social Justice*, Oxford: Oxford University Press.

Jorgenson, A. K. (2006) "Unequal ecological exchange and environmental degradation: a theoretical proposition and cross-national study of deforestation, 1990–2000," *Rural Sociology*, 71(4): 685–712.

Kütting, G. (2003) "Globalization, poverty and the environment in West Africa: too poor to pollute?," *Global Environmental Politics*, 3(4): 42–60.

—— (2004) *Globalization and the Environment: Greening Global Political Economy*, Albany: State University of New York Press.

Kymlicka, W. (1996) "Concepts of community and social justice," in F. O. Hampson and J. Reppy (eds), *Earthly Goods: Environmental Change and Social Justice*, Ithaca, NY: Cornell University Press.

Lal, D. (2002) *The Poverty of "Development Economics,"* London: Institute of Economic Affairs.

Lambert Colomeda, L. A. (1999) *Keepers of the Fire: Issues in Ecology for Indigenous Peoples*, Boston: Jones & Bartlett.

Leopold, A. ([1948] 1968) *A Sand County Almanac*, Oxford: Oxford University Press.

Levy, D. L., and Newell, P. J. (2005) "A neo-Gramscian approach to business in international environmental politics: an interdisciplinary, multilevel framework," in D. L. Levy and P. J. Newell (eds), *The Business of Global Environmental Governance*, Cambridge, MA: MIT Press.

Lomborg, B. (2001) *The Skeptical Environmentalist: Measuring the Real State of the World*, Cambridge: Cambridge University Press.

Low, N., and Gleeson, B. (1998) *Justice, Society and Nature: An Exploration of Political Ecology*, London: Routledge.

—— (2001) "Introduction – the challenge of ethical environmental governance," in B. Gleeson and N. Low (eds), *Governing for the Environment: Global Problems, Ethics and Democracy*, Basingstoke: Palgrave.

—— (2002) "Ecosocialization and environmental justice," in J. Byrne, L. Glover, and C. Martinez (eds), *Environmental Justice: International Discourses in Political Economy, Energy and Environmental Policy*, New Brunswick, NJ: Transaction.

Luper-Foy, S. (1988) "Introduction: global distributive justice," in S. Luper-Foy (ed.), *Problems of International Justice*, Boulder, CO: Westview Press.

Martinez-Alier, J. (2002) *The Environmentalism of the Poor: A Study of Ecological Conflicts and Valuation*, Cheltenham: Edward Elgar.

Meadows, D. H., Meadows, D.L., Randers, J., and Behrens, W. W. (1972) *The Limits to Growth*, New York: Universe Books.

Meyer, J. M. (2005) "global liberalism, environmentalism and the changing boundaries of the political: Karl Polanyi's insights," in J. Paavola and I. Lowe (eds), *Environmental Values in a Globalising World*, London: Routledge.

Mies, M., and Shiva, V. (1993) *Ecofeminism*, Halifax, NS: Fernwood.

Miller, D. (1976) *Social Justice*, Oxford: Oxford University Press.

Mol, A. P. J. (2002) "Ecological modernization and the global economy," *Global Environmental Politics*, 2(2): 92–115.

Morvaridi, B. (2008) *Social Justice and Development*, New York: Palgrave Macmillan.

Naess, A. (1973) "The shallow and the deep, long-range ecology movements," *Inquiry*, 16: 95–100.

Newell, P. J. (2007) "Trade and environmental justice in Latin America," *New Political Economy*, 12(2): 237–59.

Nussbaum, M. (2000) *Women and Human Development: The Capabilities Approach*, Cambridge: Cambridge University Press.

O'Connor, J. (1998) *Natural Causes: Essays in Ecological Marxism*, New York: Guilford Press.

Okereke, C. (2008) *Global Justice and Neoliberal Environmental Governance: Ethics, Sustainable Development and International Co-operation*, New York: Routledge.

Orr, D. W., and Soroos, M. S. (eds) (1979) *The Global Predicament: Ecological Perspectives on World Order*, Chapel Hill: University of North Carolina Press.

Paavola, J. (2005) "Seeking justice: international environmental governance and climate change," *Globalizations*, 2(3): 309–22.

—— (2008) "Science and social justice in the governance of adaptation to climate change," *Environmental Politics*, 17(4): 644–59.

Paavola, J., and Lowe, I. (eds) (2005) *Environmental Values in a Globalising World*, London: Routledge.

Page, E. A. (2006) *Climate Change, Justice and Future Generations*, Cheltenham: Edward Elgar.

Parks, B. C., and Roberts, J. T. (2006) "Environmental and ecological justice," in M. M. Betsill, K. Hochstetler, and D. Stevis (eds), *International Environmental Politics*, New York: Palgrave Macmillan.

Payne, A. (2005) *The Global Politics of Unequal Development*, New York: Palgrave Macmillan.

Pellow, D. N. (2007) *Resisting Global Toxins: Transnational Movements for Environmental Justice*, Cambridge, MA: MIT Press.

Pellow, D. N., and Brulle, R. J. (eds) (2005) *Power, Justice, and the Environment: A Critical Appraisal of the Environmental Justice Movement*, Cambridge, MA: MIT Press.

Rawls, J. ([1971] 1999) *A Theory of Justice*, Cambridge, MA: Belknap Press.

Rees, W. E., and Westra, L. (2003) "When consumption does violence: can there be sustainability and environmental justice in a resource-limited world?," in J. Agyeman, R. D. Bullard, and B. Evans (eds), *Just Sustainabilities: Development in an Unequal World*, Cambridge, MA: MIT Press.

Reus-Smit, C. (1996) "The normative structure of international society," in F. O. Hampson and J. Reppy (eds), *Earthly Goods: Environmental Change and Social Justice*, Ithaca, NY: Cornell University Press.

Rice, J. (2007) "Ecological unequal exchange: consumption, equity, and unsustainable structural relationships within the global economy," *International Journal of Comparative Sociology*, 48(1): 43–72.

Richardson, J. L. (2001) *Contending Liberalisms in World Politics: Ideology and Power*, Boulder, CO: Lynne Rienner.

Ringquist, E. (1998) "A question of justice: equity in environmental litigation," *Journal of Politics*, 60(4): 1148–65.

Roberts, D. (2003) "Sustainability and equity: reflections of a local government practitioner in Southern Africa," in J. Agyeman, R. D. Bullard, and B. Evans (eds), *Just Sustainabilities: Development in an Unequal World*, Cambridge, MA: MIT Press.

Rollin, B. E. (1988) "Environmental ethics and international justice," in S. Luper-Foy (ed.), *Problems of International Justice*, Boulder, CO: Westview Press.

Sachs, W. (2002) "Ecology, justice, and the end of development," in J. Byrne, L. Glover, and C. Martinez (eds), *Environmental Justice: International Discourses in Political Economy, Energy and Environmental Policy*, New Brunswick, NJ: Transaction.

Schlosberg, D. (2007) *Defining Environmental Justice*, Oxford: Oxford University Press.

Sen, A. (1999) *Development as Freedom*, New York: Anchor Books.

Shrader-Frechette, K. (2002) *Environmental Justice: Creating Equality, Reclaiming Democracy*, Oxford: Oxford University Press.

Shue, H. (1992) "The unavoidability of justice," in A. Hurrell and B. Kingsbury (eds), *International Politics of the Environment*, Oxford: Oxford University Press.

—— (1996) "Environmental change and the varieties of justice," in F. O. Hampson and J. Reppy (eds), *Earthly Goods: Environmental Change and Social Justice*, Ithaca, NY: Cornell University Press.

—— (1999) "Global environment and international inequality," *International Affairs*, 75(3): 531–45.

Sikora, R. I., and Barry, B. (eds) (1978) *Obligations to Future Generations*, Philadelphia: Temple University Press.

Simon, J. L. (1984) *The Resourceful Earth: A Response to Global 2000*, Oxford: Oxford University Press.

Solow, R. M. (1974) "Intergenerational equity and exhaustible resources," *Review of Economic Studies*, 41: 29–45.

Stevis, D. (2000) "Whose ecological justice?," *Strategies*, 13(1): 63–76.

—— (2005) "The globalizations of the environment," *Globalizations*, 2(3): 323–33.

Stiglitz, J. E. (2006) *Making Globalization Work*, New York: W. W. Norton.

Taylor, P. J., and Buttel, F. H. (1992) "How do we know we have global environmental problems? Science and the globalization of environmental discourse," *Geoforum*, 3: 405–16.

Vanderheiden, S. (2008) *Atmospheric Justice: A Political Theory of Climate Change*, Oxford: Oxford University Press.

Wapner, P. (1997) "Environmental ethics and global governance: engaging the international liberal tradition," *Global Governance*, 3: 213–31.

WCED (World Commission on Environment and Development) (1987) *Our Common Future*, Oxford: Oxford University Press.

Weiss, E. B. (1989) *In Fairness to Future Generations : International Law, Common Patrimony, and Intergenerational Equity*, Dobbs Ferry, NY: Transnational.

Wenz, P. S. (1988) *Environmental Justice*, Albany: State University of New York Press.

Westra, L. (2008) *Environmental Justice and the Rights of Indigenous Peoples: International and Domestic Legal Perspectives*, London: Earthscan.

Wissenburg, M. (2006) "Global and ecological justice: prioritising conflicting demands," *Environmental Values*, 15: 425–39.

Part 2

7   Climate change

Paul G. Harris

Since the 1980s, climate change has moved from being a minor, mostly scientific matter in the affairs of states to being the most prominent issue in global environmental politics. It is now a major concern of governments, international organizations, industry, nongovernmental organizations, and a growing number of people around the world. As climate change has become better understood and more prominent in the media and public discourse, so too have predictions of its adverse impacts on nature and societies. Indeed, many of the effects are being felt today. Governments have negotiated agreements to study climate change and, in the case of many developed countries, to start limiting the pollution that causes it. However, the responses of states to the problem have failed to keep up with the increasing pace of climate change; they are grossly inadequate.

In this chapter I first summarize some of the official scientific findings on the causes and impacts of climate change before describing how governments have created a regime of international agreements and ongoing diplomatic negotiations aimed at tackling the problem. I then discuss several major themes in the global politics of climate change: the underlying driving force of material consumption, the important role of transnational actors, security concerns associated with climate change, and some of the unavoidable questions of justice that arise from it.[1]

Scientific assessments of climate change and its impacts

Over the last two decades, scientists have radically improved their understanding of the causes and consequence of global warming – the warming of the Earth as a consequence of greenhouse gases building up in the atmosphere. The Intergovernmental Panel on Climate Change, a large group of experts created by governments in 1988 to study climate change, has concluded with "*very high* confidence that the global average net effect of human activities since 1750 has been one of warming" (IPCC 2007: 37). Carbon dioxide, the most influential greenhouse gas in aggregate, is emitted through the burning of fossil fuels (e.g. coal, oil, and natural gas) and by the felling of trees and the carbon that is released by their decay or burning. "Climate change" refers to changes in climate and their consequences resulting from global warming, with the United Nations Framework Convention on Climate Change including under this rubric atmospheric changes connected directly or indirectly to human activities.[2] This human-induced global warming was, until recently, viewed as a *future* problem. But it is becoming clearer that *ongoing* climatic changes are consequences of global warming (see e.g. New Scientist 2006). The impacts of climate change on natural ecosystems and on human society and economies are potentially severe, particularly in parts of the world where geographic vulnerability and poverty make adaptation difficult or impossible (Brainard *et al.* 2009). Importantly for our understanding of the global politics of climate change, the problem is intimately connected to most economic activity and modern lifestyles, thereby connecting the environment to how people live and work.

The most authoritative official reports on the causes and consequences of climate change come from the Intergovernmental Panel on Climate Change, especially its 2007 *Fourth Assessment Report.*[3] According to the assessment, since 1970 anthropogenic greenhouse gas emissions have increased globally by 70 per cent, with carbon dioxide in particular increasing by 80 per cent, especially since 1995. The intergovernmental panel reports that "atmospheric concentrations of CO_2 [carbon dioxide] and CH_4 [methane] in 2005 exceed by far the natural range over the last 650,000 years" (IPCC 2007: 37). The concentration of carbon dioxide in the atmosphere in 2005 was 379 parts per million (ppm) compared with 280 ppm before the Industrial Revolution, with the annual increase being nearly 2 ppm. Importantly, although plants and the oceans absorb carbon dioxide, global warming inhibits their ability to do so, thereby creating a feedback loop contributing to more warming and greater climate change. Perhaps seeking to counter the political influence of "climate skeptics" – who question the reality of global warming and attribute it to all manner of causes, such as sun spots – the Intergovernmental Panel on Climate Change (IPCC) has declared that "warming of the climate system is unequivocal, as is now evident from observations of increases in global average air and ocean temperatures, widespread melting of snow and ice and rising global average sea level" (ibid.: 30). What is more, in a new determination since its *Third Assessment Report* in 2001, the panel found that "discernible human influences extend beyond average temperature to other aspects of climate, including temperature extremes and wind patterns" (ibid.: 40). That is, the impacts of climate change are undoubtedly attributable to human activities.

Among many ongoing adverse impacts of climate change, the proportion of the Earth affected by drought has increased, as has the frequency of extreme weather events, heavy precipitation, the incidence of intense tropical cyclones, extreme high sea levels in a wide range of locations, and heat waves (in most regions). Meanwhile, the frequency of cool days and nights has declined. These changes are having noticeable effects on both physical and biological systems, as demonstrated by melting glaciers and sea ice; the warming of lakes and rivers; the early advent of spring and associated changes to plants and wildlife, such as earlier greening of vegetation and impacts on bird migration and egg laying; and major impacts on marine ecosystems, including changes in salinity and currents, changes in ranges of marine life and timing and locations of fish migrations, likely adverse impacts on reefs, and losses of coastal wetlands and mangroves (both crucial for healthy fisheries). The IPCC reports adverse changes to agriculture and harm to forests from more fires and pests. Human health has also been affected by, among other things, heat stresses and expanding ranges of disease vectors (e.g. mosquitoes).

The IPCC considered the influence of planned and likely national sustainable development policies and efforts to mitigate climate change. Its findings are not optimistic; even following the adoption of anticipated proactive policies, greenhouse gas emissions will climb. The panel projected out two decades, anticipating an increase per decade under most emissions scenarios of about 0.2 degree C, with future temperature increases of course depending on how the world responds. Global average temperature is predicted to rise by 1.4 to 5.8 degrees C, with the highest increase more likely without additional mitigation policies. With continued warming, expected manifestations of climate change in this century will be "larger" (i.e. usually more adverse) than those seen in the last century (IPCC 2007: 45). Among changes expected this century are generally higher temperatures over land and at high northern latitudes, reduced snow cover, thawing permafrost, shrinking sea ice, sea-level rise, more frequent heat waves, heavy precipitation events, and more intense tropical cyclones. As a consequence,

> the resilience of many ecosystems is likely to be exceeded this century by an unprecedented combination of climate change, associated disturbances (e.g. flooding, drought, wildfire, insects, ocean acidification) and other global change drivers (e.g. land-use change, pollution, fragmentation of natural systems, overexploitation of resources).
>
> (Ibid.: 48)

Positive feedbacks will increase as carbon uptake by plants reaches saturation, the risk of extinction for 20 to 30 per cent of plant and animal species will increase (based on only 2.5 degrees of warming), and changes in biodiversity and ecosystems seen in the last century will be exacerbated – adversely affecting human needs, such as water and food supplies. Coastal erosion and flooding as a result of sea-level rise will increase. Extreme weather events are expected to become more frequent and intense, with "mostly adverse effects on natural and human systems" (ibid.: 53).

The health of millions of people will be adversely affected, manifested in, for example,

> increases in malnutrition; increased deaths, diseases and injury due to extreme weather events; increased burden of diarrheal diseases; increased frequency of cardio-respiratory diseases due to higher concentrations of ground-level ozone in urban areas related to climate change; and the altered spatial distribution of some infectious diseases.
>
> (IPCC 2007: 48)

Even in affluent parts of the world, which have a greater aggregate capacity to adapt, some groups of people, notably the poor and the elderly, will suffer the risks of climate change. The upshot is that, around the world, "more people are projected to be harmed than benefited by climate change," even if temperature increases are somehow mitigated (Working Group II of the Intergovernmental Panel on Climate Change 2001: para. 2.8).

Regional affects will vary, ranging from up to hundreds of millions of people exposed to water stress in Africa, increased flooding in the coastal and delta regions of Asia, significant loss of biodiversity in Australia, the retreat of glaciers in the mountains of Europe and water shortages in Southern Europe, the loss of tropical forests and biodiversity in Latin America, water shortages and heat waves in North America, detrimental changes to natural ecosystems in polar regions, and inundations and storm surges in small islands – to list only a few of the anticipated changes in coming decades. Later in the century, the likelihood of abrupt or irreversible environmental changes increases, with some of them considered inevitable. These could include rapid sea-level rise, significant extinctions (40 to 70 per cent of species if temperature increases exceed 3.5 degrees C), large-scale, persistent changes to marine systems and fisheries, and yet more positive (i.e. harmful) feedback loops as oceans absorb more carbon dioxide. In future centuries, impacts of climate change could be truly monumental.

Climate change diplomacy

Scientific assessments from the IPCC and other scientists provided the stimulus for international agreements to address climate change (Bolin 2008). However, because the science has been intimately wrapped up with politics, climate diplomacy has often taken on a life of its own, one that is partly divorced from science. One of the earliest important international events was the 1979 First World Climate Conference, a gathering of scientists interested in climate change and its relationship to human activities. From that conference a program of scientific research was established, leading to creation of the IPCC in 1988. The intergovernmental panel's first assessment report and the Second World Climate Conference in 1990 added stimulus to initial concerns about climate change among governments. In December 1990, therefore, the United Nations General Assembly established the Intergovernmental Negotiating Committee for a Framework Convention on Climate Change. The goal of the committee was to negotiate a framework convention that would be the basis for subsequent international protocols dealing with climate change.

From that point until the 1992 United Nations Conference on Environment and Development ("Earth Summit"), representatives of over 150 states negotiated the Framework Convention on Climate Change. The stated aim of the convention is:

> stabilization of greenhouse gas concentrations in the atmosphere at a level that would prevent dangerous anthropogenic interference with the climate system. Such a level should be achieved within a time-frame sufficient to allow ecosystems to adapt naturally to climate change, to ensure that food production is not threatened and to enable economic development to proceed in a sustainable manner.
>
> (United Nations 1992: art. 2)

The Framework Convention on Climate Change called on the world's most economically developed states to reduce their emissions of greenhouse gases to 1990 levels by 2000; this objective was not achieved. The convention came into force in 1994, after ratification by fifty states. Particular responsibility was also laid on the developed states to provide "new and additional" resources to developing countries to help them with their efforts to limit greenhouse gas emissions. While negotiation of the framework convention was fraught, and characterized by tensions between developed and developing states, negotiations after 1992 were even more contentious.

In 1995 parties to the Framework Convention on Climate Change established the Conferences of the Parties, which became the convention's overriding authority. Many of these conferences were held to negotiate the details of how greenhouse gas emissions limitations would be achieved. At the first Conference of the Parties (COP), held in Berlin in 1995, developed states acknowledged that they had a greater share of the responsibility for causing climate change and would act to address it first. Central to the resulting Berlin Mandate was the demand by developing countries that the industrialized states take on greater commitments to reduce their greenhouse gas emissions and to assist the poor countries with sustainable development. Thus the first COP affirmed the notion of "common but differentiated responsibilities" – meaning that, while all states have a common responsibility to address climate change, the developed states have greater ("differentiated") obligation to do so. At the second COP, which met in Geneva in 1996, governments called for a legally binding protocol with specific targets and timetables for reductions of greenhouse gas emissions by developed states. The resulting Geneva Declaration served as the negotiating basis for the Kyoto Protocol, which was agreed in December 1997 at the third COP in Kyoto (Grubb *et al.* 1999). The protocol requires most developed country parties to reduce their aggregate greenhouse gas emissions by 5.2 per cent below 1990 levels between 2008 and 2012. However, not all developed states agreed to be bound by the protocol.

The Kyoto conference proved to be especially contentious, not least because the United States seemed to be reneging on the Berlin Mandate when President Bill Clinton called for the "meaningful participation" of developing countries. Nevertheless, diplomats at the conference managed to agree to the Kyoto Protocol, which established specific emissions goals for developed states without requiring significant commitments from developing countries. The protocol also endorsed three market-based mechanisms that states could use to meet their commitments under the agreement. These mechanisms, which are related and overlap in many ways, included emissions trading (the so-called carbon market), joint implementation, and the Clean Development Mechanism. Emissions trading is a process that allows developed states to buy and sell emissions credits among themselves. If a particular state is able to reduce its emissions more than is required by the protocol, it has a surplus of unused "emissions reductions" that it is allowed to sell to other states that have not met their own reduction targets under the protocol. The price of the unused emissions reductions is determined by market demand, hence the term "carbon market." (This "carbon" market trades on other greenhouse gases as well. All greenhouse gas emissions are converted to a carbon equivalent to standardize trading.) One ongoing contentious issue among all states is whether the use of carbon sinks, which are processes such as planting trees (afforestation) and land-use changes that can remove greenhouse gases from the atmosphere, should be counted alongside concrete reductions in emissions.

Among other market-based mechanisms that states are allowed to use to meet their commitments under the Kyoto Protocol is joint implementation, whereby developed states that are required to reduce their greenhouse gas emissions under the protocol can earn emissions credits when investing in one another's emissions-reduction projects. This mechanism allows these countries to work together to find the most efficient and least expensive means of reducing their collective greenhouse gas emissions. The Clean Development Mechanism is similar in that it allows developed country parties with emissions commitments under the Kyoto Protocol to meet those commitments, or receive saleable emissions credits in the carbon market, for emissions-reduction projects in developing countries (i.e. those countries without emissions-reduction commitments under the protocol). This has created a rapidly expanding market for emissions credits that come from investments in China, India, and other developing countries that have expanding industrial sectors with opportunities for building new, less polluting factories – or for cleaning up old factories – than would exist without the protocol-inspired investment from wealthy states. The argument made in favor of these projects is that they produce a win–win situation: developed states are able to reduce their emissions at much less cost by implementing cuts in developing countries through Clean Development Mechanism projects, and the developing countries also benefit from new investment that they might not otherwise enjoy. The cleaner facilities in these countries often mean less local, national, and regional air pollution. But these projects are not without their critics, in particular those who argue that many of them would go ahead anyway. What is really needed if climate change is to be mitigated adequately are cuts in both developed and larger developing countries.

Some of the means by which the Kyoto Protocol's 5.2 per cent goal would be reached were codified at the fourth COP, held in Buenos Aires in 1998. At the fifth COP, which met in Bonn during October 1999, diplomats agreed to a timetable for completing outstanding details of the Kyoto Protocol by the sixth COP and, in an effort to speed up negotiations, gave the conference president the power to "take all necessary steps to intensify the negotiating process on all issues during the coming year" (United Nations 1999). The sixth COP began in November 2000 in The Hague, but the talks broke down because of disagreements among delegates, particularly on the question of carbon sinks. The Kyoto Protocol's ratification was put into doubt with the advent in the United States of President George W. Bush, who withdrew all US support for it. The sixth COP resumed in Bonn during July 2001. The resulting Bonn Agreement clarified plans for emissions trading, carbon sinks, compliance mechanisms, and aid to developing countries. The seventh COP negotiations were conducted in 2001 in Marrakech, where parties to the Framework Convention on Climate Change agreed to a long list of ways to meet the Kyoto commitments. The result was the Marrakech Accords, a complicated mix of proposals for implementing the Kyoto Protocol, largely designed to garner ratification from enough states to allow the protocol to enter into force. Parties agreed to increase funding for the convention's financial mechanism, the Global Environmental Facility, as well as to establish three new funds that would provide additional aid to poor countries: the Least Developed Countries Fund, the Special Climate Change Fund, and the Adaptation Fund.

At the eighth COP in New Delhi in October 2002, a tacit agreement was arguably reached between the United States, a few other developed states, and several large developing countries, notably China and India. What emerged was a shift of focus away from *mitigating* greenhouse gas emissions and climate change toward *adaptation* – wealthy countries agreeing to help developing countries adapt to the effects of climate change, rather than the former having to reduce their greenhouse gas pollution more substantially or the latter having to do so in the future. One might argue that this shift toward adaptation was a sort of deal with the Devil insofar as it effectively renounced major cuts in greenhouse pollution in favor of adaptation strategies, but the intervening years have seen this agenda develop into something more serious and central to international responses to climate change. Because greenhouse gas concentrations in the atmosphere are already approaching – or, more likely, have already gone beyond – safe limits, and because carbon dioxide and some other greenhouses gases remain in the atmosphere for decades, substantial climate change is inevitable. The kinds of adverse impacts from climate change described earlier – such as rising sea levels, more severe storms, drought, landslides, forest fires, and the spread of disease-causing pests, to name a few – are inevitable regardless of whether governments can agree to the substantial cuts in greenhouse pollution necessary to mitigate their effects. This means that developing countries, especially the poorest among them, will need help to adapt. This will have to come in the form of technological assistance and new funding to help people and communities cope with the impacts of climate change, as well as in the form of additional aid to help developing countries move toward low-carbon economies so that they can limit and, in the case of the large developing countries such as Brazil, China, and India, eventually reduce their own greenhouse gas emissions (Adger *et al.* 2006).

At the eighth COP, as well as at the ninth, diplomats also discussed ways to implement the Marrakech Accords and prepare for the ratification of the Kyoto Protocol. The tenth COP in Buenos Aires in December 2004 was dubbed the "Adaptation COP," because discussion again focused more on adaptation to climate change than the more common efforts to mitigate it through emissions limitations. In the end, there were pledges for more assistance to aid poor countries most affected by climate change, but there were no firm commitments to make access to adaptation funds easier for developing states. Importantly, it was also in 2004 that Russia ratified the Kyoto Protocol, allowing the agreement finally to enter into force in February 2005.

One visible aspect of the climate change negotiations has been the acrimony between the developed countries – particularly the United States – and the developing world. The international negotiations have been plagued by efforts by developed states to persuade developing countries to commit to emissions limitations, on the one hand, and developing country efforts to avoid such commitments, on the other. These differences were manifested in late 2005 during the combined eleventh COP and the "First Conference of the Parties Serving as the Meeting of the Parties" to the Kyoto Protocol, held in Montreal. Despite US attempts to derail the meeting, it formalized rules for implementing the protocol (e.g. rules for emissions trading, joint implementation, crediting of emissions sinks, and penalties for non-compliance), streamlined and strengthened the Clean Development Mechanism, began negotiations for further commitments by developed country parties to the protocol beyond 2012 (when the Kyoto commitments expire), set out guidelines for an Adaptation Fund, and initiated a process for negotiating long-term action to combat climate change. Several developing countries, while still opposed to binding obligations, showed new interest in undertaking voluntary measures, in keeping with the principle of common but differentiated responsibility.

Climate negotiations in the last few years have resulted in mostly incremental progress. In his opening address to the twelfth COP in Nairobi in November 2006, United Nations Secretary-General Kofi Annan characterized the negotiations up to that point as displaying a "frightening lack of leadership" from governments (Annan 2006). At the thirteenth COP, held in Bali in late 2007, the familiar arguments between developed and developing states were manifest: European states argued in favor of deeper international commitments for greenhouse gas cuts, the United States strongly opposed them, and developing countries argued for more financial and technological assistance (Pew Centre 2007). The discussions at Bali were pushed to a substantial degree by the IPCC's *Fourth Assessment Report*, which removed any remaining doubt (among officials willing to entertain the facts) about the seriousness of the problem. The meeting was important in its widespread opposition to efforts by US diplomats to thwart negotiations on a new, post-2012 agreement that would require developed states to take on new obligations to limit greenhouse gas emissions and aid developing states with sustainable development.

In the end, developing country governments agreed that they would consider taking unspecified future actions to mitigate their greenhouse gas emissions, which was a substantial shift from their longstanding policy of refusing to agree to any commitments whatsoever. The *quid pro quo* for the developing countries' stated willingness to consider future emissions limitations was a streamlining of the Adaptation Fund and sourcing it with a new 2 per cent levy on Clean Development Mechanism projects. Developed states also agreed to new emissions targets and timetables – but, as with the developing states' agreement, nothing was specified. Diplomats instead adopted the so-called Bali Roadmap, intended to guide discussions leading to a new, comprehensive agreement, under both the Framework Convention on Climate Change and the Kyoto Protocol, to be agreed in time for a COP in Copenhagen at the end of 2009.

All of these international efforts to address climate change have been far too little when viewed in relation to the severity of the problem. Even with full implementation, the Kyoto Protocol would result in reductions of well under 5 per cent of developed countries' emissions because the manner in which those commitments are fulfilled (e.g. emissions trading and land-use changes) often will not result in significant national emissions cuts. However, scientists tell us that emissions of carbon dioxide must be ended *completely* just to stabilize their concentrations in the atmosphere and to prevent chaos in the global climate system (Mathews and Caldeira 2008). James Hansen *et al.* (2008) have shown that, because of the time lag before the full impact of emissions is felt, even *current* concentrations of carbon dioxide in the atmosphere will likely bring dangerous interference with the Earth's climate system that the Framework Convention on Climate Change was intended to prevent. Even the relatively ambitious aim of the European Union to keep global temperatures to only 2 degrees C above pre-industrial levels is far too weak a target. The current concentration of carbon dioxide (about 385 ppm) is "already too high to maintain the climate to which humanity, wildlife, and the rest of the biosphere are adapted" (ibid.: 15). Instead, what is required at minimum is an effort to bring carbon dioxide concentrations down, very quickly, to about 350 ppm, meaning a near total move away from any use of fossil fuels if carbon cannot be captured and permanently stored – something that is not practically possible at present. According to Hansen *et al.* (ibid.),

> present policies, with continued construction of coal-fired power plants without CO_2 [carbon dioxide] capture, suggest that decision-makers do not appreciated the gravity of the situation. We must begin to move now toward the era beyond fossil fuels. Continued greenhouse gas emissions, for just another decade, practically eliminate the possibility of near-term return of atmospheric composition beneath the tipping level for catastrophic effects.

Consequently, the Kyoto Protocol has been, at best, a very tiny step toward greater action. In the meantime, global greenhouse gas emissions will continue to rise precipitously, notably because large developing countries (especially China and India) will be increasing their use of fossil fuels as their economies grow. Climate change will continue, virtually unabated, short of new, *much more aggressive* collective action to reduce greenhouse gases. However, strong signals of the more robust action needed are conspicuous by their absence. The IPCC, in a typically guarded understatement, characterizes the failure of the Kyoto Protocol this way: "To be more environmentally effective, future mitigation efforts would need to achieve deeper reductions [than the protocol] covering a higher share of global emissions" (IPCC 2007: 62). International legal instruments intended to avert dangerous interference with the Earth's climate – the stated aim of the Framework Convention on Climate Change – are increasingly about mitigating and adapting to that dangerous interference rather than averting it.

Themes in the global politics of climate change

The reason that climate change has found its way onto the international environmental agenda is primarily because its causes and consequences have become so evident and prudentially important. The underlying driving force has been material consumption, modern lifestyles, and associated industrial pollution – and the world's reliance on carbon-based fuels for most of its energy. Transnational actors have played a central role in highlighting the problem (as in the case of scientific groups and communities), in pushing for government action (by environmental non-governmental organizations), and – especially in the United States – in using domestic political processes to prevent or slow action (as in the case until very recently of a number of American business and industry groups). These roles have routinely been premised on maintaining the economic status quo: fossil-fuel intensive economic development and growth. But they have been politically juxtaposed against growing concerns about the many ways in which climate change might undermine national and human security in coming decades. All of these themes have been wrapped up in disparate conceptions of how to achieve fair agreements and action to address climate change – how to achieve ecological justice in this context.

The driving force behind climate change is consumption. Nearly everything that people consume leads to the emission of greenhouse gases, whether directly, as with the burning of fossil fuels for transportation, or indirectly, as when fossil fuels are burned to produce material "goods" that people consume by necessity or for pleasure, or when other greenhouse gases are emitted, such as methane that comes from animals (e.g. cattle) that are consumed for food. The vast bulk of the historical consumption of material goods and energy has occurred in the developed, industrialized world of the Global North. This is changing as people in developing countries adopt lifestyles and consumption habits similar to those in the West, but, even today, average per capita energy use and consumption in Western countries is many times that in the developing world. The developed world's disproportionate impact on the global environment, manifested in its greater historical pollution and higher average per capita greenhouse gas emissions, explains why many developed states were the first to commit to start reducing their emissions.

However, trends are shifting, with China overtaking the United States to become the largest national source of greenhouse gas emissions (Netherlands Environmental Assessment Agency 2008), and millions of people in China and a number of other developing countries moving into the global middle class, thereby enabling them to consume and pollute as much as Westerners have done for a century or more (Myers and Kent 2004). Thus the globalization of modern lifestyles is having a profoundly damaging impact on the Earth's atmosphere, placing new demands for more widespread and comprehensive action if the very worst effects of climate change are to be mitigated.

As holds true in the case studies of global environmental politics described in other chapters, climate change demonstrates the importance of transnational actors, notably groups of scientists and environmental non-governmental organizations (Raustiala 2001). The underlying scientific understanding of climate change, which feeds into national policy and international negotiations on climate change, was developed by scientists who routinely collaborate internationally, attempt to influence domestic policy-makers, disseminate their views for the use of diplomats involved in the climate change international negotiations, and even in some cases serve on national delegations at conferences of the parties. Scientists may also work in collaboration with non-governmental organizations, which in turn attempt to influence public opinion and government officials.

Non-governmental organizations active in pushing for stronger action on climate change include those in favor of more robust action to cut back on greenhouse gas emissions and to help poor countries and people cope with climate change, such as Greenpeace, Oxfam and WWF. These and similar organizations have been prominent and visible in their public relations and direct-action campaigns to persuade developed country governments and members of their national legislatures to support greenhouse gas emission cuts, subsidies for green programs and industries, and international aid for climate change-related projects in the developing world (Carpenter 2001). Many of these groups have large memberships that garner the attention of national legislators, expertise that can be brought to bear in climate change debates, and the moral high ground as news about the impacts of climate change become more prominent and widespread. Environmental non-governmental organizations work at both the grassroots level to muster public support and with like-minded groups in other countries to pool resources and expertise. Many of these groups, notably Greenpeace, routinely show up at international conferences to shame diplomats and governments publicly for not agreeing to bigger cuts in greenhouse gases.

Other groups, such as the American Chamber of Commerce and (during the 1990s) the Global Climate Coalition, have lobbied legislators and governments to avoid climate-related laws, particularly those that would require businesses to comply with new regulations or that would lead to "green taxes" or "carbon taxes" on activities that lead to greenhouse pollution. Among those industries in developed states most opposed to action on climate change have been petroleum companies, electric utilities, and automobile manufacturers. By appealing to legislators' concerns about jobs and economic growth, and through their donations of funds to politicians' election campaigns (as in the United States), these industries were able to block robust regulations and laws to bring about reductions in greenhouse gases. As time goes by, however, some of these industries are following the lead of new science and public opinion, slowly reducing their opposition to climate change-related laws while looking for new business opportunities in alternative energy and "green" products. These more environmentally inclined businesses are diluting the influence of the traditional energy producers that often maintain their support for fossil fuel-based and carbon-intensive economic systems, providing an opening for less polluting industries to gain influence with governments (Falkner 2008).

In the last few years there has been a tectonic shift in the global politics of climate change away from scientific skepticism to recognition that it is a real problem requiring action by governments and other actors. The debate is no longer about whether to act but how to do so. A central reason for this shift is the realization by officials and even publics that climate change presents them with very real challenges to prudential interests. Put another way, climate change is a matter of *security* (Lacy 2005; Campbell 2008). Indeed, the security challenges of climate change were salient enough to encourage the United Nations Security Council in 2007 to hold a debate on the issue. While there remain disagreements about whether climate change is a bona fide *national* security concern in the traditional sense – some (albeit not the small island states most vulnerable to sea-level rise) will debate whether it is an existential threat to states – there is no longer any doubt that it is a major threat to human and economic security, especially in the developing world. The environmental changes that result from climate change leave people who are already vulnerable to drought, storms, and pestilence even more vulnerable than before.

This in turn raises profound questions of justice, both international and global (Page 2006; Vanderheiden 2008). Concerns about international justice have been expressed by developing states from the beginning of the climate change negotiations. As they argue, it is the developed countries of the world that are most responsible for historical emissions of greenhouse gases, and it is the developing countries that will suffer the most from the environmental changes brought on by those emissions. Thus the developed countries are responsible for reducing emissions of greenhouse gases and helping developing countries to adapt to the inevitable changes that cannot be avoided. This is an unassailable argument. Consequently, at the first COP, governments agreed upon the principle of common but differentiated responsibility. It followed from this principle that the Kyoto Protocol would not require developing countries to reduce their emissions of greenhouse gases. But, as we have seen, the actual cuts in emissions by developed countries have barely begun, and the amount of funding that these countries have given to developing countries for adaptation to climate change has been tiny compared to the need (see Muller 2006).

Climate change also presents us with potentially even more profound questions of *global* justice. As millions of people in developing countries join the world's affluent classes, calls will grow for them to unite with Americans, Germans, and Japanese in limiting and eventually reducing their greenhouse gas pollution. It may be too soon to demand that Brazil or India agree to binding limitations on their own emissions, but it may also be past time to demand that wealthy Brazilians and Indians do so. The failure to implement climate justice among states ought not to hide the need for climate justice among people (see Harris 2010).

Conclusion

News about the latest science of climate change – or about the most recent "natural" disaster that may be a manifestation of global warming or made worse by it – is now daily fare for everyone with access to newspapers, television, or the World Wide Web. The science has improved to the point where it is now impossible for policy-makers to deny the reality of the problem or its seriousness for most of the world. Consequently, climate change has become one of the most prominent issues in global politics, now routinely attracting the attention of presidents and prime ministers. Nevertheless, despite the heightened pace of international negotiations that have resulted from the growing amount of high-level and public attention to climate change, emissions of greenhouse gases continue to grow at an alarming pace. While it is very likely that governments will be able to agree to more action, and specifically to more cuts in atmospheric pollution at the root of the problem, there is little real prospect for the scale of cuts globally that scientists say are needed. Global warming will continue. Even if the developed world cuts back substantially on its greenhouse gas emissions, the developing world's emissions will grow for decades more. Without radical changes in government policies and the rapid deployment of environmentally friendly technologies, the best we can expect in the near and medium term are modest limitations in pollution resulting in somewhat lesser impacts later this century and beyond. Fundamentally, however, climate change and its various painful manifestations are unavoidable. Sadly, therefore, climate change reveals the limits of global environmental politics. This demonstrates the great need for all capable individuals to do whatever we can to reduce our greenhouse gas pollution, and ideally to help those people who suffer the most from climate change – the world's poor – while states work toward agreement on the vastly more aggressive action that will be required of them if the worst effects of climate change are to be limited in the future.

Notes

1 Parts of this chapter, notably the next two sections, are adapted from Harris (2007a, 2007b, 2008a, 2008b, 2009a, 2009b, 2010) and works cited therein.
2 'Climate change' in the lexicon of the IPCC refers to changes from both natural processes and human activities, whereas the Framework Convention on Climate Change addresses only the latter.
3 Here I summarize findings of the *Fourth Assessment Report*, the four volumes of which are available at www.ipcc.ch.

Recommended reading

Giddens, A. (2009) *The Politics of Climate Change*, Cambridge: Polity.
Hulme, M. (2009) *Why We Disagree about Climate Change: Understanding Controversy, Inaction and Opportunity*, Cambridge: Cambridge University Press.
Kolber, E. (2006) *Field Notes from a Catastrophe: Man, Nature, and Climate Change*, New York: Bloomsbury.
Rosencranz, A., Schneider, S. H., and Mastrandrea, M. (eds) (2010) *Climate Change Science and Policy*, Washington, DC: Island Press.
Stern, N. (2009) *The Global Deal: Climate Change and the Creation of a New Era of Progress and Prosperity*, New York: Public Affairs.

References

Adger, W. N., Paavola, J., Huq, S., and Mac, M. J. (eds) (2006) *Fairness in Adaptation to Climate Change*, Cambridge, MA: MIT Press.
Annan, K. (2006) "Citing 'frightening lack of leaders' on climate change," available: www.un.org/News/Press/docs/2006/sgsm10739.doc.htm.
Bolin, B. (2008) *A History of the Science and Politics of Climate Change: The Role of the Intergovernmental Panel on Climate Change*, Cambridge: Cambridge University Press.
Brainard, L., Jones, N., and Pervis, A. (2009) *Climate Change and Global Poverty: A Billion Lives in the Balance?*, Washington, DC: Brookings Institution.
Campbell, K. M. (2008) *Climate Cataclysm: The Foreign Policy and National Security Implications of Climate Change*, Washington, DC: Brookings Institution.

Carpenter, C. (2001) "Business, green groups and the media: the role of non-governmental organizations in the climate change debate," *International Affairs*, 77(2): 313–28.

Falkner, R. (2008) *Business Power and Conflict in International Environmental Politics*, Basingstoke: Palgrave Macmillan.

Grubb, M., Vrolijk, C., and Brack, D. (1999) *The Kyoto Protocol: A Guide and Assessment*, London: Royal Institute of International Affairs.

Hansen, J., Sato, M., Kharecha, P., Beerling, D., Berner, R., Masson-Delmotte, V., Pagani, M., Raymo, M., Royer, D. L., and Zachos, J. C. (2008) "Target atmospheric CO_2: where should humanity aim?," *Open Atmospheric Science Journal*, 31 October. Available: http://arxiv.org/pdf/0804.1126v2.

Harris, P. G. (2007a) "Collective action on climate change: the logic of regime failure," *Natural Resources Journal*, 47(1): 195–224.

—— (ed.) (2007b) *Europe and Global Climate Change: Politics, Foreign Policy, and Regional Cooperation*, Cheltenham: Edward Elgar.

—— (2008a) "Constructing the climate regime," *Cambridge Review of International Affairs*, 21(4): 671–2.

—— (2008b) "The glacial politics of climate change," *Cambridge Review of International Affairs*, 21(4): 455–64.

—— (2009a) "Climate change in environmental foreign policy: science, diplomacy and politics," in P. G. Harris (ed.), *Climate Change and Foreign Policy: Case Studies from East to West*, London: Routledge.

—— (ed.) (2009b) *The Politics of Climate Change*, London: Routledge.

—— (2010) *World Ethics and Climate Change: From International to Global Justice*, Edinburgh: Edinburgh University Press.

IPCC (Intergovernmental Panel on Climate Change) (2007) *Climate Change 2007: Synthesis Report*, Cambridge: Cambridge University Press. Available: www.ipcc.ch.

Lacy, M. J. (2005) *Security and Climate Change: International Relations and the Limits of Realism*, London: Routledge.

Mathews, H. D., and Caldeira, K. (2008) "Stabilizing climate requires near-zero emissions," *Geophysical Research Letters*, 35. Available: www.agu.org/pubs/crossref/2008/2007GL032388.shtml.

Muller, B. (2006) *Montreal 2005: What Happened, and What it Means*, Oxford: Oxford Institute for Energy Studies. Available: www.oxfordenergy.org/pdfs/EV35.pdf.

Myers, N., and Kent, J. (2004) *The New Consumers: The Influence of Affluence on the Environment*, London: Island Press.

Netherlands Environmental Assessment Agency (2008) "China contributing two thirds to increase in CO_2 emissions," 13 June. Available: www.mnp.nl/en/service/pressreleases/2008/20080613ChinacontributingtwothirdstoincreaseinCO2emissions.html.

New Scientist (2006) "Climate change is all around us," *New Scientist*, no. 2543, 18 March. Available: http://environment.newscientist.com/channel/earth/mg18925432.600-editorial-climate-change-is-all-around-us.html.

Page, E. A. (2006) *Climate Change, Justice and Future Generations*, Cheltenham: Edward Elgar.

Pew Center on Global Climate Change (2007) *Summary of COP13*. Available: www.pewclimate.org/docUploads/Pew%20Center_COP%2013%20summary.pdf.

Raustiala, K. (2001) "Nonstate actors in the global climate chang regime," in U. Luterbacher and D. F. Sprinz (eds), *International Relations and Global Climate Change*, Cambridge, MA: MIT Press.

United Nations (1992) *Framework Convention on Climate Change* Available: http://unfccc.int/resource/docs/convkp/conveng.pdf.

—— (1999) "Ministers pledge to finalize climate agreement by November 2000," press release (5 November). Available: www.unis.unvienna.org/unis/pressrels/1999/env75.html.

Vanderheiden, S. (2008) *Atmospheric Justice*, Oxford: Oxford University Press.

Working Group II of the Intergovernmental Panel on Climate Change (2001) *Climate Change 2001: Impacts, Adaptation and Vulnerability*, Cambridge: Cambridge University Press. Available: www.grida.no/CLIMATE/IPCC_TAR/wg2/010.htm.

8   Marine pollution

Peter Jacques

Introduction

The World Ocean – that ensemble of oceans around the globe – is riddled with complex and persistent pollutants, most of which come from inland sources. These pollutants include toxic chemicals, fertilizers, garbage, hydrocarbons, and carbon dioxide, among many other contaminants.[1] On the other hand, most marine pollution regimes focus on ocean dumping, or pollution added to the ocean deliberately from ships or land-based structures. This chapter will explain the disconnect between most pollution that reaches the ocean and the policies the international community has devised through Ulrich Beck's notion of the "risk society" to understand marine pollution better. The risk society proposes that modern industrial systems have begun to create ubiquitous and irreversible problems that the same systems cannot address. From this chapter we come to understand that some modern problems may not have modern solutions, but rather may require much more difficult political choices. Ultimately, marine pollution cannot effectively be addressed through dumping regulations, even though these may help with the dumping of pollutants. Effective policy for international marine pollution requires the reduction of pollution from the sources of larger social systems, such as the world economy, and ecological systems, such as inland and marine space.

In the theoretical section of this book, we saw that there are several different ways to conceive of and explain global environmental politics. Central to our understanding of marine pollution will be the ideas of international political economy, environmental security, nongovernmental actors, and, of course, the use of state-led institutions or regimes. This chapter provides the case of marine pollution in global environmental change as a surprising counterpoint to some of our normal understandings of environmental management. Our normal – that is to say, modern – understanding of environmental problems is that the more environmental pollution we create, the more effective and efficient regimes we need to control it. This management almost always employs "end-of-the-pipe" controls and restrictions to reduce the impact of industrial processes. Thus, one political purpose of environmental management, both on the domestic and on the international scale, is to preserve the current economic and political systems that produce pollution while reducing what comes out of the pipe or what happens to this pollution when it does. End-of-the-pipe solutions are seen in ocean dumping. But what does it mean that we cannot control the majority of "pipes," or what happens to the vast majority of marine pollutants once they are produced or once they are used?

Ahistoric (or new to human history) global environmental changes have become a pressing reality. Humans have changed approximately half of the world's land space, appropriated about half of the world's available surface water, and have led the extermination of non-human life in the Sixth Great Extinction, where extinction rates are some 100 to 1,000 times greater than background rates (Vitousek *et al.* 1997: 494). Meanwhile, we tinker with the chemistry of the world's soils, waters, and atmosphere with profound and unknowable results. Unfortunately, all of these changes intertwine in frightening complexity, and we are unable effectively to single out one thing and "fix it." Take biodiversity as an example. Biodiversity is driven principally by the consumption of habitat land-use changes, which themselves are produced by a series of political-economic and social contexts through property law, agriculture, and urbanization, to name a few. Fishery declines and collapses are a specific part of biodiversity loss and occur through overfishing, but will be fundamentally affected by rising sea-surface temperatures (Lehody *et al.* 2006), and this chapter will show that climate change is forcing ocean acidification that will affect fish physiology. We will also see that industrial inputs of soil nutrients from agriculture and land-use changes lead to one of the more important oceanic pollutant issues that permanently or sporadically eradicate marine life. We therefore find ourselves at the threshold of major ecological shifts that provide an important moment to reconsider the nature of world politics.

This chapter will highlight and explore the fact that marine pollution has grown along with industrial production and expanding populations, but there are no significant regimes that address the vast majority of marine pollution, most of which is arguably far more destructive than the pollution for which we do have regimes. Ulrich Beck's (1992) idea of the "risk society" will be used to understand the nature of new global marine pollution threats. This idea poses the prospect of consequences from the era of modernity, which has grown out of a simultaneous impulse of control over people and the expansion of liberal freedoms. These dual impulses are in the freedoms of expanding individual rights in welfare states and the forces of increasing control over nature, economy, and people.

Beck indicates some of this irony of modern politics when he observes that the efforts of control have resulted in a series of interrelated crises, or the opposite of control. This set of crises then creates a crisis of legitimacy for the modern institutions that generated the problems because these problems are a normal result – not an aberration or exception to the rule. Consequently, the forces that generated our marine pollution problems will theoretically not be able to solve them. If this is the case, then our study of global environmental politics will have to go beyond thinking just of the nation-state as a sovereign policy-maker, science and technology as an answer to the hardest questions, and economic growth as an unambiguous value. Thus, marine pollution offers an opportunity really to question some core assumptions about global environmental politics.

This chapter will proceed by explaining the standard evolution of marine pollution and some state-led regimes that have followed as a way of managing standard problems of ocean *dumping*, followed by a juxtaposition of marine problems that are relatively irreversible, diffuse, and escape control because they never involve dumping. Instead, this class of pollutant is carried by airsheds and the atmosphere, the hydrological cycle, and wind – all things which are well outside of the control of state bureaucrats. These are marine pollutants characteristic of a world risk society – nutrient pollution, plastic pollution, persistent organic pollutants (see Chapter 12 in this volume), and ocean acidification. All of these problems are life threatening on a large scale but are results of states, economies, and industrial science's *normal* operation, and none are subject to international regimes. Worse, even if there were relevant state-led institutions, there is little theoretical hope of ameliorating these problems without changing the production systems that generate them, the political systems that subsidize and legislate processes of production and consumption, and the goals of industrial science. However, the chapter will start by outlining important marine history to contextualize the progression of marine pollution into the twenty-first century.

Marine history

We can cover only a cursory view of ocean history here, but some major themes and eras stand out as exceptionally important. The first part may seem trite to modern readers, but it precedes all life on the planet, where the ocean served as the most important birthing ground of all time, perhaps the vital amniotic fluid for Planet Earth. All life began in the saline water – and even after some animals evolved on land, some chose to return to the oceans – cetaceans, such as whales, porpoises, and dolphins are the most obvious. Blood in our bodies may be present to mimic this primordial condition, and it retains a remarkable mineral composition, such as salinity, similar to ocean water. The ocean may, indeed, be in our blood.

As human societies built their lives around the ocean, different histories played out, but one thing is clear – the ocean was and continues to be a social space, despite the tendency for some peoples to see it as a socially empty space (Steinberg 2001).

To Western peoples, who may form the most fundamentally *anthropocentric* set of societies known (Hay 2002), the ocean is more of an instrument where the main limits to its use come from what people can get from it. For example, in fishery politics, the principal concern is the total allowable catch for each state, but the International Commission for the Conservation of Atlantic Tuna does not extend consideration for what might be the *tuna*'s interests. While understanding non-human interests may be difficult, the political theorist Paul Wapner (2002) suggests that the minimum expectation would be to allow a species to exist, and Atlantic tuna appear to be losing this simple consideration.

Non-Western peoples have typically had a more expansive view of who and what are recognized as agents. Physical and spiritual worlds are commonly seen as inseparable in indigenous institutions. Makere Stewart-Harawira (2005) describes the Maori idea of *Te Aho Tapu*, or the "sacred thread," as a requirement to recognize more than just the human agents in the world. All existence has a life-force, or *mauri-ora*:

> This concept of *mauri* as the unique living force that is present in all kingdoms of existence extends to inanimate as well as animate objects and, indeed, to concepts and forms of knowledge. Within the natural world, each individual rock and stone, each individual animal and plant, as well as every body of land and water, is recognized as having its own unique life-force.
>
> (Stewart-Harawira 2005: 39)

In this schema, the oceans have a unique life force of their own. But the dominant notions of the oceans do not permit this arrangement. This is exemplified in the first global regime, articulated by Hugo Grotius, who argued that no single country could possess the ocean and therefore it could not belong to any. *Mare liberum*, or "freedom of the seas," started out as a way of legitimizing Dutch navigation for trade and colonialism, along with the Portuguese and Spanish, at the same time that the British were also acquiring colonies. The idea was that the ocean was free to be used as a highway for Christian European kings[2] to trade with other countries – something Grotius believed was a "natural" or inalienable right. Note how this contrasts with *Te Aho Tapu*.

It is important to point out in this history that *mare liberum* created an open-pool regime in the oceans, minus the first 3 miles from the coastline. These were territorial zones controlled by nations. Open-pool regimes have no rules for access or use, and this permits nearly any behavior on the oceans. This means at least two things. First, open-pool regimes are a recipe for disaster, because they create a collective action problem that is very difficult to solve. This is the notorious "tragedy of the commons," where individual interests under- mine the common good by depleting or despoiling a common resource. One user takes as much as they can before other users can do so, and more and more users may enter – driving the resource to collapse and tragedy. Second, it creates a very long and well-established legacy for intensive and even wanton use of the oceans.

Even if the agency of the ocean is not restored, however, the era of *mare liberum* is truly over. It retains some legacy on the high seas, but we are now in the era of the Law of the Sea. The Law of the Sea establishes a number of international principles that significantly change the open access of *mare liberum* and grant wide jurisdictions for coastal states that cover some of the most important marine habitat. It is at this point that Ernst Haas poses the following question:

> The ocean regime for centuries was based on the norm of maximum open access: out- side the territorial sea – whose boundary floated inexorably outward after 1945 – any state could do anything. What caused the change toward fisheries conservation zones, pollution-free zones, restrictions on transit, and international controls on the mining of the deep sea? What is responsible for the norm that the oceans are "the heritage of mankind," a public good par excellence?
>
> (Haas 1983: 24)

Haas believes that our ideas of nature changed, and it was this shift in knowledge that changed our regimes on the ocean. As our ideas of nature became more holistic, seeing nature as interdependent and fragile, our rules for the ocean became more restrictive.

This era began at the end of World War II. At this time it was clear to US President Truman that oil was going to be a major site of power, and he issued two declarations. First, he proclaimed the right of coastal states to minerals on the coastal shelf, primarily for oil prospecting. Second, he argued for national control over fisheries adjacent to territorial zones out to 200 miles, with deference to historical fishing fleets, so that US fleets could keep plying foreign coasts.

The Truman declarations appear to have triggered in 1958 the first of three conferences of the Law of the Sea, where the international community of states met to codify *mare liberum*, the right to fish, and a few other rights of states. The second United Nations Conference of the Law of the Sea in 1960 ended in no agreements because there was conflict over how to set jurisdictions for coastal states. The third conference began in 1973, ended in 1982, and went into force in 1994. This final conference produced the Convention on the Law of the Sea, establishing a 12 mile territorial sea (states have sovereignty over this area) and a 200 mile exclusive economic zone (EEZ). States have control over EEZs but hold them in trust for the international public interest. Beyond these areas were still "high seas," though the sea soil and minerals there were declared the "common heritage of mankind," to be used for the uplift of the poor in lesser industrialized countries.

In sum, we have progressed through at least three major periods of ocean history, each with its own politics and dangers. The first was the pre-colonial period, when many coastal peoples interacted with complex marine systems as an extension of a living world. The second was the colonial era, where colonialism and mercantile capitalism dominated and the institution of *mare liberum* defined global ocean space and potential. The current era is that of the Law of the Sea, beginning after World War II, which established clear jurisdictions and an expectation for conservation of the marine world from industrial, including military, uses. Note that the industrial period spans the colonial and postwar periods, while the emergence of a world risk society fits in the latter era.

The idea of the risk society

In this section, the German sociologist Ulrich Beck's (1999) notion of the risk society, which he says is always a "world" risk society, is explained in order to frame contemporary ocean problems. Within the risk society, the actors with whom we are most concerned are leaders of nation-states, leaders of industrial and financial firms, and industrial scientists as representatives of their respective modern institutions in the state–economy–science triad. One final group consists of the transnational citizens that realize these modern institutions are generating deadly risks, and these individuals form coalitions to change the way decisions of risk are supposedly made. Beck refers to the development of transnational civic groups – non-governmental organizations (NGOs) – that attempt to develop a *sovereignty of their own* beyond nation-states as a "reflexive" or critical modernity.

Industrial society calculates risks and manufactures hazards that it attempts to insure and control through economic logic. Industrial societies[3] have established the power and rationality to prioritize wealth produced through systems of extraction–production–distribution–consumption–waste. The nation-state organizes and legitimates, principally through legislation, these systems to govern the economic systems, and insures against the risks through welfare and protective policies such as environmental policies. Importantly, environmental management and environmental policies have exploded upon the world in a patchwork of laws and management schemes. However, Peter Dauvergne (2008) has shown that, even as environmental bureaucracy and management has increased manyfold, the scope of environmental damage is outpaced by extensive, largely invisible (to consumers), and devastating "shadows of consumption" that threaten sustainability in local areas as well as in the global environment. This irony of intensified management in a world of broadening environmental crisis and change fits perfectly with the theory of the risk society, because states are moving to manage environmental impacts without changing the political-economic and ideological systems that have created the problems.

Within the risk society, industrial science produces the knowledge and technology to extract, produce, distribute, and tacitly control the hazards of wastes. Firms – either nationalized or private – manage and drive the extraction, production, distribution, and demand for products, such as through advertising, public relations, and propaganda. They also figure in the distribution and types of wastes. Individuals and societies have basic necessities, provide labor, consume, and produce wastes. The globalizing industrial and modern Western society attempt to calculate, anticipate, understand, and insure against the risks produced by the entire system described above. Beck names this "first modernity."

There are two aspects that follow to produce a risk society. The first Beck believes is impossible to stop – industrial society produces risks that defy control:

> The entry into risk society occurs at the moment when the hazards which are now decided and consequently produced by society *undermine and/or cancel the established safety systems of the welfare state's existing risk calculations*. In contrast to early industrial risks, nuclear, chemical, ecological and genetic engineering risks (a) can be limited in terms of neither time nor place, (b) are not accountable according to the established rules of causality, blame and liability, and (c) cannot be compensated for or insured against.
>
> (Beck 1999; emphasis in original)

The second, which is more contingent, is that the industrial institutions of state–economy–science face a crises of legitimacy that undermines their future in "reflexive modernity." This stage is reflexive because transnational citizens see how first modernity produced global existential threats. This development is more contingent because industrial powers in world politics may move to obstruct the reflexivity and questioning through the repression of dissidents and activists or the suppression of information. One first move is to deny that environmental problems exist in the first place or to demobilize social movements through dismissing or discrediting activists and scholars who point out such threats.

Here we will explore pollution in the World Ocean in the context of a first and a second modernity.

Episodes of modern marine problems and modern solutions

After World War II, regulations on the sea proliferated, and the right of innocent passage and free navigation of ships began to be increasingly qualified by requirements for ship safety and protection of the marine environment (Tan 2006).

While some pollution is declining, such as oil pollution, deliberate and accidental incidents have continued in a way that raises questions about the effectiveness of the marine pollution institutions. Tan writes that the "inescapable conclusion appears to be that the prevailing international rules and standards, principally those enacted by the International Maritime Organization (IMO), have not been adequately enforced or complied with" (Tan 2006: 5). Ironically, Tan contends that even marine pollution that theoretically *can* be controlled is not being effectively managed in the world political economy of shipping.

The IMO is the principal international organization that handles international marine shipping standards. It was created in 1948, and originally named the International Maritime Consultancy Organization, to manage technical problems from shipping. However, the shipping business is extremely competitive, and this provides an incentive for shipowners, ports, and oversight agencies toward less costly substandard ships and a lack of compliance with some important pollution laws. Such a system disadvantages shipowners and operators who observe regulations and safety measures that raise costs. While the IMO focuses tightly on the technical standards for safety and pollution, it often ignores the broader political and economic system in which these standards fit; meanwhile, the shipping industry has actively worked to slow or obstruct more strict pollution safeguards. Inside the shipping system of industry and states, owners often collude with port inspectors and classification agencies, all in an effort to avoid costly observance of pollution restrictions. As these conditions worsen and political pressure mounts from specific accidents, such as the *Exxon Valdez* spill in 1989 off the coast of Alaska, North America and the European Union have moved toward more unilateral and strict rules as a way of avoiding the international tangle of negotiations. However, this means that many of the worst polluting offenders keep to regional shipping outside the US and the EU, endangering the rest of the world's marine ecosystems and coastal people where the bulk of marine biodiversity and sensitive habitat is situated – and where human population growth, industrialization, and coastal development/urbanization is growing.

Despite the lack of enforcement and observation of marine pollution laws, dumping of oil and other hazards in the oceans has been reduced by some 60 per cent since the 1970s (Tan 2006). This reduction has been through state-led regimes meant to reduce the impact of industrial production at the same time that the state–economy–science order has intensified these activities, such as through oil production and shipping, globally. Many of the banned or regulated materials in these regimes themselves defy control – for example, nuclear waste or toxic chemicals – but *dumping* them from ships or coastal point sources is controllable.

The earliest international regime to control oil dumping is the 1954 London Oil Pollution Convention (OILPOL). This attempted to mitigate *intentional*, or operational, oil pollution from the release of slops. Slops are the comingled water and oil mixtures that remain inside a tanker after it uses sea water for ballast (stability) on a return trip with empty cargo holds. Before the convention came into force, ships used to release these slops wantonly. OILPOL limited the dumping of oil to 50 miles offshore, where previously there were few limits at all, but the oil still floated onshore and caused heavy pollution in the ocean. Also, the regime did not recognize gasoline as oil pollution and did not address accidental oil spills. OILPOL was later replaced with the 1973/78 International Convention for the Prevention of Pollution from Ships (MARPOL), which provided mechanical restraints and engineering changes to ships to control intentional oil pollution from tankers. The fact that the problem being addressed is "intentional" oil pollution, deliberate restrictions seem appropriate and have significantly reduced pollution from slops (Mitchell 1994). A linear problem – dumping oil into the ocean – is addressed by a linear solution – that is, to stop dumping as much oil into the ocean.

States agree, or not, to the limits imposed by these marine regimes, and can decide to enforce them, or not, through several outlets. One outlet is through its flagging policies. All ships on the sea must fly a flag; a ship attains a flag from a state, and that state is responsible for enforcing national and international ocean laws, such as labor laws and pollution laws. Some states flag ships and have much more lenient labor or environmental laws or commitments to enforcing these laws. The problem of "flags of convenience," also known as "open registration," riddles many ocean regimes – mostly fishing – that do not have enforcement measures outside of flagging states. Some pollution management occurs through port state inspections, but these inspections are often rushed, completed by ports that are understaffed and are pressed by their real goal – to get ships in and out quickly.

One fairly successful marine pollution regime is the 1972 London Dumping Convention, which globally restricted "deliberate disposal of wastes and other matter at sea by ships, aircraft, and man-made structures … and is widely regarded as one of the most successful treaties addressing marine pollution" (Hunter *et al*. 2006: 732). This early convention managed a "black" list of banned substances, such as high-level radioactive waste, and a "gray" list of controlled substances that required a permit for dumping, such as low-level radioactive waste. However, in 1996 the London Dumping Convention experienced an important transition when it turned the "onus," or burden of proof, around and indicated that only materials on its Annex I list could be dumped. This move embodies the precautionary principle, which attempts to err on the side of caution through dumping only those materials the states and the IMO deem "safe." Thus, the state–economy–science triad produces risks and then uses state-based regulation to address the hazards, to the extent that Annex I is an authentic list of hazards that the regional seas can absorb without damaging marine systems. However, the new rules of the convention did not go into force until ten years later, and still only has thirty-seven parties that have agreed to it (out of about 200 nations in the world).

The fact that these regimes are state-based should not discount the role of civil society – those associations of people that are neither the government nor business. Certainly, the publicity and scandal produced by the *Stella Maris* incident is a good example. The *Stella Maris* was a Dutch ship that left the port of Rotterdam in 1971 amid protests because the crew's mission was to dump 650 tons of toxic chlorinated hydrocarbons into the North Sea, but it had to return under the blunt force of public outcry combined with foreign government objections. As a direct result of this scandal, a year later Europe produced a regional accord, the Oslo Convention for the Prevention of Marine Pollution by Dumping by Ships and Aircraft (Hunter *et al.* 2006).

Lessons from accidental oil spills

Note that the *Stella Maris* incident created a reactionary agreement to limit the intentional dumping of toxic waste – and to limit a legitimacy crisis for nations involved, such as the Netherlands. This *post hoc* structure is the historical pattern found in state-led oil-spill regimes, where notable spills result in public and international outcry and the states respond by creating or amending the accidental oil spill laws, either domestically or, when a spill is recognized as a crisis, internationally. One of the largest oil spills in US history, however, was not recognized as a crisis and garnered no such reaction. This was Unocal's operation at California's Guadelupe Dunes and lasted for thirty-eight years. It was allowed to build for nearly forty years because regulators, workers, and corporate heads refused to identify the slow leak into the ocean as a problem and therefore did nothing about it until one worker finally called in to report it as a problem – and when he did he was confronted by peers as threatening their jobs. So, one advantage of oil spills from shipping is that they trigger a response that identifies them as problems needing to be addressed. A "tanker on the rocks" motivates actors to do something, whereas to the "crescive" or growing nature of some environmental problems inspire little or no response at all (see Beamish 2002).

The *Exxon Valdez*, for example, spilled just under 11 million gallons of oil that spread slowly across 2,500 miles of flat, calm Alaskan coastline while the corporation and the government argued over who should clean it up. The cataclysm forced President George H. W. Bush to abandon hopes of drilling for more oil in the Alaskan National Wildlife Refuge and to pass the Oil Pollution Act of 1990. This act requires, among other things, corporations to be prepared to pay to clean up oil spills and obliges all tankers in US waters to have two hulls by 2010 to stem spills; international law requires tanker hulls be doubled by 2015. Interestingly, the *Exxon Valdez* was banned from Prince William Sound, but the tanker was renamed the *Sea River Mediterranean* and still plies the waters.

But the spill from the Exxon *Valdez* is only one in a string of crises that were met with *post hoc* policy reactions to answer public and international demands. One of the best-known cases was the *Torrey Canyon*, which on 18 March 1967 struck Seven Stones Reef in Cornwall. It initially spilled half of its 120,000 tons of oil, which eventually contaminated almost 200 miles of English and French coastline. The government and the shipping industry were so ill-prepared for a tanker accident that the response lasted well into April 1967, and in many respects made the spill much worse through the use of bombing and damaging detergents; this accident thus remains one of the most important oil disasters in British history.

John Sheail explains that the stranding of the leaking *Torrey Canyon* off the Cornish coast of the UK was unprecedented in its political consequences:

> The tourist-trade was ruined – the damage to marine life incalculable. The government appeared overwhelmed, as it became increasingly caught up in the political and economic repercussions. One minister was reported by the telegram to have described it as "the greatest peace-time menace" ever to have confronted Britain's shores. All the extra men and equipment in the world would be insufficient to cope with it. The Prime Minister held on-the-spot conferences. Five ministers were assigned to specific duties.
> (Sheail 2007: 486)

Oil spills had occurred before, but by 1967 a new era of environmental concern was developing, and heightened awareness surrounded some pollution issues. The *Torrey Canyon* spill had occurred in another era as well, though – intensification of the oil-based political economy in the Global North. The ship itself had been enlarged to accommodate more oil as fuel imports in the affluent countries increased in the 1960s. As yet, governments had considered only their need for oil, and less so their abilities to prepare for its consequences on the marine environment. Some government officials recognized the nuisance of the spill but still refused to admit that government had any responsibility in cleaning it up. Of course, government did intervene, but in a surprising way. The response to the stranded ship was eventually to try and blow it up in order to ignite the oil in the sea. In so doing, the Royal Air Force jets introduced more pollutants than they removed, adding to the ocean "160,000 pounds of high-explosives, 10,000 gallons of aviation kerosene, 3000 gallons of napalm," as well as over 800,000 gallons of detergent (really these detergents were solvents) (Sheail 2007: 494). While the effort destroyed some 40,000 tons of oil, in bombing the ship to the bottom of the sea, the rest of the cargo slipped out to sea. In addition, one-third of the bombs did not explode, and what sea life survived the oil slick was killed by the detergent, which turned the ocean into a milky-white color. This detergent was produced by British Petroleum (BP), which also owned the oil to which the detergent was applied. This meant the British government was pressed into paying BP for the clean-up of its own oil. In order to ensure that BP paid the British government, a sister ship was detained in Singapore until £3 million was paid to the British and French governments.

Given cooperative weather and other lucky breaks, the *Torrey Canyon* incident could have been much worse than it was. But several lessons appear to stand out. One is that government, science, and industry were concerned first with the delivery of basic energy for the industrialized post-World War II economy, and much less prepared to think about the consequences of either the economic structure of massive increases in oil production–distribution–consumption or the common-sense expectation that sometimes oil tankers will be wrecked. Second, the political demands to put state-led institutions to respond to and handle the legalities of oil tanker accidents only occurred after this catastrophe, which pressed the international community into some form of action. In fact, the British government could not even begin to work on containing the disaster with confidence until the captain of the Liberian tanker legally abandoned the ship. Thus, neither Britain nor France even had plans for how to handle the inevitability (somewhere) of a tanker accident, and neither did the rest of the international community. After the *Torrey Canyon*, new international agreements regarding the liability of tanker owners were increased through the Protocol to Amend the International Convention on Civil Liability for Oil Pollution Damage. The liability caps, however, are still considered favorable for shipowners and had been limited to the salvage value of the ship – which for the *Torrey Canyon* was the value of one lifeboat. It also became painfully obvious that OILPOL was inadequate (remember that it had no conditions for accidental spills). From the *Torrey Canyon*, pressure to amend the convention to include provisions for accidental spills helped force a new agreement in MARPOL (see above). Consequently, lessons from oil spill history indicate that global environmental politics are rarely preventative or proactive when confronted with the prospect of limiting economic activity.

The worst imaginable accident, everyday

Between the regional Oslo Convention (and later Paris Convention, which focused on land-based dumping) and the progression of the London Convention, it is clear that there is a growing general international aversion to dumping at sea. What to do with toxic waste such as chlorinated pollutants appears to be a more complex problem that fits in the following section, but it is *comparatively* easy to identify the boats containing nasty things and stop them from putting these into the ocean.

But what happens when this is not the case?

Beck identifies four pillars of calculus that live in modernity but are abolished in a world risk society:

> First, one is concerned here with global, often irreparable, damage that can no longer be limited; the concept of monetary compensation therefore fails. Second, precautionary after-care is excluded for the worst imaginable accident in the case of fatal hazards; the security concept of anticipatory monitoring of results fails. Third, the "accident" loses its delimitations in time and space, and therefore its meaning. It becomes an event with a beginning and no end; an "open-ended festival" of creeping, galloping and overlapping waves of destruction.
>
> (Beck 1999: 53–4)

Consider that, while we have significantly reduced the dumping of oil and hazardous wastes even in a system with low enforcement and observance, *we do not do anything for the vast majority or the most important ocean pollution*. It is clear that the most pernicious and destructive pollution comes from inland sources:

> Almost all of the problems of the oceans start on land. It is here that virtually all of the pollution originates, whether from factories and sewage works at the coasts, from fertiliser or pesticides washed into rivers and down to the sea, or from metals and chemicals emitted from car exhausts and industry and carried by the winds far out to the oceans.
>
> (GESAMP 2001: 19)

One group of scientists indicate that 44 per cent of marine pollution comes from inland sources, 33 per cent from atmospheric sources, and only 12 per cent from shipping (GESAMP 1990) – and of course much of the atmospheric sources come from activities on land such as burning coal. Almost all marine pollution regimes have focused on that 12 per cent, probably because it is easier to pick out definitive ships than diffuse non-shipping sources, and land-based pollution has traditionally been considered a domestic issue for coastal states. However, inland and atmospheric pollutants are not just domestic issues. One study (Halpern *et al.* 2008) shows that humans impact every part of the World Ocean – over 40 per cent of it intensively – and much of this results from pollution: coastal run-off, nutrient pollution, warming water temperature as a result of human-induced climate change, sonar (sound pollution) that harms whales, and many others. Inland pollutants are a global threat.

Many of the attempts to mitigate these "creeping, galloping and overlapping waves of destruction" are futile inasmuch as they ignore the origination of the threats. Let us explore a few cases of these types of marine pollution. All of them have several things in common:

1   They are fairly irreversible and devastating.
2   They originate from diffuse and comingled sources. To the extent that more pollution is contributed by more people, the more impossible it is to assign a command structure to stop it.

3   They are global in scope, and there is neither ability for compensation for the type of damage done nor any one agent who is responsible who could offset this damage.
4   These pollutants are not accidents, but are "operational" in the sense that they occur during the normal running of the global economy.

The United Nations Environmental Programme (UNEP) operates the Regional Seas Programme, which is a "best practices"-type institution that attempts to build capacity for coastal regions to improve marine quality. It provides a cooperative setting for building regional relationships and managerial capacity but does not dictate terms, standards, or outcomes. As such, the program has suffered from the weaknesses of bureaucratic under-funding, commitment, and related issues (Kütting 2000; VanDeveer and Dabelko 2001). By and large, the "soft law" of the Regional Seas has not shown enormous promise in dealing with the problems we are going to discuss because they are fighting against the larger goals of the state–economy–science triangle that produces, sanctions, and funds the pollution to begin with. Below are four brief examples – fertilizers, micro-plastics, persistent organic pollutants, and ocean acidification – each of which is diffuse and once unleashed has consequences modern science or the state have been unable to control and state-led regimes have ignored.

Nutrient/fertilizer pollution

Fertilizers cause a pollution of bitter irony. Nutrients from fertilizers end up in deltas and spur algae growth (life) so intensively that it kills much of the remaining sea life around it (the algae use the dissolved oxygen in the water). These anoxic and hypoxic (low in oxygen) areas become so reduced or devoid of life they are called "dead zones."

The problem occurs when farmers turn to industrial techniques of the Green Revolution, which industrialized agriculture through the increased use of petro-chemical inputs, high-yield varieties, and mechanization usually for monocultural crops. One key aspect to indus-trialized agriculture is the use of nitrogen and phosphates and other related chemical fertilizers. These chemicals filter through the dirt or accumulate through run-off into tribu-taries, then streams, then rivers. The rivers empty into the World Ocean through deltas or submarine groundwater discharge.[4]

Since the 1960s, when these techniques were internationalized beyond the trials in Mexico and India (1940s, 1950s), there has been an exponential growth in dead zones all around the world, and they are now reported in over 400 systems, primarily as a result of this fertilizer pollution (Diaz and Rosenberg 2008). These dead zones are the result of worst imaginable "accidents" that occur every day. They are now global in scope and cannot be reversed once the pollution is applied *to the land*. Fertilizers are ironically used to extend control over the agricultural process and the life of plants, but they result in a crisis of plant and animal death and migration. Since the pollution is produced by diffuse and multiple farmers up and down riparian systems, the more pollution there is, the harder it is to identify individual causality. One potential policy could be to ban or significantly reduce agricultural phosphates, but the state–economy–science triad supports this process with policy, funds, and growth in revenue for industry and epistemic developments in agronomy that focus on yield-per-acre that have undoubtedly increased with this approach.[5] Nonetheless, even though the risk is manufactured, the cost of this pollution is incalculable because entire areas of life are being lost, and it is very likely that the growth of dead zones is a "key stressor on marine ecosystems" (ibid.).

Persistent organic pollutants

Biocides have left their mark as well (see Chapter 12 in this volume, which focuses specifically on POPs worldwide), transported through surface water, through atmospheric currents, and even through plastics in the ocean (see below). Some of the biocides used, such as DDT and other organochloride chemicals used to treat inland areas for pests, are persistent organic pollutants (POPs). These have been found in marine life throughout the World Ocean. POPs become increasingly concentrated in the fatty tissue of predators (such as people and sharks), and samples of people in the Arctic show high levels of POPs *never* used in that region. Notably, Arctic native people have made the case that they are suffering the burden of chemicals that they did not have a say in using or benefit from using. For example, an international claim of substantive injustice is lodged by the Cree, who are concerned not only for themselves but for wildlife such as whales and caribou. Perhaps this is one reason for the development of the 2001 Stockholm Convention on Persistent Organic Pollutants, which attempts to regulate the use of these hazards. That being said, these pollutants operate at minute levels and have spread all around, to be found in molluscs and sediment in China, the Ross Sea in Antarctica, and the eggs of gulls in the Arctic. It is found in Adelaide penguins, pacific herring, bottle-nosed dolphins, and, of course, polar bears. Polar bears are threatened by multiple problems, such as the loss of summer sea ice needed for hunting, but increased POPs in their blood is also thought to hurt their ability to bring a cub to maturity. POPs spread through every major ecological medium – ocean currents, the food web, and air currents. They affect hormones, birthing survival, and disease. They do not degrade easily in the environment and will be aroundfor a very long time, diffusing all around the world beyond the point when we stop making and using them.

Micro-plastic pollution

Another diffuse and devastating marine pollutant is micro-plastic. There are at least two types of plastic pollution. One is simply refuse, which makes its way to the ocean and accumulates in gyres, for example, the North Pacific gyre, which holds the "Great Pacific Garbage Patch" – a giant soup of plastic bits "twice the size as continental United States" (Marks and Howden 2008). This is not like a solid island to which you could travel to and easily scoop up floating toys in a matter of a few days; rather, these bits are continuously photodegrading into brittle, smaller (micro-plastic) bits that do not even sit directly on top of the water. Much of this pollution breaks down to resemble zooplankton consumed by many marine animals, and so finds its way into the food chain. Even if the plastic, such as bags found to threaten the critically endangered leatherback turtle (Mrosovsky *et al.* 2009), does not fully obstruct the animal's gastrointestinal tract and kill it, it may remain inside the animal and constrain essential calories. As far as some animals are concerned, there is a narrow margin between the energy gained through the food they forage and the energy they use to obtain it. If plastic takes up vital space in such an animal, it can push its energy budget far enough to starve it. This is known to occur in turtles and probably happens in other animals as well.

The second kind of plastic pollution comes from "nurdles," which form the pre-production raw material for plastic manufacturers. These resemble the fish eggs consumed by many marine mammals. Like the micro-plastic fragments, nurdles can absorb carcinogenic toxic pollution from the water. They have been shown to have as much as a *million* times the levels of persistent organic pollution than the ambient water because they chemically attract and absorb them (Mato *et al.* 2001). These nurdles become diffuse transports of concentrated marine toxins, eaten by fish and other animals.

It turns out that Annex V of MARPOL, which went into force in 1988, specifically bans the dumping of all forms of plastic into the sea from ships. While it probably has reduced the amount of plastic garbage *dumped* while at sea, it misses most of the plastic that finds its way into the ocean, and this type of pollution is not slowing. Using the modern ideals of control and rationality through state–economy–science, we produce plastic products that have innumerable uses. Ironically, once these products are made through the exacting control of this science, we have little control over where they end up once they are set free into the world. Rationality evolves into irrationality, and control into chaos, as a normal condition – not as an exception to the rule – of the principle modern institutions. While some plastic accumulates in gyres, this pollution is found globally on some of the most remote beaches and is known to be a mechanism for harmful compounds to enter the food chain (Teuten *et al.* 2007).

Ocean acidification

Out of the four ocean pollutants discussed here, the results of CO2 absorption into the World Ocean from a diffuse and well-mixed atmosphere may be the most threatening (see Miles 2009). This pollution, like fertilizers and plastic, is a result of the normal operations of modernity through state-sponsored and industrial use of hydrocarbon (mainly coal and oil) energy, developed through modern science and technology. Like fertilizers and plastic, hydrocarbons are a core part of modern life and form the very base of industrial states and their political economy. The legacy of burning so very many hydrocarbons in the process of generating energy for goods and services (such as cement and transportation) is pursued as the height of rationality and control. Control of energy in hydrocarbons is central to modern ideas of "development," and control of or access to oil is now recognized as a key foreign policy goal for any state – especially the Global North and the United States, which burns more per capita than any other country.

In addition to adding greenhouse gases to the atmosphere, which raise the Earth's mean temperature, most of this CO^2 will end up being absorbed into the ocean, with likely unpleasant effects on marine life. As the CO^2 is absorbed, it lowers the pH of the water. One study found that, with a few possible exceptions, "oceanic absorption of CO^2 from fossil fuels may result in larger pH changes over the next several centuries than any inferred from the geological record of the past 300 million years" (Caldeira and Wickett 2003). While pH varies between oceanic basins and zones, ocean acidification is and will be globally distributed, and it will impact the *basic physiology* of fish and invertebrates, especially organisms such as coral that require calcium carbonate to build skeletons. Ocean acidification change is therefore one of the more extensive and fundamental changes to the marine water column, yet this pollution has only recently gained some attention. There will be no way to stop ocean acidification short of changing modern energy production.

Legitimacy and subpolitics

Command regimes that limit the dumping of oil and nuclear waste have a theoretical reason for working. State-led regimes were able to solve collective action problems and reduce the damage done by *dumping*. But with whom do you negotiate when you find a continent-size swirl of microscopic plastic pollution in the ocean, or when the basic chemistry of the oceans is being changed? Inasmuch as the ideals of control and modernity drove the production of these hazards, they likely are incapable of controlling the output of risks and changes that occur as a result. These land-based pollutants are some of the most severe risks faced by marine communities, but they are produced by the *normal* operation of a world capitalist system and economy. How can effective regimes be built by states to counteract the very conditions upon which the states and economies and sciences themselves live upon?

Further, to the extent that the normal operation of states, economies, and science are meant to improve or secure our lives through these industrial products, they also create death, destruction, and insecurity. The very logics of modernity consume the modern system itself as it erodes the critical ecological life-support systems. In this way, the lessons of this text on ecological security, regimes, and consumption meet a somewhat different interpretation when we are confronted with these problems.

This is where Beck notes the modern world order begins to crumble through a crisis of legitimacy of the state–economy–science institutions. Instead, subpolitics supposedly emerges to generate near sovereign actions by transnational civic groups that attempt to change the actions of the legal-rational, or bureaucratic, institutions in the international system.

Greenpeace is one notable NGO operating in a transnational way that resembles a "reflexive" approach. Its strategy is to document and then confront states and firms and industrial science[6] to create transnational outrage against uses of nuclear technology in the oceans, unsustainable fishing, whaling, and ocean dumping. Greenpeace operates in a way that creates its own legitimacy and sovereignty, mostly by generating the support and alliances from other states willing to oppose a particular practice *with* them. For example, normally the pursuit of pirates would be a policing action reserved for national powers, but Greenpeace has dedicated some of its fleet to monitoring the Pacific for illegal fishing and pursuing boats it feels are "pirating" fish until national coastguards arrive to take the presumed thieves into custody.

Confrontations such as these work to generate a more reflexive social sphere where hazards are *purposefully* produced and distributed. One of the first major changes, then, for marine pollution is to unmask the manufactured risks. This unmasking also exposes how marine pollution is a product of the successful operation of industrial systems that enforce, then ignore, then deny, then perhaps change the structure of political economy so that plastic, trace chemical poison, fertilizers, and CO_2 are not wantonly produced. Once these things exist, the modern systems have no way to stop them from ending up in the ocean as major threats to a system full of life and which continues to support human communities around the world. A reflexive modernity would confront this economic production, its power and logic, and exert pressure for systematic reform in *how pollution is manufactured in the first place*. In the industrial period, our main pollution policy responses – in oil, nuclear waste, and toxics – was simply to ban them from being dumped, but, as Barry Commoner (1971) writes, "everything must go somewhere."

Notes

1   In campaigns to undermine public policy that might attempt to reduce CO_2 as a way to mitigate climate change, some climate "skeptics" have argued that it is not a pollutant. However, this point is misdirected. Not all pollutants are toxic. Pollutants, rather, are inputs and additions that consume ecological sinks (resources that absorb and ameliorate the input) or are simply undesired. For example, saltwater is not a pollutant in the ocean, but it is a pollutant when it infiltrates freshwater

aquifers. As CO^2 disrupts the chemical dynamics of the ocean, it becomes a critical stressor – a pollutant – in marine systems.

2 Grotius believed the natural law was universal and extended to everyone in the world, but he expected mostly the Christian European monarchs to be the ones who would most freely accept this as law.

3 William Hipwell (2004, 2007) notes that industrial societies are really connected through a network of urban areas and transit lines that draw in resources from peripheral and less powerful regions. This single network is referred to as "industria" and includes important innovations on Wallerstein's (2004) ideas of a world capitalist system.

4 This is where aquifers meet coastal waters and push out the nutrient pollution into them. This process can delay the effects of nutrient pollution on land by eighty years or more, so the effects of much of the Green Revolution are yet to be observed through this mechanism.

5 This calculus changes, though we might think about a return of around 1 calorie of food for every 10 to 15 used in industrial agriculture (Mushita and Thompson 2007).

6 For example, Greenpeace confronts the idea that science is produced from Japanese whaling because Japan has claimed a scientific exception to the International Whaling Commission's moratorium on commercial whaling.

Recommended reading

Borgese, E. M. (1998) *The Oceanic Circle: Governing the Seas as a Global Resource*, New York: United Nations University Press.

Earle, S. (1995) *Sea Change: A Message of the Oceans*, New York: Fawcett Columbine.

Prager, E., and Earle, S. (2000) *The Oceans*, New York: McGraw-Hill.

Safina, C. (1998) *Song for a Blue Ocean: Encounters along the World's Coasts and beneath the Seas*, New York: Henry Holt.

Van Dyke, J., Zaelke, D., and Hewison, G. (eds) (1993) *Freedom for the Seas in the 21st Century: Ocean Governance and Environmental Harmony*, Washington, DC: Island Press.

References

Beamish, T. (2002) *Silent Spill: The Organization of Industrial Crisis*, Cambridge: MA: MIT Press.

Beck, U. (1992) *The Risk Society: Towards a New Modernity*, Newbury Park, CA: Sage.

—— (1999) *World Risk Society*, Cambridge: Polity.

Caldeira, K., and Wickett, M. E. (2003) "Anthropogenic carbon and ocean pH," *Science*, 425: 365.

Commoner, B. (1971) *The Closing Circle: Nature, Man, and Technology*, New York: Knopf.

Dauvergne, P. (2008) *The Shadows of Consumption: Consequences for the Global Environment*, Cambridge, MA: MIT Press.

Diaz, R. J., and Rosenberg, R. (2008) "Spreading dead zones and consequences for marine ecosystems," *Science*, 321: 926–9.

GESAMP (Joint Group of Experts on the Scientific Aspects of Marine Environmental Protection) (1990) *The State of the Marine Environment*, London: International Maritime Organization.

—— (2001) "A sea of troubles," in *Editorial Board of the Working Group on Marine Environmental Assessments*, The Hague: GESAMP and Advisory Committee on Protection of the Sea.

Haas, E. (1983) "Words can hurt your; or, who said what to whom about regimes," in S. Krasner (ed.), *International Regimes*, Ithaca, NY: Cornell University Press.

Halpern, B. S., Walbridge, S., Selkoe, K. A., Kappel, C. V., Micheli, F., D'Agrosa, C., Bruno, J. F., Casey, K. S., Ebert, C., Fox, H. E., Fujita, R., Heinemann, D., Lenihan, H. S., Madin, E. M. P., Perry, M. T., Selig, E. R., Spalding, M., Steneck, R., and Watson, R. (2008) "A global map of human impact on marine ecosystems," *Science*, 319: 948–52.

Hay, P. R. (2002) *Main Currents in Western Environmental Thought*, Bloomington: Indiana University Press.

Hipwell, W. (2004) "A Deleuzian critique of resource-use management politics in industria," *Canadian Geographer*, 48(3): 356–77.
—— (2007) "The industria hypothesis: 'The globalization of what?,'" *Peace Review*, 19(3): 305–13.
Hunter, D., Zaelke, D., and Salzman, J. (eds) (2006) *International Environmental Law and Policy*, Boulder, CO: West Group.
Kütting, G. (2000) *Environment, Society, and International Relations: Towards More Effective International Environmental Agreements*, New York: Routledge.
Lehody, P., Alheit, J., Barange, M., Baumgartner, T., Beaugrand, G., Drinkwater, K., Fromentin, J.-M., Hare, S. R., Ottersen, G., Perry, R. I., Roy, C., Lingen, C. D. V. D., and Werneri, F. (2006) "Climate variability, fish and fisheries," *Journal of Climate*, 19: 5009–30.
Marks, K., and Howden, D. (2008) "The world's rubbish dump: a tip that stretches from Hawaii to Japan," *The Independent*, 5 February.
Mato, Y., Isobe, T., Takada, H., Kanehiro, H., Ohtake, C., and Kaminuma, T. (2001) "Plastic resin pellets as a transport medium for toxic chemicals in the marine environment," *Environmental Science & Technology*, 35: 318–24.
Miles, E. L. (2009) "On the increasing vulnerability of the world ocean to multiple stresses," *Annual Review of Environment and Resources*, 34(1): 17–41.
Mitchell, R. (1994) *International Oil Pollution at Sea: Environmental Policy and Treaty Compliance*, Cambridge, MA: MIT Press.
Mrosovsky, N., Ryan, G. D., and James, M. C. (2009) "Leatherback turtles: the menace of plastic," *Marine Pollution Bulletin*, 58: 287–9.
Mushita, A., and Thompson, C. B. (2007) *Biopiracy of Biodiversity: Global Exchange as Enclosure*, Trenton, NJ: Africa World Press.
Sheail, J. (2007) "Torrey Canyon: the political dimension," *Journal of Contemporary History*, 42: 485–504.
Steinberg, P. E. (2001) *The Social Construction of the Ocean*, Cambridge: Cambridge University Press.
Stewart-Harawira, M. (2005) *The New Imperial Order: Indigenous Responses to Globalization*, New York: Zed Books.
Tan, A. K.-J. (2006) *Vessel-Source Marine Pollution: The Law and Politics of International Regulation*, New York and Cambridge: Cambridge University Press.
Teuten, E. L., Rowland, S. J., Galloway, T. S., and Thompson, R. C. (2007) "Potential for plastics to transport hydrophobic contaminants," *Environmental Science & Technology*, 41: 7759–64.
VanDeveer, S., and Dabelko, G. (2001) "It's capacity stupid: international assistance and national implementation," *Global Environmental Politics*, 1: 18–29.
Vitousek, P. M., Mooney, H. A., Lubchenco, J., and Melillo, J. (1997) "Human domination of Earth's ecosystems," *Science*, 277: 494–9.
Wallerstein, I. (2004) *World-Systems Analysis: An Introduction*, Durham, NC: Duke University Press.
Wapner, P. (2002) "The sovereignty of nature: environmental protection in a postmodern age," *International Studies Quarterly*, 46: 167–87.

9 International forest politics

David Humphreys

Introduction

The conservation and sustainable management of forests became a politically important environmental issue in the mid-1980s, when international concern over deforestation grew to such an extent that the first tentative international initiatives to tackle the problem were established. This chapter begins by explaining deforestation as an international political issue using public goods theory. It then presents an analytical overview of international forest politics, beginning with the negotiations that took place at the 1992 United Nations Conference on Environment and Development in Rio, before tracking the aftermath of the Rio process, which has seen the establishment of a series of international forest bodies within the UN system. These bodies have agreed to several non-legally binding agreements but, despite several attempts, there is still no consensus as to whether a global forests convention should be negotiated.

The absence of such a convention explains in part why international forest policy is spread over several international organizations. It is argued that an understanding of neoliberal discourse is needed in order to comprehend fully the international policy responses to deforestation. Neoliberalism promotes certain types of environmental policy, in particular those that are voluntary, business-led, and market-based. In this respect neoliberalism establishes the parameters of international forest policy. This chapter concludes by arguing that the World Trade Organization (WTO) has served as a powerful driver in the expansion of global neoliberalism, providing neoliberal principles with a political and legal force that environmental objectives lack in global governance. Using forests as a case study, therefore, I aim to draw out some broader points of relevance to the politics of global environmental governance.

Forests as public goods

Like other international environmental issues, deforestation is politically significant because it has a public goods element. Public goods are those that benefit a broader public – a publicum. Depending on the public good in question, the publicum may vary considerably, extending from the local to the global. In the case of global public goods, all humanity is the publicum. Forests play a major role in the regulation of the Earth's climate – a classic global public good, as everyone benefits from a clean and stable atmosphere – by absorbing carbon dioxide, a major greenhouse gas, from the atmosphere, breaking it down by photosynthesis and storing it in trees and plants. Public goods have two attributes in common. First, they are non-excludable. For example, no one can be excluded from the benefits of a clean and stable atmosphere. Second, public goods are non-rival in consumption: the consumption of a public good by one person will not affect what is left for others. So, because one "consumes" clean air does not mean that there is less available for others to consume.

Forests serve as habitats for as much as 80 per cent of the world's terrestrial species. They thus contribute to the global public good of biological diversity conservation and the maintenance of the diverse global gene pool that is necessary for resilient and adaptable species and ecosystems (Perrings and Gadgil 2003). At a local level, forests may satisfy recreational or spiritual needs for a local *publicum*, such as a village of indigenous peoples or a local community, and supply local and regional soil conservation and watershed management functions. Forests thus provide a range of public goods for both proximate and distant users. In this sense forests can be seen as shared, not in a spatial or ownership sense, but in the sense that they provide life support functions for all humanity.

When deforestation takes place, especially from burning, carbon dioxide is released back into the atmosphere, which contributes to anthropogenic climate change. The main source of carbon dioxide is the burning of fossil fuels, such as coal and oil. Other greenhouse gasses are methane, nitrous oxide, and chlorofluorocarbons (CFCs). Anthropogenic climate change is a public bad. Like public goods, public bads are non-excludable (ultimately no one on Earth will be able to escape the risks and hazards that will accrue from climate change) and non-rival (the suffering of some people from climate change will not reduce the suffering for others). When serious or widespread deforestation occurs, other public bads may involve the siltation or drying up of rivers and streams, soil erosion, landslides, and desertification.

Part of the problem of deforestation as an international political issue is that, while forests contribute to the maintenance of global public goods, such as atmospheric regulation and biodiversity conservation, in international law forests are a sovereign resource of the state. Some tropical countries are particularly assertive about this. For example, successive Brazilian governments have made it clear that no other country has any right to say how the Brazilian Amazon should be used; only the government of Brazil has this right. Since the 1960s successive governments in Brazil have sought to develop the Amazon for economic development, exploiting the forests for the harvesting and mining of private goods. Private goods are those that can be bought and sold in markets. In contrast to public goods, private goods are rival in consumption (for example, the more timber that a business extracts from an area of forest, the less is available for others) and excludable (since those who own a private good can, legally at least, prevent others from using it). Among the private goods that forests provide are timber, nuts, berries, rattan, and rubber.

In neoclassical economic theory the provision of private goods is best realized through markets. But, because markets work best when goods are both rival and excludable, they undersupply public goods or do not supply them at all. Furthermore, the overharvesting of private goods can lead to public good depletion. This is particularly the case with deforestation, which is often the result of clearance to harvest timber or to free land for alternative land uses, such as cattle ranching, crop agriculture, or the mining of minerals or oil. The degradation of public goods is an example of what economists call market failure, when the routine functioning of markets fails to bring about an allocation of resources that maximizes the welfare of society. Forest politics is, in large part, an attempt to manage the tension between conserving the public good attributes of forests and exploiting the private goods that forests, and forest land, can realize. This tension runs in different guises throughout all forest policy and forest-related political conflicts, from the global level to the local. Conceptually, at least, the tension has been overcome by the idea of sustainable forest management. Sustainable forest management, which has served as a guiding concept in international cooperation for nearly two decades, may be defined as the maximization of the yield of the private goods that forests can provide, but only to the extent that this does not deplete forest-related public goods.

There are divided views on how forest public goods can best be realized. Some argue that, like private goods, the provision of public goods should take place through the creation of a new generation of environmental markets. (This claim is examined below.) Others maintain that the supply of public goods requires intervention in markets and tough regulatory action from publicly accountable authorities, such as states and intergovernmental organizations. In the negotiations that took place before the 1992 United Nations Convention on Environment and Development, the so-called Earth Summit in Rio de Janeiro, it was suggested that forests should be governed by a global convention that would aim to prevent deforestation, conserve forests, and achieve sustainable forest management. It is to these negotiations that we now turn.

An unconventional approach to international forest politics

The two most significant outputs from the 1992 United Nations Conference on Environment and Development (UNCED) were the Convention on Biological Diversity and the Framework Convention on Climate Change. Because forests are a major sink of carbon dioxide and an important habitat of biodiversity, it was suggested by developed country governments and the UN Food and Agriculture Organization that a third convention should be agreed, a global forests convention, that would support the forest-related provisions of the biodiversity and climate change conventions and promote the conservation and sustainable management of forests. However, states failed even to commence negotiations for a convention, eventually agreeing only to a non-legally binding instrument commonly called the Forest Principles (United Nations 1992a).

The main reason for this is that the UNCED forest negotiations were characterized by a clear division between the developed countries of North America, Europe, and Japan and the developing countries of Asia, Latin America, and Africa. North–South differences are often overstated in international relations literature. However, at the UNCED all the developed countries of the North argued for a forests convention while all the developing countries of the South – speaking through its UN caucus group, the Group of 77 Developing Countries (G77) – argued against. The EU, the US, Canada, and Japan declared that the concept of sovereignty should be linked to two other principles: stewardship (the principle that countries with forests should manage them for the common good of humanity) and common responsibility (the notion that all countries share a common responsibility to manage their forests sustainably). Some delegates from the North suggested in the corridors, though not in the formal negotiations, that forests themselves could be seen as a common heritage of mankind, or a global common. This was a clumsy attempt to recognize the contribution that forests make to global public good provision, but it drew forth a retort from the Malaysian delegation, speaking on behalf of the G77, that concepts such as global commons had a supranational character and were an attempt by the North to erode the sovereignty of developing countries over their forests (Humphreys 1996: 95). The G77 asserted that sovereignty should not be delimited by linkage to other principles.

Timothy Ehresman and Dimitris Stevis argue in this volume (Chapter 6) that the governments of the South view international negotiations through the lens of justice. This was the case during the UNCED forest deliberations, when many G77 position statements centered on issues of equity and responsibility. The G77 held that the countries of North America and

Europe bear a disproportionate responsibility for deforestation, as they have not only reduced forest cover significantly since the Industrial Revolution, but they continue to drive deforestation through high levels of consumption of forest products. Hence, maintained the G77, states should agree not to the principle of "common responsibility" but rather to "common but differentiated responsibilities," thus denoting that some states have more responsibility than others for causing the problem in the past and, therefore, more responsibility for paying for future conservation measures. But, while the developed countries agreed to include "common but differentiated responsibilities" in the Framework Convention on Climate Change, thus recognizing that those countries that had industrialized first bore primary responsibility for global warming, they refused to recognize the principle in the context of forests.

The G77 also introduced the concept of "compensation for opportunity cost foregone." The concept of opportunity cost has its origins in neoclassical economic theory; if an economic resource is used in one way, the opportunity cost is the value of the next best alternative for which the resource could have been used. The opportunity cost of conserving forests is that they cannot be used for economic gain. The G77 used the concept of opportunity cost foregone to signify that utility-maximizing forest owners and the governments of forested states will rationally opt for forest conservation if they can receive a financial sum that makes it at least as beneficial for them to conserve their forests as to cut them down. The G77 also introduced the issue of external indebtedness, noting that payments from developing to developed countries for debt servicing and repayment exceeded official development assistance transfers from developed to developing countries, resulting in net South to North financial transfers. The G77 argued that any agreement on forest conservation should be tied to debt relief, greater financial assistance, and increased transfers of environmentally sound technology. The negotiating strategy of the G77 was summed up by the Malaysian prime minister, Mahathir bin Mohamad, shortly before the UNCED: "If it is in the interests of the rich that we do not cut down our trees then they must compensate us for the loss of income" (Mahathir 1992: 3). The UNCED forest negotiations did not, therefore, focus exclusively on forests, and saw protracted deliberations on broader economic concerns of salience to the developing countries.

Two theoretical explanations may be offered for the failure of the UNCED forest negotiations to lead to a forest convention. The first relates to cognitive theories of international cooperation. Cognitive theories focus on the role that shared ideas, beliefs, norms, and values can play in fostering international agreement (Jönsson 1993; Hasenclever *et al.* 2000). International agreement is more likely when states can agree on a formula, a principle, or a set of ideas that informs the negotiations and around which actors' expectations converge. However, there was no agreement on core concepts to guide the Rio forest negotiations: instead different states invoked different concepts. But these conceptual differences exposed deeper differences between North and South over past and future responsibilities and distributive justice, in particular what constitutes a fair and equitable distribution of the world's natural, financial, and technological resources. The negotiations may also be viewed as a crude price negotiation in which the North pressed the South to implement strong forest conservation policies in the form of a global forests convention, while the G77 responded by introducing its economic concerns, arguing that all issues needed to be settled in a comprehensive package. So the G77 raised the price of forest conservation, a price that the North was unwilling to pay (Humphreys 1996).

This leads to a second explanation that centers on power. Powerful states possess the material capabilities to block the aspirations of other states. The neorealist view of international politics introduced by John Vogler in Chapter 1 of this volume – according to which states will seek to preserve their relative advantages over other states and, where possible, to achieve relative gains – is relevant here. Both tropical and developed states have the power to grant or, alternatively, to thwart the aspirations of each other. Tropical states possess resources in the form of their rainforests, which produce private goods (such as tropical timber) and public goods (such as carbon sinks) valued by other actors. Meanwhile the North has the power to satisfy the aspirations of the South for increased financial and technological transfers and debt relief. The enhanced value that the developed countries now attach to tropical forest conservation has provided the governments of tropical forested countries with enhanced bargaining leverage.

Realizing this, the G77 attempted to translate the concerns of the developed countries over tropical deforestation into hard economic gains. But the developed countries of the North could not conceivably meet the G77's bargaining demands without eroding their relative advantages in international trade and finance. The costs that would be borne by taxpayers and businesses in the North to meet the G77's demands on, say, financial and technological transfers would be extremely high. While Northern-based governments have been prepared to make modest increases of aid on a bilateral basis, they are unwilling to agree to large-scale transfers on a multilateral basis that would enable developing countries to realize relative economic gains. In any case, donor countries are likely to agree to significant North to South resource transfers only if they can extract some binding commitments from the South on forest conservation targets, and this would touch upon the sensitivities of many developing countries on sovereignty. From this gridlock the non-legally binding and heavily caveated statement of Forest Principles was agreed as a compromise between the pro- and anti-convention states (United Nations 1992a).

The UNCED negotiations on forests were fractious and divisive. Two years later, representatives from the governments of Canada, which had lobbied more strongly than any other state for a forests convention at Rio, and Malaysia, which led the G77 against a convention, initiated a confidence-building dialogue to which select other countries were invited. The eventual result of this initiative was the creation under the auspices of the UN Commission on Sustainable Development of an Intergovernmental Panel on Forests with a two-year life span. This met four times between September 1995 and February 1997. It negotiated a series of non-legally binding proposals for action, namely suggestions and policy recommendations for consideration by governments and other actors. With most developing countries remaining wary of international forest commitments, most of the proposals were for actions that could be taken at the national level. Indeed one of the main areas of agreement of the Intergovernmental Panel on Forests was the recommendation that all states should formulate and implement national forest programs, which should be holistic, intersectoral, and iterative and recognize and respect the rights of local communities (Humphreys 2003).

The twin issues of financial aid and technological transfer which had dominated the UNCED negotiations were also raised on several occasions by the G77, especially during the final session of the panel, when states returned to the question of whether there should be a forests convention. There had been some significant shifts in position on this issue since 1992. First, the United States was now opposed to a convention. The US appears to have favored a convention at Rio as an instrument that would be focused principally on tropical forests. It did not envisage a convention as an instrument that would entail significant costs for the US, for example in the form of financial assistance to developing countries or raised standards for the American forest industry (Davenport 2006: 131). Following Rio, the US shifted against a convention once it became clear that this could be achieved only if there were major North to South aid transfers. Second, Malaysia, the strongest voice against a convention at Rio, now argued in favor. As with the United States, the reason for this lies with domestic factors. Malaysia's shift of position followed a change in the ministry with lead responsibility for forests, from the Ministry of Foreign Affairs, which viewed forests strategically as a sovereign resource, to the Ministry of Primary Resources, which saw a convention as an instrument that could promote the international trade in forest products to Malaysia's advantage (Kolk 1996: 162). Indonesia and most of the Central American states also changed position to support a convention. Meanwhile Brazil and its Amazonian Pact allies remained resolutely opposed. With no agreed view among the developing countries, the G77 formulated the common line that the desirability of a convention should be assessed later. The EU remained in favor.

With no consensus for a convention, but with increased confidence between countries on the forests issue, the decision was taken to replace the Intergovernmental Panel on Forests with another temporary body, also reporting to the Commission on Sustainable Development. This was the Intergovernmental Forum on Forests – to all intents and purposes the panel with a slightly changed name and revised agenda. During its three years of existence, the Intergovernmental Forum on Forests met four times between October 1997 and February 2000. Its activities were very similar to those of its predecessor. It negotiated further proposals for action (it is generally agreed that, between them, the panel and the forum agreed approximately 270 proposals for action; the exact number is slightly unclear, as there are areas of duplication and overlap between different proposals), and it reconsidered once more the question of whether a convention should be agreed, where the breakdown of countries "for" and "against" was more or less the same as when the panel had considered the question three years previously.

During this period another international forest initiative took place, namely the formation of a World Commission on Forests and Sustainable Development. World commissions usually comprise an elitist "eminent persons" membership of between twenty and thirty who set out to examine an international problem with a humanitarian or public goods dimension that is either being ignored in international politics or requires some innovative thinking. The World Commission on Forests and Sustainable Development was the brainchild of a former prime minister of Sweden, Ola Ullsten. The organizing committee for the commission was convened shortly after the UNCED, but it was not until 1995 that the full commission first met. Its final report was issued in 1999. The commission made a serious effort to broaden the international discourse on forests and to emphasize the public interest, both global and local, in forest conservation. It argued that the custodial role that local communities play in maintaining and conserving forests is not always valued and made a commendable effort to rehabilitate the public goods values of forests in international politics (WCFSD 1999).

However, the impact of the commission on mainstream international politics was negligible. There are three reasons for this. First, the organizing committee started from the assumption that a forests convention was necessary. This led many developing countries to question the objectivity of the initiative, which was seen as starting work with a preordained political agenda. Second, and related to this first point, the commission did not achieve formal endorsement from within the UN system. The approval of the UN secretary-general, Boutros Boutros-Ghali, was sought but not given. This is in comparison to the Brundtland Commission, which had been called for by the General Assembly. Finally, the initiative was eclipsed by the creation of the Intergovernmental Panel on Forests and the Intergovernmental Forum on Forests (Humphreys 2006: 48–65). Overall the commission failed to gather a critical mass of support from the world's governments, with only a few – Canada, Sweden, and the Netherlands – expressing any support.

A summary report of the commission's recommendations that circulated at the final session of the Intergovernmental Forum on Forests had no impact. By now states were poised to elevate the international forest policy dialogue within the UN system. In 2000 the decision was taken to create a new body, the United Nations Forum on Forests (UNFF), to report directly to the UN Economic and Social Council rather than the lower-level Commission on Sustainable Development. In addition to its elevated position within the UN system, there were two further differences between the UNFF and its predecessors. First, a multi-stakeholder dialogue segment was introduced during which stakeholders such as forest business, indigenous peoples, farmers, and scientific organizations could engage both with each other and with government delegates. Second, some UNFF sessions included a ministerial segment. Throughout 2002 to 2004, the UNFF negotiated resolutions on a number of forest-related issues, such as forest health and productivity, maintaining forest cover, scientific knowledge, and the economic aspects of forests. However, there was little evidence that the multi-stakeholder dialogues and ministerial segments had any real bearing on the negotiation of the resolutions. By now UN forest institutions had entered a phase of diminishing marginal returns, and the UNFF resolutions added little, if anything, that was new.

In an effort to rejuvenate itself, UNFF set out in 2005 to agree a new international forests instrument. Before the text was negotiated, there was discussion on whether it should be a convention or non-legally binding. By now there was a weary familiarity to the proceedings. Brazil, supported by other Amazonian Pact countries such as Bolivia, Peru, and Ecuador, again opposed a convention. These were joined by the US, which now opposed a convention on ideological grounds; under Bush junior the US agreed to no new international environmental commitments on the basis that this would constitute another, undesirable, layer of international regulation that would interfere with international markets and impose costs on US industry. For these very different reasons, Brazil and the US formed what was, in effect, a veto coalition.

With no consensus for a convention, states agreed to negotiate the unimaginatively named "Non-Legally Binding Instrument on All Types of Forests," which was concluded in 2007. During the negotiations the EU, Canada, Costa Rica, Mexico, Norway, South Korea, and Switzerland pressed hard for time-bound and quantifiable targets – for example, that states would commit toward reducing their rate of deforestation by x per cent, or increasing their forest cover by y thousand hectares, by a stipulated date. However, the anti-convention states, principally the US and Brazil, opposed any mention of time-bound or quantifiable targets, or even of voluntary commitments to such targets. The instrument contained only four generalized "global objectives" and stated that countries agreed "to achieve progress toward their achievement by 2015," namely (in abbreviated form) to:

- reverse the loss of forest cover worldwide through sustainable forest management;
- enhance forest-based economic, social and environmental benefits, including by improving the livelihoods of forest-dependent people;
- increase significantly the area of protected forests worldwide and other areas of sustainably managed forests; and
- reverse the decline in official development assistance for sustainable forest management and mobilize significantly increased, new and additional financial resources from all sources for the implementation of sustainable forest management.

(United Nations 2007: para. IV)

With the exception of these objectives there is no new commitment of any sort in the non-legally binding instrument that is not contained in the 1992 Forest Principles, the proposals for action agreed between 1995 and 2000, and the UNFF resolutions. Once again developed states vetoed any language suggesting they had a mandatory or legal responsibility to transfer finance and technology to their counterparts in the South. The pro-convention states pressed unsuccessfully for mention in the instrument that a convention or "legally binding instrument" was a future option.

In summary, a body of non-legally binding law (or soft law) on forests has been agreed at the UNCED and by various UN forest bodies, of which the United Nations Forum on Forests is the current incarnation, as the best possible option in the absence of any international consensus for a convention. But international forest politics is not confined just to the UNFF. It is also scattered across a wide range of public and private international organizations, as the next section shows.

Neoliberalism and the fragmentation of international forest policy

Apart from the failure to agree a forests convention, there are two other reasons why the coordination of international forest policy has proved to be so difficult. The first relates to the nature of forests as a political issue. Because forests provide such a wide range of public and private goods, international forest politics inevitably encroaches upon the jurisdictions of several international legal agreements with a forest-related mandate, in particular the Framework Convention on Climate Change, the Convention on Biological Diversity, the Convention to Combat Desertification, and the International Tropical Timber Agreement. An important dimension of international forest politics is a form of institutional "turf war" in which the UNFF, which has no budget for forest policy implementation, both collaborates and competes with other international organizations.

The second reason concerns the broader international political and economic context. This is not unique to forests and is relevant for other international environmental issues too. Forests became an item on the international political agenda in the 1980s, the same decade that neoliberal economic policies were in the ascendant. The theoretical origins of neoliberalism can been traced to Friedrich von Hayek (1944), who asserted that a strong role for the state in the economy would destroy individual and economic freedoms, and to the monetarist Milton Friedman (1962, 1963), who argued for deregulation, privatization, government spending cuts, and the control of the economy through the money supply. The prefix "neo" (for "new") indicates that neoliberalism is a contemporary variant of liberalism. Neoliberalism has adopted the liberal belief in free international trade that underpinned nineteenth-century laissez-faire economic policies, and it draws from neoclassical economics, in particular the notion that the common collective good is best realized when individuals compete in the marketplace. According to David Harvey (2005), the first country to implement neoliberal policies was Chile, in 1973–4, although it was only when the United States under Reagan and the United Kingdom under Thatcher adopted programs of privatization, government spending cuts, deregulation, and marketization that neoliberalism became ascendant internationally. The US and the UK, backed over time by other developed countries and international organizations such as the World Bank and the International Monetary Fund, have successfully promoted neoliberal ideas such as trade and investment liberalization in developing countries.

Neoliberalism has structured how policy-makers think about and interpret the world (Castree 2008a, 2008b; Heynen *et al.* 2007; Larner 2000). Neoliberalism is a discourse in the sense that Michel Foucault (1994) employed the term, as a more or less coherent set of understandings and ideas that shape the boundaries of thought, and thus of action. Proponents of neoliberalism favor certain environmental policy responses – market-based policies, voluntary commitments, and business-based solutions – that the UNFF or, indeed, any single international forest organization is poorly equipped to handle. Neoliberalism has influenced international environmental policy in three important respects. The first is the emphasis on market-based solutions. Neoliberals argue that natural resources are most likely to be conserved when their functions are valued and priced through market mechanisms. A central difference between liberalism and neoliberalism is that, under the latter, the state uses its agency to leverage open new spaces where market forces can operate. One example is the creation under the Kyoto Protocol of an international system of tradeable emission permits, under which some states are granted permits to emit an agreed level of carbon dioxide. These permits can be traded between countries; states that wish to exceed their emissions quota need to purchase permits from low-polluting states with unused permits to sell.

Second, neoliberals advocate an enhanced role for the private sector; natural resources will be more effectively managed when placed under private, rather than state, ownership. Developed countries have argued, in the UNFF and other international organizations, that the forests of developing countries will be more effectively managed if privatized. However, developing countries, most of which view their forests as sovereign natural resources, have been reluctant to privatize, as under current international trade and finance rules any business would have the right to bid to purchase forests in other countries, and developing countries could over time expect to lose control of their forests to powerful business corporations from the developed world. However, private businesses have a major role in developing countries through forest concessions. This is a mechanism under which a public authority hands over an area of state-owned forests to a private business for management or for logging for a prescribed time period.

Finally, neoliberals emphasize voluntary action rather than regulation. To neoliberal orthodoxy, public regulation creates market distortions, and is thus burdensome and inefficient. Deregulation frees markets, enabling them to work more effectively. Instead of the public sector setting environmental targets and standards, any targets adopted should be those to which business itself agrees, for example in voluntary codes of conduct. Where regulation is necessary, it should be soft and optional if markets are to work most effectively. The emphasis in neoliberalism on deregulation helps explain the aversion of some states to time-bound and quantifiable targets for forest protection.

As a result of these two contextual factors – the large number of international institutions with a forest-related mandate and the neoliberal international policy environment – international forest policy is highly fragmented among a diversity of international organizations, as the following four examples illustrate.

Forest certification and labeling

In the late 1980s, with concern about tropical deforestation growing, an attempt was made to introduce an international timber labeling scheme through the International Tropical Timber Organization (ITTO). Created in 1985, the ITTO is the first, and so far the only, international commodity organization with a conservation mandate. In 1989 Friends of the Earth in London lobbied the UK delegation to the ITTO to table a proposal for a timber labeling scheme that would not have banned the international trade of unsustainably managed timber, but would have provided for the labeling of timber from verified sustainably managed forests. The proposal was rejected after opposition from the tropical timber producer caucus, in particular Malaysia, Indonesia, and Brazil, which saw it as a veiled attempt both to infringe upon national sovereignty and to interfere with the international market for tropical timber. However, even if the proposal had been agreed, it is unclear whether it would have been consistent with international trade rules, in particular the provision in the General Agreement on Tariffs and Trade (GATT), which prohibits discrimination between "like products" on the basis of manufacture – a provision that could be interpreted to mean that discriminating between sustainably and unsustainably sourced timber is GATT-illegal. There was also a concern that the ITTO scheme would have discriminated between tropical and non-tropical timber in international trade.

The ill-fated ITTO timber labeling proposal made it clear that any international timber labeling scheme would need to apply to all timber, not just tropical timber, and that any such scheme would need to be consistent with international trade law. In the early 1990s the World Wide Fund for Nature, which had supported the Friends of the Earth proposal, worked with other environmental NGOs, including the Rainforest Alliance, and several environmentally concerned businesses to create in 1993 the Forest Stewardship Council (FSC) (Cashore *et al.* 2004). The FSC is a voluntary, non-state, private scheme for the certification of forest products harvested from well-managed sources. It is governed by a novel institutional structure with three chambers – social, environmental, and economic – each of which has one-third of voting rights, with equal representation between developed and developing countries. As a voluntary, non-state, private organization, the FSC does not admit governments as member organizations. This exclusion is necessary for the FSC to avoid charges that it is a form of intergovernmental organization, and thus bound by international trade law, which since 1995 has been administered by the WTO.

The FSC, and other international timber labeling schemes that have subsequently been created, such as the Programme for the Endorsement of Forest Certification, has thus been deliberately constructed to be compatible with international trade law, which has, in effect, set the boundaries within which all certification and labeling schemes must operate if they wish to avoid a WTO challenge. This is also the case with respect to the European Union's efforts to address the international trade of illegally logged timber.

International measures to curb illegal logging

Illegal logging and the international trade in illegally logged timber pose an increasing threat to tropical forests. There is no multilateral agreement to ban the trade in illegally logged timber. Such a ban is possible in principle, although there would likely be technical difficulties, as different countries have different definitions of illegal logging. A multilateral ban would need to be agreed either through an international environmental agreement or through the WTO. There are several precedents for multilateral trade bans on environmental grounds, including ozone-depleting substances (the 1987 Montreal Protocol to the 1985 Vienna Convention for the Protection of the Ozone Layer), hazardous wastes (the 1989 Basel Convention on the Control of Transboundary Movements of Hazardous Wastes and Their Disposal), and endangered species (the 1973 Convention of International Trade in Endangered Species of Wild Fauna and Flora, or CITES).

With no multilateral ban on the international trade in illegally logged timber, no state can impose a unilateral ban without falling foul of the WTO. Somewhat ironically, therefore, a unilateral ban on the import of illegally logged timber would itself be illegal under international trade law. Since 2003 the European Union has taken an international lead in promoting policies to counter the international trade in illegally logged timber, and has opted to take the only action that is available to it consistent with international trade law, namely voluntary action. Under its Forest, Law Enforcement, Governance and Trade action plan (European Commission 2003), the EU is looking to conclude voluntary but legally binding, bilateral partnership agreements with timber-producing countries which undertake to export to the EU only timber from verifiable legally logged sources. Trade between such countries and the EU will be licensed and monitored. The obvious weakness in this scheme is that criminals can circumvent it by exporting illegally logged timber to the EU via a third country that does not have such a voluntary agreement. The EU concluded its first (and, at the time of writing, its only) voluntary partnership agreement with Ghana in 2008. Over time the EU aims to create a network of such agreements. With no multilateral support for a comprehensive worldwide ban on the international trade of illegally logged timber, the EU's voluntary partnership scheme is the strongest permissible under current international trade law.

A third long-running dispute in international forest politics is whether knowledge of the properties of individual species should be patented. Here, too, the WTO plays a central role.

Knowledge patenting and benefit-sharing

Over time local communities and indigenous peoples have accumulated knowledge of the properties – for example, as foodstuffs and medicines – of the planet and tree species that form part of their environments (Berkes 1999). For example, indigenous forest peoples have developed knowledge on which plants can be used to treat burns and abrasions, which can be used to treat migraines and stomach ailments, and so on. This knowledge, usually called traditional knowledge, has been passed on from generation to generation, often orally, and comprises what is, in effect, a public good that is freely available to all. However, under intellectual property rights law, and especially under the WTO's Agreement on Trade-Related Intellectual Property Rights (TRIPS), business corporations have the right to patent knowledge on biological species (providing that no prior patent has been filed) and to charge royalties to other businesses that wish to use this knowledge for commercial ends. Dozens of such patents have been filed by agricultural, pharmaceutical, and biotechnology corporations. One argument that the proponents of patents make is that, by assigning economic value to biological resources, patents make it more likely that these resources will be conserved and sustainable managed.

Under the TRIPS Agreement, financial benefits from the commercial use of knowledge flow to patent holders. The TRIPS Agreement is opposed by two main groups of actors. First, the governments of biodiversity-rich countries, principally tropical forest states, argue that a share of the financial benefits from patenting should accrue to the government of the country where the species grows. Second, indigenous peoples and local communities have opposed the TRIPs Agreement. Two different views have been expressed by these actors. The first is that knowledge on biological species should be freely available and there should be no patenting of such knowledge. The second accepts patenting as a practice, but insists that, when a patent is based on traditional knowledge, a share of the royalties should flow to those communities and indigenous peoples who originally discovered or developed the knowledge.

Given that traditional knowledge has developed over many generations and has been passed on to many different social groups, there are clear definitional problems with agreeing who the traditional knowledge holders are and, therefore, who should receive a share of the benefits. However, it can be argued that this does not invalidate the general principle. Indeed the principle that the financial benefits from patenting should be shared has status in international law: the Convention on Biological Diversity provides for "the equitable sharing of the benefits" that arise from the utilization of knowledge with the original knowledge holders (United Nations 1992b: article 8(j)). However, while the Convention on Biological Diversity upholds equitable benefit-sharing as a principle, it does not indicate a formula by which the benefits should be shared between the three main claimant groups: commercial patent holders, governments, and local communities/indigenous peoples.

The politics of patent rights to biological resources is thus played out between different legal instruments – the TRIPS and the Convention on Biological Diversity. Not surprisingly, different political actors favor the instrument that best promotes their interests. The TRIPS Agreement reflects the interests of those actors that were instrumental in its negotiation, namely developed states and corporations seeking to promote the commodification of nature and the private ownership of knowledge on biological resources; these actors wish patent rights, like other "trade-related" issues, to be kept firmly under the purview of the WTO. Meanwhile, the governments of biodiversity-rich countries and community and indigenous peoples' groups argue that this debate should be settled by parties to the Convention on Biological Diversity. Pending a resolution of this issue, royalties from patent rights continue to accrue to commercial patent holders, although the governments of tropical forested countries assert their sovereign right to decide which corporations may have access to their biological resources and which may not.

Valuing the carbon sink function of forests

The role of markets occupies a central place in neoliberal thinking and has been key to international climate policy since the agreement of the 1997 Kyoto Protocol. In 2007, parties to the Framework Convention on Climate Change initiated a policy debate on how to reduce carbon emissions from deforestation and forest degradation, especially in developing countries (United Nations 2008). The debate was initiated by Papua New Guinea and Costa Rica and later attracted support from Bolivia, the Central African Republic, the Dominican Republic, Nicaragua, and the Solomon Islands. The decision was premised on the idea that financial incentives should be put in place to encourage developing countries to reduce their deforestation rates.

The incentivizing of conservation through valuing the carbon that is stored in forests in order to prevent deforestation has become known as "reducing emissions from deforestation and forest degradation" (REDD). The basic idea is that countries which reduce their deforestation above a certain baseline will create carbon credits that can be sold to countries which wish to exceed their agreed emission levels in a post-Kyoto market-based global carbon-trading scheme. The baseline is the background (or "business-as-usual") rate of deforestation. Such a scheme has the potential to restructure international forest and climate politics. When emissions from deforestation are included, then, after the United States and China, Indonesia and Brazil become the world's third and fourth largest emitters of carbon dioxide (*The Economist* 2006).

In addition to the methodological and technical issues that will inform baseline measurement, there is a potential political problem: developing countries may bargain for generous deforestation baselines before agreeing to participate. The European Union's Emissions Trading Scheme (ETS) illustrates the problems that an international REDD scheme might face in this regard. In order to establish the ETS scheme, the EU allocated permits to some businesses with high levels of carbon dioxide emissions. The EU was accused of agreeing generous baselines by overestimating the past emissions levels of these businesses in order to secure their participation. Businesses that had taken measures to reduce their emissions prior to the implementation of the ETS scheme were not rewarded. Against this, it can be argued that more stringent emissions baselines would have attracted fewer businesses, thus compromising the long-term effectiveness of the ETS. How baselines are agreed thus has a bearing upon both participation and effectiveness. Similar considerations will inform any REDD scheme. A tropical forest country will have greater incentive to participate in such a scheme when its baseline of estimated future deforestation is generous, as that country would then be able to claim a higher level of reduced deforestation than has actually been achieved. In such circumstances countries could gain financially, as they would generate additional carbon credits for sale to high-emitting states (Humphreys 2008).

In environmental terms this is clearly self-defeating. Not only would the developing country have less incentive to take proactive policies to reduce future deforestation, but lenient baselines would lead to an oversupply of REDD credits, which could depress the price of credits worldwide. High-emitting countries would thus be able to purchase credits at a lower price than if more accurate baselines had been used, and would consequently have less incentive to invest in clean technology to reduce their emissions at source. Generous baselines will thus lower the incentives to lessen deforestation in developing countries and to reduce carbon emissions in high-polluting countries.

The REDD debate also brings to the fore the question of justice. It might be argued that, provided the baselines are accurate, a REDD scheme can promote the principle of intergenerational equity, which holds that environmental risks and harms should not be passed on to future generations. A counter-argument is that REDD focuses only on the carbon stock value of forests, which will promote a narrow emphasis on one forest-related public good – climate regulation – at the expense of others, such as biodiversity habitat, watershed services, sociocultural values, and so on. Furthermore, it may be argued that REDD violates another dimension of justice, namely intra-generational equity. This is the principle of fairness between different groups and countries in the present generation, according to which all people within any one generation have a fair and equal claim to the world's ecological space, including the atmospheric commons (Dobson 2003). Under the principle of intra-generational equity, REDD can be viewed as a morally unjust mechanism that enables some states to continue polluting by purchasing carbon sequestration in other countries, in effect colonizing the ecological space of other people. Indigenous forest peoples' groups, such as the Forest Peoples' Programme, are critical of REDD, claiming it will lead to elite control over nature, with most of the financial benefits flowing to national treasuries rather than to communities (Griffiths 2007).

Conclusion

It is often suggested that a forests convention would rationalize and harmonize global forests governance. According to VanderZwaag and MacKinlay (1996: 2), a convention would promote a more effective and holistic approach to global forests governance and address the increasing fragmentation in the activities of international forest-related organizations. Against this it can be argued that there is no legal reason why a forests convention should rank higher than any other freestanding legal instrument. Indeed, a forests convention could, by adding another layer of international regulation, lead to further legal uncertainties and complications. As Skala-Kuhmann (1996: 23) has argued, "the notion of a 'superconvention', designed to serve as a kind of umbrella over existing conventions and harmonize the areas they cover, is unprecedented in international law." In any case, there is no political will for a convention; key states, notably the Amazonian Pact countries and the United States, have long been opposed to such an instrument.

Like its predecessors in the UN system, the United Nations Forum on Forests has been unable to provide a coordinating focus for international forest management issues. Global forest policy has developed not according to any rational design, but incrementally across several international institutions. It has been argued in this chapter that international forest policy has been strongly guided by neoliberalism, which favors voluntary action and business-led, market-based initiatives while eschewing regulation and a strong role for the state. Both forest certification and the idea of REDD are based upon the principle of voluntary action through international markets. States have no role in forest certification. In the case of international tradeable emission permits, the role of states has been confined solely to creating a new generation of property rights – the right to pollute – and establishing the conditions for the international trading of these rights, after which the state stands back and allows the market to set a price for carbon that, it is hoped, will reduce carbon emissions and incentivize forest protection. Similarly, states have created the intellectual property right to patent knowledge on biological resources. Voluntary action characterizes the EU's policy to counter illegal logging; however, in this case it is fair to conclude that EU member states would have taken stronger action to tackle illegal logging had they been able to do so. They have not done so because they were constrained by WTO rules. Overall, therefore, neoliberal principles have been absolutely central to contemporary international forest policy.

This leads on to a broader point that is relevant not just to international forest politics but, more broadly, to international environmental politics. International environmental law is considerably weaker than the international legal instruments that promote neoliberal principles. International legal instruments on trade, investment, and intellectual property rights are now consolidated under the auspices of a single international organization – the WTO (Larner 2008). Stephen Gill (1995, 2002) has argued that there is now a "new constitutionalism" that codifies not the rights of people and publics, but the rights of business and investors. To Gill, the WTO promotes what he calls "disciplinary neoliberalism," namely neoliberal principles that are backed by powerful developed states which exert influence and control over international organizations. International environmental law is scattered across several legal instruments and international organizations, whereas the WTO agreements are administered by one body. For business corporations and other proponents of neoliberalism this has an advantage, as the WTO has stronger enforcement mechanisms than international environmental law. States are required to implement WTO law, including making any necessary changes to domestic law, on pain of sanctions. International forest policy has been constructed so as not to fall foul of the WTO. On other environmental issues, too, governments have become increasingly self-censorious, avoiding any trade restriction measures that might not survive a WTO challenge (Eckersley 2004). The WTO agreements have a stronger normative force than international environmental law, and in this respect they have established the limits of international environmental policy.

Recommended reading

Cashore, B., Auld, G., and Newsom, D. (2004) *Governing through Markets: Forest Certification and the Emergence of Non-State Authority*, New Haven, CT: Yale University Press.

Humphreys, D. (2006) *Logjam: Deforestation and the Crisis of Global Governance*, London: Earthscan.

Smouts, M. C. (2003) *Tropical Forests, International Jungle: The Underside of Global Ecopolitics*, New York: Palgrave Macmillan.

Tacconi, L. (ed.) (2008) *Illegal Logging: Law Enforcement, Livelihoods and the Timber Trade*, London: Earthscan.

References

Berkes, F. (1999) *Sacred Ecology: Traditional Ecological Knowledge and Resource Management*, Philadelphia and London: Taylor & Francis.

Cashore, B., Auld, G., and Newsom, D. (2004) *Governing through Markets: Forest Certification and the Emergence of Non-State Authority*, New Haven, CT: Yale University Press.

Castree, N. (2008a) "Neoliberalising nature: the logics of deregulation and regulation," *Environment and Planning A*, 40(1): 131–52.

—— (2008b) "Neoliberalisng nature: processes, effects, and evaluations," *Environment and Planning A*, 40(1): 153–73.

Davenport, D. S. (2006) *Global Environmental Negotiations and US Interests*, New York: Palgrave Macmillan.

Dobson, A. (2003) *Citizenship and the Environment*, Oxford: Oxford University Press.

Eckersley, R. (2004) "The big chill: the WTO and multilateral environmental agreements," *Global Environmental Politics*, 4(2): 24–50.

The Economist (2006) "So hard to see the wood for the trees," 19 December. Available: www.economist.com/world/international/displaystory.cfm?story_id=10329203 (accessed 27 May 2009).

European Commission (2003) "Communication from the Commission to the Council and the European Parliament: Forest Law Enforcement, Government and Trade (FLEGT), proposal for an EU action plan," COM (2003) 251 final, Brussels, 21 May.

Foucault, M. (1994) *The Archaeology of Knowledge*, London: Routledge.

Friedman, M. (1962) *Capitalism and Freedom*, Chicago: University of Chicago Press.

—— (1963) *Inflation: Causes and Consequences*, New York: Asia.

Gill, S. (1995) "Globalisation, market civilisation and disciplinary neoliberalism," *Millennium: Journal of International Studies*, 24: 399–423.

—— (2002) *Power and Resistance in the New World Order*, London: Palgrave Macmillan.

Griffiths, T. (2007) *Seeing "RED"?: "Avoided Deforestation" and the Rights of Indigenous Peoples and Local Communities*, Moreton-in-Marsh, Glos.: Forest Peoples Programme.

Harvey, D. (2005) *A Brief History of Neoliberalism*, Oxford: Oxford University Press.

Hasenclever, A., Mayer, P., and Rittberger, V. (2000). "Integrating theories of international regimes," *Review of International Studies*, 26(1): 3–33.

Hayek, F. von (1944) *The Road to Serfdom*. Chicago: University of Chicago Press.

Heynen, N., McCarthy, J., Prudham, S., and Robbins, P. (eds) (2007) *Neoliberal Environments: False Promises and Unnatural Consequences*, London: Routledge.

Humphreys, D. (1996) *Forest Politics: The Evolution of International Cooperation*, London: Earthscan.

—— (ed.) (2003) *Forests for the Future: National Forest Programmes in Europe – Country and Regional Reports from COST Action E19*, Luxembourg: European Communities.

—— (2006) *Logjam: Deforestation and the Crisis of Global Governance*, London: Earthscan.

—— (2008) "The politics of "avoided deforestation": historical context and contemporary issues," *International Forestry Review*, 10(3): 433–42.

Jönsson, C. (1993) "Cognitive factors in explaining regime dynamics," in V. Rittberger (ed.), *Regime Theory and International Relations*, Oxford: Clarendon Press.

Kolk, A. (1996) *Forests in International Environmental Politics: International Organizations, NGOs and the Brazilian Amazon*, Utrecht: International Books.

Larner, W. (2000) "Neo-liberalism: policy, ideology, governmentality," *Studies in Political Economy*, 63: 5–26.

—— (2008) "Neoliberalism, Mike Moore and the WTO," *Environment and Planning A*, 41(7): 1576–93.

Mahathir, M. (1992) "Speech by the prime minister of Malaysia, Dato' Seri Dr Mahathir bin Mohamad, at the official opening of the Second Ministerial Conference of Developing Countries on Environment and Development, Kuala Lumpur, on Monday, 27 April 1992" (mimeo).

Perrings, C., and Gadgil, M. (2003) "Conserving biodiversity: reconciling local and global benefits," in I. Kaul, P. Conceição, K. Le Goulven, and R. U. Mendoza (eds), *Providing Global Goods:*

Managing Globalization, Oxford and New York: University Press and United Nations Development Programme.

Skala-Kuhmann, A. (1996) "Legal instruments to enhance the conservation and sustainable management of forest resources at the international level," paper commissioned by the German Federal Ministry for Economic Cooperation and Development and GTZ, July.

United Nations (1992a) "Non-legally binding authoritative statement of principles for a global consensus on the management, conservation and sustainable development of all types of forests," A/CONF.151/6/Rev.1, Rio de Janeiro.

—— (1992b) *Convention on Biological Diversity*, New York: United Nations.

—— (2007) "Non-legally binding instrument on all types of forest" A/C.2/62/L.5, New York: United Nations.

—— (2008) "Reducing emissions from deforestation in developing countries: approaches to stimulate action," in *Report of the Conference of the Parties on its Thirteenth Session, held in Bali from 3 to 15 December 2007*, FCCC/CP/2007/6/Add.1, Decision 2/CP.13, 14 March. Available: http://unfccc. int/resource/docs/2007/cop13/eng/06a01.pdf#page=3 (accessed 27 May 2009).

VanderZwaag, D., and MacKinlay, D. (1996) "Towards a global forests convention: getting out of the woods and barking up the right tree," in Canadian Council on International Law (ed.), *Global Forests and International Law*, London: Kluwer Law International.

WCFSD (World Commission on Forests and Sustainable Development) (1999) *Our Forests, Our Future: Report of the World Commission on Forests and Sustainable Development*, Cambridge: Cambridge University Press.

10 Biodiversity

Antje Brown

The term "biodiversity," though used widely and liberally by researchers and practitioners, refers to a complex and under-researched environmental policy area. Deforestation, habitat destruction, wildlife conservation, overfishing, species extinction, and the introduction of genetically modified organisms (GMOs) have all necessitated the adoption of a biodiversity regime at the UN level in the form of the Biodiversity Convention of 1992 and subsequent Biosafety Protocol of 2000, as well as various ad hoc working groups and thematic programmes.[1] This chapter explores the different aspects involved in the biodiversity debate and identifies key actors and their interests involved. It also provides an overview of the UN policy to date and highlights unresolved issues that are likely to occupy stakeholders in the near future. Ultimately, biodiversity is positioned at the policy periphery and is not integrated properly into political and economic paradigms of societies. This neglect is somewhat surprising, considering that biodiversity involves – in true "think global act local" fashion – both local communities and intergovernmental organizations such as the UN, the EU, and the WTO. Biodiversity has caused much controversy over the years and continues to throw up a number of economic, political, and ethical questions.

In policy terms, biodiversity refers to the notion that the access and use of shared natural resources should be regulated carefully and in a sustainable manner following centuries of unsustainable resource exploitation and degradation. More importantly, worldwide biodiversity loss suggests that the problem needs to be solved at the international level through regime-building and a system of global governance.

The objective of the UN policy is threefold: conservation, the sustainable use of natural resources, and benefit-sharing. These three objectives should ensure that natural resources benefit both current and future generations. In order to be effective, however, the policy has to be applied evenly in every part of the world, and this, in turn, suggests that the UN policy affects (or interferes with) the sovereignty and decision-making powers of national and local governments. Member states are meant to ratify an international agreement through a vote in their parliaments and arrive at a democratic policy; however, complex negotiations at the international level involve many trade-offs. It is therefore inevitable that policies raise questions of equity and justice. Furthermore, in light of modern GM technology and intellectual property rights, biodiversity increasingly affects relationships between transnational actors representing environmental and economic interests. In a climate where economic actors are allowed to patent natural processes, the lines between nature and business become ever more blurred. This obfuscates the supposed open-access, common character of "natural processes" and transforms them into private property, denying universal access. In addition, policies influence relations between environmentally rich and economically poor countries in the South and economically rich and environmentally poor countries in the North. It therefore touches upon issues such as multilevel governance, economic relations, development, and environmental justice.

The chapter explores the different aspects of the biodiversity debate and identifies key actors and their interests involved in regime formation. Biodiversity is an area that makes it particularly clear that the traditional state-centric way of organizing and regulating an environmental problem is facing severe limits. It also assesses to what extent international relations and environmental theory can explain policy developments while also considering the lessons that can be learned from the biodiversity case study for the discipline of international environmental politics.

Defining biodiversity

According to the UN Convention on Biological Diversity of 1992, biodiversity can be defined as: "variability among all living organisms from all sources … ; this includes diversity within species, between species and of ecosystems." Put simply, biodiversity is about diversity in species, ecosystems, landscapes, and genetic resources. This means it is not just about endangered animals or plants but also about their genetic material and about the relations between species, plants, and humans in particular areas. Scientists estimate the total number of species as somewhere between 5 and 15 million, 1.75 million of which have been formally identified worldwide, and that there remain a greater number than this that are unknown.[2] Ecosystems vary from forests, deserts, rivers, mountains, oceans, swamps, and more – all consisting of carefully balanced and interdependent components. Ecosystems and species have come under increasing pressure in recent decades. Pressure can occur in many forms, predominantly man-made, and can be caused by hunting, overfishing, logging, industrial pollution, climate change, intensive farming, and the commercial exploitation of particular regions. The current number of species officially recognized as threatened is large. One just needs to look at the list provided by the Convention on International Trade in Endangered Species of Wild Fauna and Flora (CITES) to realize that the rate at which ecosystems and species are destroyed is alarming.

CITES is an international treaty on endangered species which was signed by eighty parties in March 1973 in Washington, DC. It entered into force in July 1975 and now has 175 parties. The convention is a voluntary agreement to "ensure that international trade in specimens of wild fauna and flora does not threaten their survival." This is achieved by identifying different types of endangered species and regulating (and, if necessary, banning) their trade worldwide. Endangered species – to date, CITES has formally identified 5,000 animal species and 28,000 plant species – are listed in three appendices according to the level of the threat against them. It has to be noted that these lists include whole groups of species, such as primates, therefore increasing the actual number of species covered by the convention. Endangered species are the most visible form of biodiversity loss and were recognized as an environmental problem earlier than other biodiversity issues.

Biodiversity loss as a whole is projected to accelerate tenfold by 2050. A recent UN report, *Global Environmental Outlook GEO-4* (UNEP 2007), pointed out that many animal and plant species have seen a dramatic decline both in terms of numbers *and* in terms of geographical spread. For example, in regions with a dense population of diverse species, such as areas threatened by deforestation, there is an acute danger of losing substantial numbers of species and genetic material for good. One-quarter of mammal species are currently threatened by extinction. Loss of biodiversity is no longer a problem limited to local communities or regions; it has become a global problem which requires collective action at the international level on account of the nature of the global political economy and also the interconnectedness of ecosystems.

The problem of biodiversity loss is therefore recognized not only as a scientific fact but also as a "human-made" problem that calls for collective action. It is at this point that biodiversity moves beyond pure *science* and becomes a matter of *politics* and *international relations*. Collective action starts with the premise that biodiversity requires a regime that seeks to regulate the conservation, access, and use of shared natural resources. This should be conducted in a sustainable and fair manner after centuries of resource exploitation and degradation. Indeed, UN documents confirm and emphasize this train of thought. According to the UN, current biodiversity loss is not only unprecedented but it takes an entirely new form: "all available evidence points to a sixth major extinction event currently under way. Unlike the previous five events, which were due to natural disasters and planetary change, the current loss of biodiversity is mainly due to human activities" (UNEP 2007). These human impacts are either the result of direct intervention, for example through deforestation by large timber companies, or the indirect result of wider developments such as climate change and its effects on flora and fauna.

Facing political conundrums

One might assume that the objective of preserving the diversity of our species and ecosystems is simple and straightforward. However, in reality, regime-building at the UN level and compliance on the ground has produced a number of conundrums in a similar yet unique way compared with other attempts to curb and regulate environmental problems.

First, the UN convention seeks to ensure the *sensible* and sustainable use of resources and thereby provide for biodiversity for generations to come. In other words, it establishes an intergenerational responsibility. However, in order to be successful in the long term, the policy has to be applied *evenly* and effectively in every country and at every level of government. It is therefore inevitable that the UN policy touches upon the sovereignty and decision-making powers of national and local governments. In this case, biodiversity is an excellent example of how the term "think global, act local" should be understood. Indeed, the policy is dependent on the commitment of national and local actors. Or, as Le Prestre (2002) puts it, "the policy succeeds or fails at the national level." In other words, it takes cooperation and commitment at the international level, but the action then has to follow at the national and subnational level to implement what was agreed. However, this commitment toward biodiversity in every part of the world is difficult to achieve. Many researchers have documented variations in environmental policy commitment[3] and have discussed the ever apparent "tragedy of the commons," which suggests that individuals will always seek to maximize their short-term (economic) interests even if this is to the long-term detriment of the environment and society at large.[4] Biodiversity is no exception to these observations; indeed, in many respects the biodiversity regime illustrates the "tragedy" in following short-term profits rather than long-term goals.

So part of the reason why the international community has failed to establish an effective biodiversity regime is because of actors' interests and their relationships. At first glance it may not be immediately obvious, but biodiversity touches upon vital economic interests, particularly in the areas of modern GM technology and intellectual property rights. Here the UN policy seeks to mediate between economic and preservation interests – that is, between actors who aim to control and use animal and plant species for economic profit (e.g. pharmaceutical companies) and actors who seek to protect species and ecosystems for their own sake and with them wider environmental values (e.g. non-governmental organizations). While there are instances where economic interests and environmental protection can be combined in line with sustainable development – eco-tourism is just one example – there are many other instances where economic and environmental interests clash, as will be discussed further below.

Another complexity concerns *intra*-generational relations and responsibilities: the UN policy raises questions regarding equity and justice, as it challenges the already tense relationship between developed and developing countries. Paradoxically, developing countries tend to be rich in terms of natural resources but economically poor while developed (industrial) countries tend to be comparatively poor in terms of natural resources but economically rich.[5] In other words, potentially profitable natural or genetic resources tend to be located in developing countries, while the large economic players able to take advantage of them tend to be based in developed countries. Over the years, actors from the developed world have proven to be better equipped for UN negotiations than their counterparts from developing countries. While actors from developing countries (e.g. representatives from indigenous communities) have started to improve their participation and representation skills in biodiversity regime-building, they are still lagging behind actors from the developed North.[6]

The above complexities and diverse interests have contributed toward a rather cumbersome regime-building process and a UN policy that is far from being effective.

Regime-building among a diversity in interests

There is no doubt among the international community that biodiversity loss is real and man-made, and that its prevention requires collective action. The international community also acknowledges the responsibility of the current generation to ensure biodiversity for future generations. However, in light of the above conundrums, there are major questions regarding sovereignty, equity, and interest representation that prevent actors from agreeing on common or shared policy details which in turn would contribute toward an effective regime. In essence, differences exist in terms of:

- the prioritization of the problem;
- a commitment to regulate the use of natural resources and, if necessary, to make (economic) adjustments;
- accepting concessions with regard to national sovereignty for the sake of the wider international good.

To date these differences have contributed toward a somewhat ineffective international regime,[7] and it is unlikely that, under current systems of political and economic governance, the international community will adopt a system that will halt the trend of biodiversity loss in the long term. In order to understand the shortfalls, it is necessary to look at the regime-building process so far and the interests involved in shaping the policy.

Despite biodiversity loss being an ongoing process spanning several centuries, it was not until the early 1980s that the international community saw a consensus among scientists that it was under threat. After a number of initiatives – one of which, interestingly, came from the US[8] – the UN Environment Programme (UNEP) set up a working group to formulate an international convention on biodiversity. The working group at this stage had already encountered a North–South divide over genetic resources and intellectual property rights. This would resurface during the 1992 Rio Summit negotiations.

Basically, the main obstacle in agreeing on a collective plan of action concerned the issue of *ownership of genetic resources*: governments and actors in the developing world wanted to protect their (sovereign) rights over the access and use of their natural resources, while governments and actors in the developed North argued that these resources formed part of a "common heritage of mankind" or were simply "owned by no one." In other words, the developed countries' perspective considered natural resources as common or shared resources that should be freely accessible to all. Previously, representatives from developed countries had won the argument and had benefited economically from this arrangement. This time, however, the South sought to regain control over their natural resources and thereby tackle what they perceived to be "biopiracy" and "genetic robbery."[9] Decision-makers trying to develop good, coherent, consistent policy on genetic resources continue to be faced with a multitude of interconnected issues. Even discerning which are relevant to conserving and managing these resources, and integrating them into policy, is extremely difficult.

A fundamental area of dispute is who should share the benefits derived from the exploitation of genetic resources and biotechnology. The lines are usually drawn between developed and developing countries and, within countries, between local communities – usually rural and indigenous peoples – and their better-off, more powerful compatriots.

The concerns are numerous. Some people, for example, consider that the expanded scope of intellectual property rights and their extension to biological materials enable institutions and researchers to appropriate and limit access to the resources and knowledge of farmers and indigenous communities without compensation or consent, especially in the developing world. Others point to the practices of multinational seed companies that are developing, implementing, and promoting a variety of technological tools to restrict the rights of farmers to save and reuse seeds from their harvests. This is taking place against a backdrop of accelerating loss of biological diversity, as forests are felled for timber or to make way for agriculture, fisheries collapse, and the number of plant and animal species facing extinction grows.

Not far from this ownership debate was the debate over the distinction between "old" and "new" species. Here, representatives from the North insisted on a clear distinction between "old" and "new" in their favor. They argued that any species identified recently were effectively the private property of those who had discovered them (often large transnational corporations), while species that had been long established and formed part of traditional knowledge were common and therefore shared (or free) property. In other words, while those from developed countries (e.g. large pharmaceutical companies) wanted free access to long-established genetic resources, they sought control over (and to benefit from) newly identified resources. This approach led to some astonishing decisions, the most publicized one being the US decision of 1995 to grant a patent for turmeric (a herb) to two US doctors even though turmeric's anti-inflammatory properties had been known for centuries as part of the Indian Ayurvedic tradition.[10] Understandably, actors from the South tried to rebalance this approach at the time of negotiation. And, equally understandably, those from the North tried to resist the pressure and focus instead on less controversial but media-friendly issues such as the protection of mammals and the conservation of rainforests.

What actors, including UN officials, national governments, and transnational actors (transnational corporations and environmental NGOs), had to thrash out was a UN convention that would ensure not only the *sustainable* use of natural resources but also the *fair and equitable* use of these resources. However, influenced by their respective "rational" self-interests, the majority of governments stayed well clear of quantifying specific and binding targets of biodiversity conservation and regulation, as had been suggested by some governments and NGOs. Setting watertight targets and thereby committing all sides to clear objectives proved to be a step too far for key actors in both North *and* South.

The actual convention document reflects the attitudes and interests of the main negotiators. It is essentially about good intentions regarding biodiversity but also about maintaining the existing economic paradigm. It advocates economic incentives to encourage biodiversity conservation rather than imposing tough regulation. Signed in 1992 by 150 governments at the Rio Earth Summit, the convention consists of a preamble, forty-two short articles, and three annexes covering identification and monitoring, arbitration, and conciliation. The protocol is a compromise between divergent interests. It also highlights the paradox between national sovereignty and international responsibility and cannot hide its undercurrent economic agenda:

> The objectives of this Convention ... are the conservation of biological diversity, the sustainable use of its components and the fair and equitable sharing of the benefits arising out of the utilisation of genetic resources, including by appropriate access to genetic resources and by appropriate transfer of relevant technologies, taking into account all rights over those resources and to technologies, and by appropriate funding.
> (Convention on Biological Diversity, 1992, Article 1)

Furthermore, Article 3 states the following:

> States have ... the sovereign right to exploit their own resources pursuant to their own environmental policies, and the responsibility to ensure that activities within their jurisdiction or control do not cause damage to the environment of other states or of areas beyond the limits of national jurisdiction.

To put it bluntly, the convention offers something for everybody. The document goes on to outline the "intrinsic ecological, genetic, social, economic, scientific, educational, cultural, recreational and aesthetic values" inherent in biodiversity and argues that biodiversity strengthens friendly relations among states and contributes toward peace for humankind. These objectives would be met through (loosely formulated) policy tools such as national strategies, plans, and programs as well as biodiversity identification, monitoring, conservation, and impact assessment.

Beyond good intentions, and in more practical terms, the convention appeals to governments and their economic actors to consider the environment first, *before* exploiting natural resources. Further, they should take into account what their local or national actions might do to the *international* environment. And, as far as access to genetic resources is concerned, the convention manages to find a compromise between North and South by leaving decision-making to the parties involved: they should regulate the access and use of resources on "mutually agreed terms." In effect, this compromise does not limit resource exploitation; it simply calls upon interested parties – often governments in the South and transnational corporations from the North – to act *sensibly* (whatever this may entail) and work out a deal between themselves.

Apart from the questions of ownership and access to natural resources, two other issues had to be resolved: technology transfer and funding. First, negotiators from the United States expressed concern that the inclusion of *technology transfer* from North to South would jeopardize intellectual property rights and therefore economic interests in the North.

India, on behalf of the South, represented the other side of the argument and settled in the end for a compromise: the convention acknowledges intellectual property rights but also insists that these should not contradict the aims and objectives of biodiversity.

The second issue surrounded the question of whether or not the convention deserved its own *funding mechanism*. The North insisted that funding should be provided through the already existing Global Environment Facility (GEF). From a Northern point of view, a new funding mechanism might have involved more financial commitment and less control over the policy itself, and this was an option the developed countries could not accept. It was the then executive director of UNEP, Mostafa Tolba, who put pressure on negotiators to accept a "take it or leave it" compromise. He proposed the GEF as funding mechanism in the first instance but also a concession for the South in the form of more transparency. To date the GEF is still involved in biodiversity funding; in fact, biodiversity now constitutes its largest portfolio (Le Prestre 2002).

While Tolba's proposals were duly adopted by 150 governments, interpretations of convention details continued to differ after the event depending on actors' respective sets of interests. Notably, the document was not signed by the then US president, George H. W. Bush, because the points of funding and intellectual property rights were still deemed unacceptable. While his successor, Bill Clinton, signed at a later stage, the US has not to date ratified the convention and is therefore not party to it. Considering that, by 2005, 188 countries had ratified, it can be argued that the US stands very much alone and isolated on the issue of biodiversity.

Of course, the convention signalled a starting point. Over the years, the various parties have had to fill in policy gaps with details in the form of protocols and follow-up work programs. To date we have seen only one protocol, the Cartagena Protocol of 2000, which focuses on living modified organisms and their regulation vis-à-vis biodiversity. The first work program was adopted in 1998, and so far such programs have proven to be rhetoric at best.

One major obstacle in filling the convention's gaps with effective policy details constituted the formation of so-called veto coalitions that pursue their own specific economic interests. For instance, on the issue of deforestation, the parties saw a veto coalition made up of Brazil, Canada, and Malaysia, whose governments made sure that any follow-up policies would not interfere unnecessarily with their large timber and logging industries (Chasek *et al.* 2006: 163).

A welcome distraction from the above controversies of ownership and access to natural/ genetic resources was biosafety, more specifically the regulation of genetically modified organisms. The resulting Cartagena Biosafety Protocol of 2000, however, was not free of controversy either. The protocol consists of a preamble, forty articles, and three annexes, which cover information required in notifications concerning *living modified organisms* (LMOs) as well as risk assessments. Initially intended to regulate the trade in GMOs and their impacts on biodiversity, the document is, yet again, a watered-down compromise between transnational actors. Much to the disappointment of environmental NGOs, it effectively legitimizes the use and trade of GMOs for transnational corporations. Its key policy tool is the Advanced Informed Agreement (AIA), which comprises a prior notification and consent procedure. This procedure is applied mainly to LMOs such as GM seeds. During the formulation stage of the protocol, controversy flared up regarding the inclusion of other GMOs and the question of whether or not to integrate the precautionary principle in addition to the issue of clarifying the relationship between this UN protocol and relevant WTO rules. Not surprisingly, these issues would be resolved with a watered-down compromise in the final version of the protocol (outlined below).

Apart from typical divisions between environmental and economic transnational actors, two large groups of states were formed in the course of negotiations. To a certain extent, these two groups adopted the roles of environmental and economic advocates. The so-called Miami Group, consisting of the US, Canada, Australia, Chile, Argentina, and Uruguay, pursued a lenient policy approach by keeping the number of GMOs to be included under the protocol to an absolute minimum while at the same time opposing the precautionary principle. At the opposite end of the negotiating table was the Like-Minded Group, consisting of developing countries and EU member states; this group pursued a more regulated approach, with more GMOs to be included, and insisted on the precautionary principle.

It is striking how the protocol was shaped not only by government representatives and environmental NGOs (which operated very much in the background) but also by transnational corporations, such as Monsanto, DuPont, and Sungenta (formerly Novartis and Zeneca), with vital interests in GM technology. These transnational corporations went on to create a Global Industry Coalition which would achieve a more coordinated voice and a strong force during negotiations. The coalition, chaired by BioteCanada, involved some 2,200 companies, thereby forming an unprecedented, united, and proactive economic front. This observation is similar to Jennifer Clapp's "enhanced lobby power," described in Chapter 3.

Considering the different forces in biodiversity regime-building, it is not surprising that the final version of the protocol was a compromise solution. It does cover a number of GMOs; however, these are put in different categories and governed by different criteria and, more importantly, exemptions. LMOs come under the formal AIA procedure for first international boundary movement. Other GMOs exempted from AIA are processed through a separate Biosafety Clearing House, which is a simplified notification mechanism through an internet database. As a concession to the Like-Minded Group, the precautionary principle is included in the document; however, the principle is considered only if scientific evidence can be presented to justify its application and only if the matter of cost-effectiveness is taken into consideration. The protocol also leaves existing WTO rules intact. It could be argued that it has, in effect, given transnational corporations more certainty and stability rather than providing a "green obstacle" in the trade of GMOs.

Elsewhere, discussions still continue on the issue of access to genetic resources, which begs the question whether negotiators are truly committed to biodiversity protection or whether their real interest lies in the maximization of economic interests. In 2002, the parties to the convention agreed the Bonn Guidelines on the Access to Genetic Resources and the Fair and Equitable Sharing of the Benefits Arising out of their Utilization. Meanwhile, the great expectations on either side of the North–South divide to exploit and benefit from the "green gold" have not materialized.

In recent years, the UN has attempted to establish a link between climate change and biodiversity loss. UNEP set up an ad hoc Technical Expert Group on Biological Diversity and Climate Change, which produced a document in October 2003 titled "Interlinkages between biological diversity and climate change: advice on the integration of biodiversity considerations into the implementation of the UN FCCC and its Kyoto Protocol." The document identifies specific links between climate change and biodiversity loss – for instance, climate change impacts on species migration as well as species extinction and ecosystem changes. Furthermore, the document considers indirect impacts through human population adjustments and adaptations. Among proposals for change are policy integration, sustainable management, including *afforestation* (to counteract deforestation), and – last but not least – an effective climate change policy.

May 2008 saw the ninth official meeting of the parties in Bonn, where, again, the main themes were the interlinkage between climate change and biodiversity loss and attaching a monetary value to natural resources, thereby internalizing natural resources as part of the dominant economic paradigm. Attaching a value to biodiversity, an exercise increasingly popular since the 1990s, is currently gaining in momentum.[11] Among recent estimates are the following gains or values:

- the annual world fish catch – $58 billion;
- anti-cancer agents from marine organisms – up to $1 billion per year;
- global herbal medicine market – circa $43 billion in 2001;
- honeybees as pollinators for agriculture crops – $2–8 billion per year;
- coral reefs for fisheries and tourism – $30 billion per year.

In similar fashion, the projected costs include some very specific estimates, such as:

- mangrove degradation in Pakistan – $20 billion in fishing losses, $500,000 in timber losses, $1.5 million in feed and pasture losses;
- Newfoundland cod fishery collapse – $2 billion and tens of thousands of job losses.

(UNEP 2007)

By attaching a monetary or economic value to natural resources, it is hoped that actors use these resources, or "capital," sensibly and not as "free-for-all" commodities/common goods.[12] In its efforts to attach a monetary value to biodiversity, the UN is also looking into turning so-called carbon sinks into profitable protected areas that can be bought and traded, just like carbon permits. Already, some investors and businesses have shown an interest, as carbon-sink trading may become a convenient way of offsetting greenhouse gas emissions, which is in line with the Kyoto Protocol and its climate change targets. Yet, one all-too-familiar question is already being raised: once they have been identified as market commodities, who will own these carbon sinks – private investors, such as transnational corporations from the North, or local communities/countries from the South? There are already pilot schemes, such as the Forest Carbon Partnership Facility in the Republic of Congo, which offer interesting testing grounds. Another example is the ADB carbon sequestration project in Indonesia, which is funded by the Asian Development Bank and is intended to earn Indonesia emission reduction credits. The Global Forest Coalition, a coalition of NGOs and indigenous peoples' organizations (founded in 2000), is currently looking into these carbon-sink projects, and their initial assessment appears to be skeptical.[13] The projects have not entirely addressed the question of ownership, nor do they help remove all the obstacles that have prevented actors from establishing a proper and collective mediating and policing system.

It is, nevertheless, noticeable how developments in the climate change policy area have fed into biodiversity. There are, indeed, obvious scientific as well as political interconnections. A chapter on biodiversity in *GEO-4* (UNEP 2007) offers examples of climate change–biodiversity interlinkages. *GEO-4* reports, for instance, on extinction cases in the amphibians category as well as alterations in species distribution (e.g. Arctic foxes, mountain plants, Northern temperate butterflies, and British birds) and variations in tree distribution in Europe resulting from climate change. Furthermore, it highlights modifications in species behaviour; these include earlier flight times in insects and differences in breeding patterns of amphibians and flowering of trees. And, finally, *GEO-4* points out changes in population demography – for instance, transformation in population sex ratios in reptiles. From a slightly different angle, but conveying a similar message, the *Carbon and Biodiversity* atlas (UNEP 2008) highlights so-called biodiversity hotspots, or areas threatened by biodiversity loss, whose protection would not only help maintain biodiversity but also contribute toward the creation of carbon sinks under the Kyoto Protocol.

What is interesting about the link between climate change and biodiversity is the fact that actors have not only identified this link in scientific terms, but have also started to connect the two policy areas in very practical political and economic terms. One obvious example would be the adoption of economic policy tools such as permit trading, which is already tried and tested in the climate change area and is now being envisaged for biodiversity. A certain degree of lesson learning is evident; this can also be seen in the fact that the UN is planning to introduce a group of biodiversity experts similar to that of the Intergovernmental Panel on Climate Change (IPCC).

An assessment of biodiversity policy in international relations

The above chapter has produced a number of findings that are typical for environmental regime-building. At the outset, there is an international consensus that biodiversity loss is real (i.e. scientifically proven) and predominantly a man-made problem which requires collective action. International actors also share some common ground on good intentions, such as helping "poor" indigenous communities maintain their habitats and species. However, once negotiators venture into policy details, there are many areas where styles, priorities, and interests depart from each other or simply clash. The result of the compromise-seeking process is that the biodiversity regime is somewhat watered down and – from an environmentalist's point of view – rather disappointing. In this sense, the biodiversity regime is not much different from other international environmental regimes, such as that of climate change.

As has been mentioned, the protection of species and habitats is not a simple and straightforward environmental task. Biodiversity is complex, not just in scientific but also in political and economic terms. For a start, it affects all levels of governance – from the global to the local. Consequently, its regime covers questions of self-determination vis-à-vis collective action and international responsibility (the "commons dilemma" springs to mind). In addition, it deals with economic interests, particularly those of transnational corporations which have an interest in accessing genetic and natural resources in order to feed their new technology and pharmaceutical industries. On top of that, biodiversity has *intra-* as well as intergenerational implications and generates debates over justice, equity, and responsibility: we have learned that natural resources are distributed unevenly between populations, as are their uses and benefits, and that the current generation has a responsibility toward future generations in taking effective and collective action to ensure that endangered species and habitats do not disappear forever. This is perhaps where biodiversity departs from other environmental policy areas. It is this sense of irreversibility and finality that makes biodiversity so special. As effective *and* collective action is not forthcoming, it is unlikely that the problem of biodiversity loss will be tackled in the foreseeable future. Biodiversity therefore touches upon a number of wider and fundamental discourses in political economics, global governance, and environmental justice, be it of an *inter*generational or *intra*-generational nature; these may not be evident to such an extent in other policy areas.

One of the main problems of biodiversity policy has been the "horse-trading" between actors, which in turn has distracted them away from the actual environmental objective (i.e.

to stem the trend of biodiversity loss) and instead turned their attention toward the economic interests associated with natural or genetic resources. Since the convention's adoption, the parties have tried to live up to the official policy goal of a "significant reduction in the current rate of biodiversity loss by 2010." However, with the 2010 deadline looming, there is no scientific evidence to suggest that the goal has been achieved. The trend of biodiversity loss has not been halted or even slowed down; indeed, it continues to accelerate at an alarming rate. Strategies and plans at national levels may well exist alongside the convention, but they are evidently insufficient in stopping the trend of biodiversity loss. Alongside other government priorities and day-to-day business (such as addressing international terrorism and the global financial crisis), these strategies appear to be too small and too insignificant to make a difference. Biodiversity is positioned at the policy periphery and is not integrated properly into the political and economic paradigms of societies.

Having noted at the outset that biodiversity is a neglected research area, this chapter has (hopefully) demonstrated that this neglect is unjustified. In many respects, regime-building in biodiversity has proven to be a case of environmental regime "meddling." And yet biodiversity has also proven to be an interesting, complex, and pressing policy matter that has affected international relations. One just needs to look at the "coalitions" of states that were formed during negotiations and transnational actor groups such as the Global Industry Coalition and their increased involvement in international regime-building.

From the perspective of international relations theory, insights from biodiversity regime-building are useful for a number of reasons: biodiversity is a good example in that it highlights the involvement of different government levels (from local communities to the UN); it demonstrates how environmental and economic spheres are interconnected; and it is a policy area that illustrates how transnational actors become polarized on policy details, which in turn can have an effect on regime-building and problem-solving.

By the same token, international relations theory can help us make sense of biodiversity regime-building. At first sight, the problem of biodiversity loss may be clear to all and a solution may appear to be straightforward. However, in order to understand the discrepancy between policy ideal and reality, we need to apply an *actor-centered* approach which focuses on transnational actors, their (environmental or economic) interests, and their places in a complex global setting. One finding of this chapter is that transnational actors' commitments, policy approaches, and policy measures on biodiversity are too varied to allow for decisive collective action. An international regime may exist on paper but, when it comes to effective problem-solving, it is too weak to impose collective discipline across the board. As it stands, the biodiversity regime is merely a reflection of the lack of proper commitment on the part of global civil society. Similarly, a *policy tool* approach can provide an understanding of recent policy changes.

The chapter has described how the UN has sought to give biodiversity a new impetus by establishing a causal link between climate change and biodiversity loss. This deliberate link was established partly because of obvious scientific evidence, but also in order to raise the biodiversity profile in a highly competitive global governance setting. In this setting a multitude of policy issues compete for "ear-time" in international relations. Whether or not this strategy will bring about the desired effects remains to be seen. Another International Day for Biological Diversity was marked on 22 May 2010. However, in the light of the global financial crisis, the international community and the media hardly took note of this event. The success of a global biodiversity policy will depend on the wider international context, which includes not only economic factors but also new scientific evidence and societal changes.

Notes

1 For the full text of the Biodiversity Convention, visit: www.cbd.int. Thematic programs focus on the following habitat categories – marine and coastal areas, forests, agricultural land, inland waters, dry and subhumid lands, and mountain regions.
2 Spangenberg (2007) points out that quantifying biodiversity is a difficult if not an impossible task. The estimate of 1.75 million identified species is based on UN and EU literature.
3 For a comparison of variations in sustainability commitments, see, for instance, Baker (1997).
4 See Hardin (1968). Vogler (2000) offers a more modern version.
5 Banerjee (2003) highlights this paradox.
6 For further information on how indigenous communities seek to improve their negotiating powers, see Pachamama (2008). Also visit the Indigenous Peoples Council on Biocolonialism at: www.ipcb.org.
7 Le Prestre (2002) investigates the regime's effectiveness by focusing on policy learning, capacity-building, and norm changes. He notes that its development has been uneven, which is partly owing to a lack of proper monitoring and the slow development of common indicators that would help measure its impact.
8 This initiative is interesting because the US is one of the very few nations that have, to date, not ratified the UN convention and is therefore not party to it.
9 The term "genetic robbery" has been used by Vandana Shiva on several occasions and has been cited by many. See, for instance, Shiva *et al.* (1997) and Chamerik (2003).
10 It should be noted that the patent was issued by a non-party state, the US, three years after the adoption of the convention. The patent was later revoked. See Baker (2008) for further information.
11 The difficulty of this exercise in economic valuation of biodiversity can be seen in Nunes and van den Bergh (2001).
12 Pretty and Smith (2004) investigate the notion of environmental, economic, and social capital in greater detail.
13 For the Asian Development Bank and specifically the Indonesian carbon sequestration project, visit: www.adb.org. For information on the Global Forest Coalition, visit: www.globalforest coalition.org.

Recommended reading

Le Prestre, P. (2002) "The CBD at ten: the long road to effectiveness," *Journal of International Wildlife Law and Policy*, 5: 269–85.
Pretty, J., and Smith, D. (2004) "Social capital in biodiversity conservation and management," *Conservation Biology*, 18(3): 631–8.
Vogler, J. (2000) *The Global Commons: Environmental and Technological Governance*, Chichester: Wiley.

Online resources

Congo Basin Forest Partnership: www.cbfp.org
Convention on Biological Diversity: www.cbd.int
Convention on International Trade in Endangered Species of Wild Fauna and Flora: www.cites.org
Global Forest Coalition: www.globalforestcoalition.org
Indigenous Peoples Council on Biocolonialism: www.ipcb.org
UN Environmental Programme: www.unep.org

References

Baker, L. (2008) "Turf battles: politics interfere with species identification," *Scientific American*, 299(6): 22–4.

Baker, S. (1997) *The Politics of Sustainable Development*, London: Routledge.

Banerjee, S. B. (2003) "Who sustains whose development? Sustainable development and the reinvention of nature," *Organization Studies*, 24(1): 143–80.

Chamerik, S. (2003) "Community rights in global perspective," in X. Jianchu and S. Mikesell (eds), *Landscapes of Diversity*, Kunming: Yunnan Science and Technology Press.

Chasek, P., Downie, D. L., and Brown, J. W. (2006) *Global Environmental Politics*, 4th ed., Boulder, CO: Westview Press.

Hardin, G. (1968) "The tragedy of the commons," *Science*, 162(3859): 1243–8.

Le Prestre, P. (2002) "The CBD at ten: the long road to effectiveness," *Journal of International Wildlife Law and Policy*, 5(3): 269–85.

Nunes, P., and van den Bergh, J. (2001) "Economic valuation of biodiversity: sense or nonsense?," *Ecological Economics*, 39(2): 203–22.

Pachamama (2008) *Pachamama Newsletter*, 2(2,). Available: www.cbd.int/doc/newsletters/news-8j-02-02-low-en.pdf.

Pretty, J., and Smith, D. (2004) "Social capital in biodiversity conservation and management," *Conservation Biology*, 18(3): 631–8.

Shiva, V., et al. (1997) *The Enclosure and Recovery of the Commons: Biodiversity, Indigenous Knowledge and Intellectual Property Rights*, New Delhi: Research Foundation for Science, Technology and Ecology.

Spangenberg, J. H. (2007) "Biodiversity pressure and the driving forces behind it," *Ecological Economics*, 61(1): 146–58.

UNEP (United Nations Environmental Programme) (2007) *Global Environmental Outlook: Environment for Development (GEO-4)*, Malta: Progress Press. Available: www.unep.org/geo/geo4/report/GEO-4_Report_Full_en.pdf (accessed 17 November 2009).

—— (2008) *Carbon and Biodiversity: A Demonstration Atlas*. Cambridge: UNEP World Conservation Monitoring Centre. Available: www.unep.org/pdf/carbon_biodiversity.pdf.

Vogler, J. (2000) *The Global Commons: Environmental and Technological Governance*, Chichester: Wiley.

11 Agriculture and the environment

Marc Williams

Introduction

This chapter will explore various linkages between agriculture and the environment. The study of the relationship between the two is important for a number of reasons, among them the impact of the natural and physical environment on agriculture and food production. For example, climate change and variability can have serious repercussions for farmers and consumers (Gregory *et al.* 2005). Furthermore, agriculture is important as a source of employment and income for many people, especially in the developing world. As this chapter will demonstrate, sustainable agriculture is intimately linked with the production and consumption of food and issues related to health. In brief, agriculture and the environment are at the centre of debates on sustainability. These include considerations of environmental justice and ecological justice which underlie many of the issues that will be discussed here.

I engage in this chapter with some of the key themes developed in Part 1 of the book. I will first examine some of the important linkages between agriculture and the concept of sustainability and then focus on the relationship between agricultural production, environmental sustainability, and the global economy. I go on to analyze the debate over production methods between organic agriculture and industrial agriculture and explore the relationship between both agriculture and food security and agriculture and consumption through the lens of agricultural biotechnology and the debate over genetically modified organisms (GMOs). In the final section I consider aspects of the debate on the contours of global agricultural governance – that is, the ways in which issues relating to agriculture and environmental sustainability are governed.

Agriculture and sustainability

The concept of sustainability remains contested even though it is now more than two decades since the Brundtland Commission provided a popular definition of sustainable development. Its report (WCED 1987) raised two central issues in its definition of sustainable development. One key aspect of the commission's definition of sustainable development is intergenerational equity: the current generation must not diminish the stock of natural and human capital that is available to future generations. Following this approach, Lehman *et al.* (1993: 143) claimed that "sustainable agriculture consists of agricultural practices which do not undermine our future capacity to engage in agriculture." Also at the heart of the Brundtland Commission's definition is a linkage between ecological, economic, and social dimensions of sustainability, and this threefold approach remains central to any attempt to understand the complex relationship between agricultural production and environmental sustainability. Thus, as a starting point for this chapter, sustainable development will be conceived of in terms of balancing economic, ecological, and social needs and demands. That is, the approach to agriculture and the environment adopted here situates agriculture as a social and political practice and not simply as an economic activity.

The relationship between humans and the environment which is at the heart of agricultural sustainability is as old as human civilization, although it should be noted that the development of agricultural civilizations emerged only approximately 10,000 years ago. By necessity, agricultural activities are conducted in close connection with the environment. Here I will outline briefly the threefold aspects relevant to examining the complex issues pertinent to agricultural sustainability. At the outset it is necessary to note that, although I will discuss some of the general problems relating to environmental sustainability, agriculture across the globe is complex, dynamic, and diverse (Thompson and Scoones 2009). The national struggle for environmental sustainability in agriculture will not be the same across all societies. One common distinction in the literature is recognition of the different conditions faced by producers in developed and developing countries (World Bank 2007). As will be discussed below, the differences between these agricultural policies and the impact of different farming systems and access to food supplies is a central issue in current trade negotiations and contemporary agricultural governance. But such a dichotomy between the rich and poor should not be taken as an indication that there are no differences facing farmers and the rural agricultural sector within the two broad categories.

A number of changes in the global economy have impacted on the performance of the agricultural sector in many countries and affected the development of sustainable practices. While the economic performance of the agricultural sector is highly variable across different nation-states, in most countries agriculture has become export-oriented and open to competition on world markets (McMichael 1994). In the contemporary global political economy, market pressures and changing technology have created a number of issues relevant to the sustainable use of agricultural land. Another important development relevant to discussions of sustainability is the industrialization of agriculture, especially in the developed world, which gathered pace in the twentieth century and shows no signs of slowing. Industrialization led to the adoption of larger, more intensified operations which have played a central role in raising productivity and feeding an expanded population. These developments have not, however, been greeted with universal acclamation and have been at the center of some of the debates concerning environmental sustainability. Issues such as loss of wildlife habitat, declining water quality, and loss of biodiversity have been raised by critics of industrial agriculture (Horrigan *et al.* 2002).

The dynamic interaction between agriculture and natural resources is another key issue relating to the sustainability of contemporary agriculture. While noting that specific problems will arise in different national settings, some broad areas of concern can nevertheless be outlined. These include problems related to the use of water and water efficiency – for example, water quality in rivers and streams; the impact of chemicals and pesticides on food, water, and other products; the introduction of animals and non-native plants with an adverse impact on natural vegetation; soil erosion and the loss of soil organic matter; reduced biodiversity; and greenhouse gas emissions (Soule *et al.* 1990).

Environmental policies affecting agriculture are continually evolving. Among key areas of concern directly related to the question of sustainability are sustainable practices such as water efficiency and appropriate irrigation, economic productivity, and the income of the farm sector, especially the terms of trade between agriculture and other sectors of the economy. But these policies and regulations are not simply a response to the economic and environmental issues raised above. They also reflect the preferences of citizens and governments as attitudes to agriculture and the natural environment undergo change (see, for example Hall *et al.* 2004; Hyytiä and Kola 2005; Verbeke *et al.* 2010). As will be discussed below, such preferences are linked to issues such as food safety and sustainable consumption as much as to regulations pertaining simply to the land.

With the adoption of sustainable development as a global norm, governments and the various stakeholders in the agricultural industry have made commitments to achieving long-term environmental sustainability. As the above sketch has indicated, this commitment, while laudable, is intensely political and contested.

Agricultural production, trade, and environmental sustainability

The global political economy of agricultural production intersects with environmental concerns in a number of ways. In this section I will focus on the relationship between trade, agriculture, and the environment or, more specifically, between agricultural trade and sustainable development. The relationship between trade and the environment has been a heated topic of debate since the 1990s (Brack 1998; Neumayer 2004; Williams 2001). One of the most controversial issues centers on the role of agriculture and the extent to which trade liberalization has increased environmental damage, or whether and to what extent environmental protection measures have hindered trade liberalization (Dragun and Tisdell 1999). The impact of trade liberalization on agriculture has given rise to opposed theoretical positions, competing methodologies, and conflicting findings. Within the plethora of official reports, academic papers, and other studies, two broad positions can be discerned. These two "schools of thought" differ in their assumptions concerning the role of agriculture and the goals of trade policy reform. Supporters of trade liberalization detail the negative impact of domestic protection on the environment and emphasize the positive role that agricultural trade liberalization plays in the fight against poverty and in securing food supplies (Wilson 2002). Critics of trade liberalization emphasize the historical and political context of neo-liberal globalization in which liberalization is embedded and tend to detail social aspects of agriculture, such as its role in terms of landscape management and its failure to provide satisfactory employment, incomes, and food security (Otero 2008). Both sides in the debate claim that their preferred policies will enhance welfare, food security, and ecological sustainability.

Barriers to trade liberalization in agriculture exist in the form of direct government intervention through subsidies, as well as indirect forms of support to the agricultural sector, which affect choice of production, inputs to the production process, and outputs. Domestic support in the form of subsidies is widely used by many countries. Export subsidies, while less prevalent, are also significant in restricting agricultural trade. Both sides in the debate claim that the policies of their opponents are likely to have negative environmental consequences.

The liberal perspective takes a favorable view of the impact of trade liberalization on agriculture and of the consequent benefits for environmental sustainability. Liberal theorists contend that forms of agricultural protection reduce global welfare, damage specific communities, and result in environmental degradation. Environmental degradation follows from the creation of distorted markets, leading to inefficient and inappropriate resource use. Support for agricultural trade liberalization is applicable to developed, emerging, and developing countries. In other words, trade liberalization will enhance economic efficiency, increasing welfare gains for all (Anderson and Martin 2005).

Three key goals can be met by agricultural trade liberalization. First, the reduction of subsidies and other forms of protection given to farmers in industrialized nations will reduce production that is damaging to the environment, since the impact of subsidies is to distort comparative advantage and to maintain relatively inefficient producers who are likely to be using marginally less productive land. The elimination of developed country agricultural protection will enhance environmental sustainability, since such practices contribute to an over-reliance on pesticides and fertilizers and the overexploitation of marginal land. Moreover, subsidies tend to freeze production, which may prevent a shift to less environmentally harmful policies. The overall impact of agricultural trade liberalization will be an increase in total world output, a better distribution of world income, and enhanced environmental sustainability through diversification of production and enhanced agro-biodiversity. Second, the elimination of subsidies will increase the costs of agricultural goods that at present enter the world market at artificially low prices. The reduction in subsidies will thus create a "level playing field," thereby enabling developing countries that can compete in the supply of such products to reap the benefits of higher export earnings. That is, farmers from developing countries will be able to gain access to markets in the industrialized world, since surplus production from industrialized countries will be reduced. Third, it is argued that the increased economic gains to developing countries will assist in the fight against hunger and poverty through the promotion of economic growth. It will contribute to enhanced food security in the developing world and will also assist in combating environmental degradation, since from this perspective poverty is a key cause of environmental harm. Rising incomes will allow developing countries to give more attention to fighting environmental degradation.

These arguments are rejected by those analysts who maintain that, historically, trade liberalization has been skewed to favor the interests of the wealthy and that further agricultural trade liberalization is unlikely to achieve the aims of the liberal theorists (Sharma 2005). For these analysts, trade liberalization is a component of a neoliberal paradigm which supports industrial agriculture and the commodification of nature. They contend that, insofar as trade liberalization leads to increased economic activity, this is likely to increase rather than decrease natural resource exploitation, thus worsening environmental degradation (Gonzalez 2006).

Second, some argue that, if agricultural trade liberalization is achieved, it will not benefit all developing countries equally (Pérez *et al.* 2008; Díaz-Bonilla *et al.* 2002: 18). Those countries that are competitive will gain, but many that import food (mainly the poorest developing countries) will suffer, since they will be faced with higher import bills. Third, critics focus on intra-country equality and claim that the impact of trade liberalization within societies is likely to benefit wealthy farmers at the expense of the rural poor, since this may lead in some circumstances to depressed agricultural prices, which in turn are likely to lead to forms of land consolidation, with the poorest farmers losing their land. They also argue that depressed rural incomes will lead to further land degradation in the developing world. Fourth, it has been claimed that agricultural trade liberalization leading to increased food imports and reduced prices for domestic producers with the abandonment of food subsidies will further accelerate environmental degradation, as small farmers become increasingly uncompetitive and lose market share to large export-oriented firms more likely to rely on chemicals and pesticides. In short, critics of trade liberalization argue that further liberalization will have adverse impacts on food security, environmental sustainability, and rural livelihoods.

As ever, both of the competing approaches produce empirical studies to support their claims. It is unlikely that general conclusions can be drawn from the available evidence

(Bureau *et al.* 2005). The extent to which agricultural trade liberalization can impact the environment negatively or positively will vary and results will be inconsistent. In some circumstances trade liberalization will hinder environmental sustainability and in others it will enhance environmental protection.

This debate between proponents and opponents of greater trade liberalization is not sterile but of practical importance in the context of the stalled Doha Round of multilateral trade negotiations in the World Trade Organization (WTO). The WTO has emerged as the organizational site of the contestation over the benefits of liberal trade in agricultural products (Colyer 2003). Liberal theorists support agricultural trade liberalization as a mechanism for meeting the developmental goals of the round, and anti-trade liberalization writers contend that the costs of liberalization outweigh the benefits. The sensitivity of agriculture within the economies of the major industrialized countries ensured that the sector was exempt from the rapid postwar trade liberalization that was ushered in under the General Agreement on Tariffs and Trade (GATT). However, with the convening of the Uruguay Round of trade negotiations, which led to the creation of the WTO, agriculture was placed on the agenda. The Uruguay Round Agreement on Agriculture thus marked the first moves toward trade liberalization.

The Uruguay Agreement on Agriculture classified protectionist measures designed to protect agriculture into three categories or "boxes." The green box represents permitted subsidies; the blue box applies to direct payments under certain production-limiting programs; and the amber box indicates those that should be reduced. Apart from these three main "boxes," the agreement also covers special and differential treatment for developing countries (sometimes referred to as the S&D box), and *de minimis* support relates to subsidies that are too low to be of concern to negotiations (WTO 1994).

The Doha Declaration commits members to continue the work begun in the Uruguay Round – that is, to pursue further liberalization of agricultural trade. Member states agreed to "comprehensive negotiations aimed at: substantial improvements in market access; reductions of, with a view to phasing out, all forms of export subsidies; and substantial reductions in trade-distorting domestic support" (WTO 2001: para 13). They further emphasized the necessity of making special and differential treatment for developing countries "an integral part of all elements of the negotiations" and the importance of food security, rural development, and non-trade issues. The negotiations since that time have been characterized by unwavering demands and fundamentally different assumptions regarding the Doha mandate and work program. Agricultural issues have formed a key reason for the failure to arrive at a compromise. It is not the aim of this discussion to provide an analysis of the negotiations within the WTO, but we should note that sustainable development forms a backdrop to such negotiations, since the Doha Ministerial Declaration explicitly recognizes the environment as a key issue.

Industrial agriculture, organic agriculture, and environmental sustainability

A key contemporary issue and highly charged debate concerns the sustainability of the dominant agricultural paradigm in the developed world. Industrial agriculture, which can be defined as the application of science, technology, mechanization, and industrial organization to crops, fish, livestock, and poultry, has long held sway as the answer to the problem of food security and economic efficiency. Its success in meeting the needs of feeding a rising population left it in an unchallenged position for much of the twentieth century. There are a number of claimed benefits of industrial agriculture, including cheap and plentiful food vital to feed an ever expanding human population. One of the major benefits of industrialization has been the ability to reap considerable economies of scale. The result has been a declining number of farm workers but an increase in the availability of foods, especially high-protein food such as meat (Roberts 2008: 21–4). The development of modern agri-business has had far-reaching impacts in developed societies in shaping consumption patterns (Pollan 2006).

The success of this system is now under sustained attack, since the short-term pursuit of profit and increased yields appears to be at variance with long-term goals of sustainability. This challenge to large-scale intensive farming practices has arisen because of the perceived environmental damage and some health risks. In other words, a focus on environmental sustainability and concerns with food safety have challenged industrial agriculture's position (Lowe 1992).

The critique of industrial agriculture is wide-ranging and diverse. It has been argued that

Industrial agriculture depends on expensive inputs from off the farm (e.g. pesticides and fertilizer), many of which generate wastes that harm the environment; it uses large quantities of nonrenewable fossil fuels; and it tends toward concentration of production, driving out small producers and undermining rural communities.

(Horrigan *et al.* 2002: 445)

This sums up the two-pronged attack on industrial agriculture. In the first place it is accused of engaging in practices detrimental to the environment and the health of farm workers (Arcury *et al.* 2002), and it is built on the unsustainable use of the Earth's resources, contributing to environmental degradation. For example, industrial agriculture has been successful in producing higher yields by a reliance on monoculture, which has the unfortunate effect of reducing plant genetic diversity (Thrupp 2000: 269–73). Second, it has been argued that the social costs of industrial agriculture are unacceptable, since it breeds rural poverty and increases societal inequality. One critic has accused the system of focusing on economic success rather than on biological or social concerns (Brown 2003: 238). A third critique focuses on attendant costs to human health from some practices, a good example being the risks from bovine spongiform encephalopathy (BSE), popularly known as mad cow disease.

In contrast, critics have promoted organic agriculture as a solution to the ills of modern agriculture and a vehicle for sustainable development (Conford 1992). Although at present one can conclude that organic methods have undermined but not eroded industrial agriculture in the search for sustainability, their challenge necessitates some scrutiny. In the past decade and a half, organic agriculture has become the most dynamic and fastest-growing sector of the global food industry, attracting considerable interest and government involvement in its regulation.

One of the most persistent arguments against organic agriculture is its inability to meet the demands of feeding an expanding population. However, its proponents recently produced evidence in support of its capacity to feed the world (Badgley 2007; Scialabba 2007), and a UNCTAD/UNEP (2008) study suggests that organic agriculture has an important role to play in helping African countries attain food security. Its growth is linked to a commitment to sustainable development and the search for an alternative to dominant farming practices. Moreover, it is linked to animal rights movements, ethical concerns with the treatment of animals, and food safety concerns.

But a reliance on organic agriculture is not unproblematic. Insofar as it is nested in a system of capitalist production, organic agriculture is likely to give rise to problems relating to scale (Alroe *et al*. 2005). For example, it has been observed that many of the features of large-scale production which form part of the critique of industrial agriculture are also applicable to some sections of the organic movement (Pollan 2006). The key issues relating to sustainability are linked to differences between smallholder farmers and large corporations as well as to methods of production.

Agriculture and food security

Agriculture is at the center of debates concerning food security, which is both an individual and a national issue. The Food and Agriculture Organization notes that "Food security exists when all people, at all times, have physical and economic access to sufficient, safe and nutritious food to meet their dietary needs and food preferences for an active and healthy life" (FAO 2002: 27). Following from this definition we can claim that food security comprises four key components. At the core of most definitions is the absence of hunger or undernourishment. In 1996 the World Food Summit addressed the issue of food security and set the target of halving the number of hungry people in the world by the year 2015. In its latest comprehensive publication, *The State of Food Insecurity in the World 2009* (FAO 2009), the FAO provides an estimate of 1.06 billion undernourished people worldwide. The second component of the definition is that of the safety of the food, since a sufficient quantity that is unsafe would increase food insecurity. The third issue relates to the nutritional component of food: the feeling of satiety without accompanying nutritional benefit does not in itself contribute to food security. The final component of food security refers to the culturally appropriate nature of the food consumed. In short, food security is attained when a person has "access, at all times, to enough food for an active, healthy life" (US Department of Agriculture 2009). From the above, it can be seen that agriculture is essential to the provision of food security. Food security is thus in one sense related to improvements in agricultural yields, the promotion of environmental sustainability, and enhancement of nutritional standards. One solution to the problem, vigorously promoted by some national governments, international organizations, and the private sector, is the application of biotechnology.

The capacity of agricultural biotechnology to provide greater food security is directly linked to its revolutionary impact on crops (Krimsky and Wrubel 1996). In simple terms, the application of biotechnology to agriculture consists of a process termed "transgenesis," which alters the genetic composition of the crop in order to produce a desired outcome – for example, to create crops that are resistant to pests, disease, and drought. The widespread application of such techniques promises a revolutionary impact on agricultural production, since genetically modified crops can produce higher yields at lower cost through a decrease in the application of fertilizers, herbicides, and pesticides. Limitations to improvements in agricultural productivity using traditional methods of cultivation in terms of both increased yields and improved quality make recourse to agricultural biotechnology an attractive proposition. Similar to the Green Revolution of the 1960s, agricultural biotechnology is a concerted international attempt to move beyond traditional methods through the application of science to agriculture. Specifically the use of plant biotechnology can contribute to plant growth and development. It can speed up the breeding season, create more robust crops, and counter the ravages of nature.

Supporters of agricultural biotechnology argue that such methods promote increased efficiency in farming practices, thus resulting in higher yields, environmentally sustainable development, and food security. It can contribute to food security through the production of more food in an environmentally sustainable manner (Serageldin 1999) and promote food security through achieving higher yields and improving the use of marginal agricultural land (Victor and Runge 2002). In other words, the benefits of biotechnology extend beyond more sustainable farming practices to an improved yield per acre, thus increasing the world's food supply and making a direct contribution to food security.

It has also been argued that agricultural biotechnology can contribute to food security through the development of crops which have been nutritionally enhanced, and there have been attempts to create crops which meet this goal. To date the most successful is so-called golden rice – GM rice enhanced with vitamin A – and there is some evidence that it has the potential to alleviate vitamin A deficiency (Stein *et al.* 2008; Zimmerman and Qaim 2004).

While proponents emphasize the potential beneficial impact of biotechnology through its impact on land, water, and plants, critics maintain that it is environmentally harmful. Moreover, they claim that transgenic solutions are more expensive than conventional farming methods.

The critical perspective on agricultural biotechnology argues that there are two major dangers faced by farmers and communities which adopt such techniques (Gonzalez 2007). In the first place, transgenic biotechnology is likely to have a negative impact on ecosystems. Opponents emphasize the potential harm caused to natural habitats by the introduction of new species, which, it is claimed, will unbalance the prevailing natural order through contaminating natural species, thus leading to a decline in those species and subsequent ecosystem degradation. Critics argue that the newly introduced plants and crops are likely to dominate native species because they have been specially created to withstand naturally occurring pests and threats. Such new species, through shifting the ecological balance of ecosystems, result in damage to soils. A second argument made by critics concerns the possibility that transgenes will escape, leading to serious environmental consequences. In other words, GM crops will proliferate, thus leading to the development of superweeds which will be difficult to control. Such superweeds will lead to declines in crop yields, biodiversity losses, and disruptions to natural ecosystems.

Furthermore, the argument concerning the benefits of golden rice has been met with some skepticism. Apart from standard concerns around food safety, accessibility, and affordability, it has been suggested that golden rice by itself is unlikely to overcome vitamin A deficiency. Some researchers maintain that, while useful in assisting consumers, it can play only a supplemental role (Dawe *et al.* 2002).

Advocates of agricultural biotechnology argue that the critics have overstated the potential impact of GM crops on ecosystems. Since GM organisms are finely modified forms of existing ones, the fear of widespread systemic damage is misplaced. Moreover, given the existence of established procedures for their use, it is unlikely that harmful effects on the soil will remain undetected before preventative measures can be put in place. Similarly, claims concerning the development of superweeds are also dismissed. While the possibility of outcrossing from domesticated GM crops to weedy and indigenous wild relatives remains a possibility, proponents assert that the frequency of such events will be extremely low. Furthermore, very few domesticated plants naturalize, and almost none are weeds in natural ecosystems. Supporters argue that it is difficult to see how the traits that are currently being introduced into GMOs will improve their fitness in ways that allow these plants to pose a threat to the environment. Support for these views was given in an authoritative report prepared for the Australian government, which concluded that

> There is no scientific reason to suspect that the nature of the hazard associated with virus recombination (i.e. the formation of a new virus) will differ for transgenic and

non-transgenic plants. The transgenic plant carrying a virus-derived sequence presents an increased in risk compared to the non-transgenic plant only if the frequency with which viable recombinants are generated in the former is significantly greater.

(CSIRO 2002: 8)

Agriculture, food safety, and consumption

As noted above, the links between agriculture and the environment also relate to food safety. In this section I will discuss food safety from the perspective of the debate on agricultural biotechnology, since it is an issue of topical concern. Food safety is a core public health issue which can be clearly and starkly conveyed to every citizen (Tansey and Worsley 1995). Is the food we eat produced in a manner likely to contribute to protecting and maintaining our health? At the centre of food safety concerns are the separate but related issues of trust and risk. As consumers we have to trust the regulatory authorities, farmers, food processors, retail outlets, and all involved in the chain of bringing food, whether cooked or raw, to the table. We must be certain that risks of contamination resulting in disease and death have been kept to a minimum. In articulating fears around food safety, opponents of agricultural biotechnology invoke crucial cultural as well as economic and political sensibilities.

Are GM foods safe for human consumption? In other words, what are the long-term implications of their consumption for human beings? The public debate on GM foods is frequently conducted in the absence of calm and reasoned debate. Below I set out some of the main arguments made by their opponents and supporters.

Critics of agricultural biotechnology have advanced fears over the safety of GM foods (see for, example, Druker n.d.; Pusztai 2001). They argue that, in the light of scientific uncertainty, food standards authorities should apply the precautionary principle. Instead of further GM foods being allowed into the diet, they should be strictly controlled until conclusive evidence on safety is provided. The central argument regarding safety is concerned with the potential allergenic and toxic properties of GM food and the possibility of bacterial infection. Critics claim that there are potential direct risks to human health arising from the creation of novel toxicants. Genetic manipulation could result in higher levels of toxicity in an existing protein or a toxicologically active ingredient, leading to greater exposure than normally encountered by humans in their diet. It is also possible that GM foods can increase the naturally occurring levels of toxins in food.

Those concerned with the potential risks posed by GM foods allege that genetic modification can increase the levels of naturally occurring allergens, and that therefore there should be a moratorium until we can be sure these products are safe for both people and the environment. Campaigners point out that people with allergies now have to contend with the ready availability of GM foods, and unless these are clearly labeled may be unable to take the only preventative measure possible, namely avoidance. Moreover, they argue that the potential risk posed by transfer of allergens by genetic modification is likely to increase as more food is subject to gene transfer. Critics fear, given the difficulty of predicting the potential allergenicity of foods derived from gene technology, it is possible that the use of a transgene in a staple food may lead to higher incidence of allergic reactions to that GM protein. The British Medical Research Council was sufficiently concerned about the current state of knowledge on GM foods and allergens to recommend the need for further research (Medical Research Council 2000).

A third health issue relates to the possibility that that genes present in GM foods can transfer to the consumer's make-up with disease-causing bacteria in the digestive tract, resulting in infections that are resistant to treatment with antibiotics. Although most ingested

DNA is assimilated into the digestive system along with the rest of the food, some research has shown the movement of gene-sized DNA into cells in the gastrointestinal tract.

While opponents of GM have articulated a clear set of risks opposed by the consumption of such foods, their claims have not gone uncontested. Supporters of the regulation of GM begin from the observation that no food source can be 100 per cent safe. The search for zero risk is in this view a pointless exercise and a red herring. They contend that the key issue at stake is not whether GM foods contain health risks but rather the impact of genetic modification on already occurring allergens and toxins. While not denying the possible impact of gene technology on toxins, supporters argue that toxic substances are present in many conventional foods and, unless they are removed, will remain in the GM foods derived from the conventional product. From their perspective, the real issue concerns any increase in toxic levels as a result of the application of gene technology. It is argued that this is a problem that can be safely regulated (WHO 2005). It is not a reason to apply the precautionary principle and to ban or prohibit GM foods; rather it is a case of restricting the sale of any GM product in which the application of gene technology has increased levels of allergens and toxins.

Moreover, supporters of GM reiterate the point that conventional foods contain allergenic proteins that affect some 1 to 2 per cent of adults and 6 to 8 per cent of children. Different people are allergic to different foods – for example, nuts, wheat, and fish – and allergic reactions vary depending on the person and the nature of the allergy. The issue at stake, therefore, is not the presence of allergens in food but the impact of gene transfer on the naturally present allergen. If it can be proven that the levels of naturally occurring allergens in GM foods have risen above the natural range in conventional foods, such foods should be subject to prohibition. Supporters of GM, while accepting the importance of food safety, nevertheless argue that there is an excessive zeal to deem GM foods unsafe. For example, they claim that the application of moratoriums is excessive given the fact that, based on studies to date, there is no evidence of any commercially available GM food having induced clinical manifestations of allergenicity (Centers for Disease Control and Prevention 2001). Moreover, the British Royal Society concluded in 2002 that

> There is at present no evidence that GM foods cause allergic reactions. The allergenic risks posed by GM plants are in principle no greater than those posed by conventionally derived crops or by plants introduced from other areas of the world.
>
> (Royal Society 2002: 3)

On the issue of bacterial infection, scientists in support of the licensing of GM foods and against a moratorium conclude, while recognizing research showing DNA present in food can move into mammalian cells, that the biological impact is likely to be low. The Australian and New Zealand regulatory food agency stated: "For most of the antibiotic resistance genes currently present in GM foods, the overall threat to the therapeutic use of antibiotics in humans is effectively zero" (Odgers 2000: 10). And the British Royal Society's report mentioned above reached the decision that, "Given the very long history of DNA consumption from a wide variety of sources, we conclude that such consumption poses no significant risk to human health, and that additional ingestion of GM DNA has no effect" (Royal Society 2002: 3).

Global agricultural governance

There is no global governance institution with the specific task of linking agriculture and environmental issues. The main organization overseeing agricultural issues is the Food and

Agriculture Organization (FAO), created in 1945. A specialized agency of the United Nations, the FAO is the first major international organization to be tasked with the international coordination of agricultural policy, and a further eleven intergovernmental governance arrangements deal explicitly or implicitly with international cooperation pertaining to agriculture and agricultural resources. As Table 11.1 reveals, agricultural governance covers both agricultural inputs (e.g. land use, plant variety and diversity, and pesticides) and agricultural outputs (including international trade, food safety, and food security).

Within the literature there are different approaches to the subject of global agricultural governance. Here I will explore three different perspectives. The first is that of governance as functional cooperation. Writers in this perspective focus on the role of international organizations in helping states to solve collective action problems (Macer *et al.* 2003). Thus examination of the FAO is likely to focus on its origins and its key functions (Shaw 2007: 3–11). The FAO arose from recognition of the disruptions caused to agricultural production,

Table 11.1 International agreements and agricultural governance

Institution/agreement	Agriculture governance aspects
Food and Agriculture Organization (FAO)	A forum and expert advisory organization with aims to improve agriculture, forestry, and fishery practices and nutrition. Incorporates environmental stewardship and rural development.
Convention on Biological Diversity (CBD)/Cartagena Protocol	Aims to protect biological diversity.
Global Environment Facility	Assists with climate change adaptation, including water, sustainable agriculture, food security, and land use, and facilitating biodiversity.
International Convention for the Protection of New Varieties of Plants	Aims to protect plant varieties with intellectual property rights while encouraging the development of new ones. Has the potential to create breeds that can stand up to climate/environmental changes.
International Fund for Agricultural Development (UNIFAD)	Funds agricultural development projects in poor rural areas that depend largely on agriculture.
International Plant Protection Convention (IPPC)	Aims to prevent the spread of pests in plants and to promote measures to control pests.
International Treaty on Plant Genetic Resources for Food and Agriculture	Aims to protect, preserve, and extend plant biodiversity for food and agriculture, including the use of plant diversity to hedge against unpredictable environmental changes.
Rotterdam Convention	Relates to international trade and information-sharing in pesticides and industrial chemicals, some of which have/had agricultural applications.
UN Framework Convention on Climate Change (UNFCCC)/Kyoto Protocol	Includes the promotion of sustainable agriculture in light of climate change and climate change mitigation through agricultural adaptation technologies.
World Food Programme	Aims principally to prevent hunger and deliver food aid.
WTO Agreement on Agriculture	Aims to limit barriers to trade in agriculture and to open agricultural market access.
WTO Sanitary and Phytosanitary Agreement (SPS)	Concerned with food safety and plant and animal health standards.

trade, and distribution as the result of World War II. Agricultural production was severely curtailed as factories for the production of fertilizers, pesticides, and farm machinery were given over to the war effort, and the FAO was a functional response to this crisis. As the preamble to its constitution states, the aim of the organization is to ensure that humanity is free from hunger. To that end it has key functions such as the creation and dissemination of knowledge through research, the conservation of natural resources, and the improvement of processing, marketing, and distribution of agricultural products.

A different problem-solving perspective is that articulated by the World Bank in the *World Development Report 2005* (World Bank 2004). Agricultural governance is linked explicitly to the wider governance agenda directed at tackling poverty. Hence, whereas with the FAO the function of governance is directed at all states, within the discourse of the World Bank it is an activity directed at those states (read developing countries) lacking the capacity to govern themselves properly. Global agricultural governance, which is dependent on "fair trade rules, conserving genetic resources, controlling the spread of pandemic diseases, and managing climate change," will be provided in this vision by a mix of agencies. Central to this enterprise is a vision of good governance with its foundation at the domestic level.

Higgins and Lawrence (2005), rejecting the problem-solving and functional approaches, characterize global agricultural governance as a political response to globalization. They argue that national systems have been replaced by a mixed-actor system comprising quasi-governmental authority, private organizations, NGOs, and regional bodies. This mix of public and private regulation effectively promotes the privatization of governance in support of neoliberal globalization. Thus governance is a specific political response to globalization. This approach focuses on the ways in which governance is a response to new issues such as food safety and sustainability and also generates new non-statist forms of regulation.

Conclusion

This chapter has discussed a number of issues pertinent to current debates on agriculture and environmental sustainability. Agriculture and the agri-food system is the site of a number of controversies, among them issues relating to the benefits of agricultural trade liberalization, the sustainability of industrial agriculture, the safety of novel (GMO) food, the battle against world hunger, and the scope of governance arrangements. Key issues discussed in Part 1 of this book are applicable to this case study. They include the political economy of sustainable development, trade, and environment considerations, issues relating to justice, the politics of consumption, and the role of international organizations.

Recommended reading

McMichael, P. (ed.) (1994) *The Global Restructuring of Agro-Food Systems*, Ithaca, NY: Cornell University Press.
Pollan, M. (2006) *The Omnivore's Dilemma: A Natural History of Four Meals*, New York: Penguin.
Shaw, D. J. (2007) *World Food Security: A History since 1945*, Basingstoke: Palgrave Macmillan.
Weiss, T. (2007) *The Global Food Economy: The Battle for the Future of Farming*, London: Zed Books.

References

Alrøe, H. F., Byrne, J., and Glover, L. (2005) "Organic agriculture and ecological justice: ethics and practice," in N. Halberg, H. F. Alrøe, M. T. Knudsen and E. S. Kristensen (eds), *Global Development of Organic Agriculture: Challenges and Promises*, Wallingford: CAB International, pp. 75–112.

Anderson, K., and Martin, W. (eds) (2005) *Agricultural Trade Reform and the Doha Development Agenda*, Washington, DC: World Bank.

Arcury, T. A, Quandt, S. A., and Russell, G. B. (2002) "Pesticide safety among farmworkers: perceived risk and perceived control as factors reflecting environmental justice," *Environmental Health Perspectives*, 110(2): 233–9.

Badgley, C. (2007) "Organic agriculture and the global food supply," *Renewable Agriculture and Food Systems*, 22(2): 86–108.

Brack, D. (ed.) (1998) *Trade and the Environment: Conflict or Compatibility?* London: Earthscan/RIIA.

Brown, A. D. (2003) *Feed or Feedback: Agriculture, Population Dynamics and the State of the Planet*, Utrecht: International Books.

Bureau, J.-C., Jean, S., and Matthews, A. (2005) *The Consequences of Agricultural Trade Liberalization for Developing Countries: Distinguishing between Genuine Benefits and False Hopes*, Working Paper 5, Paris: CEPII.

Centers for Disease Control and Prevention (2001) *Investigation of Human Health Effects associated with Potential Exposure to Genetically Modified Corn: A Report to the US Food and Drug Administration from the Centers for Disease Control and Prevention*, available: www.cdc.gov/ncen/ehhe/Cry9cReport/complete.htm.

Colyer, D. (2003) "Agriculture and environmental issues in free trade agreements," *Estey Centre Journal of International Law and Trade Policy*, 4(2): 123–43.

Conford, P. (ed.) (1992) *A Future for the Land: Organic Practice from a Global Perspective*, Bideford, Devon: Green Books.

CSIRO (Commonwealth Scientific and Industrial Research Organization)(2002) *Environmental Risks associated with Viral Recombination in Virus Resistant Transgenic Plants: Final Report*, Canberra: CSIRO.

Dawe, D., Robertson, R., and Unnevehr, L. (2002) "Golden rice: what role could it play in alleviation of vitamin A deficiency?," *Food Policy*, 27: 541–60.

Díaz-Bonilla, E., Robinson, S., Thomas, M., and Yanoma, Y. (2002) *WTO, Agriculture, and Developing Countries: A Survey of Issues*, Washington, DC: International Food Policy Research Institute.

Dragun, A. K., and Tisdell, C. A. (1999) *Sustainable Agriculture and Environment: Globalisation and the Impact of Trade Liberalisation*, Cheltenham: Edward Elgar.

Druker, S. M. (n.d.) "Why concerns about health risks of genetically modified food are scientifically justified," available: www.biointegrity.org/health-risks/health-risks-ge-foods.htm.

FAO (Food and Agriculture Organization) (2002) *The State of Food Insecurity in the World 2001*, Rome: FAO.

—— (2009) *The State of Food Insecurity in the World 2009*, Rome: FAO.

Gonzalez, C. G. (2006) "Markets, monocultures, and malnutrition: agricultural trade policy through an environmental justice lens," *Michigan State Journal of International* Law, 14: 345–82.

—— (2007) "Genetically modified organisms and justice: the international environmental justice implications of biotechnology," *Georgetown International Environmental Law Review*, 19(4): 583–642.

Gregory, P. J., Ingram, J. S. I., and Brklacich, M. (2005) "Climate change and food security," *Philosophical Transactions of the Royal Society: Biological Sciences*, 360: 2139–48.

Hall, C., McVittie, A., and Moran, D. (2004) "What does the public want from agriculture and the countryside? A review of evidence and methods," *Journal of Rural Studies*, 20: 211–25.

Higgins, V., and Lawrence, G. (eds) (2005) *Agricultural Governance: Globalization and the New Politics of Regulation*, London and New York: Routledge.

Horrigan, L., Lawrence, R. S., and Walker, P. (2002) "How sustainable agriculture can address the environmental and human health harms of industrial agriculture," *Environmental Health Perspectives*, 110(5): 445–56.

Hyytiä, N., and Kola, J. (2005) *Citizens' Attitudes towards Multifunctional Agriculture*, Discussion Paper no. 8, University of Helsinki, Department of Economics and Management.

Krimsky, S., and Wrubel, R. (1996) *Agricultural Biotechnology and the Environment: Science, Policy and Social Issues*, Urbana and Chicago: University of Illinois Press.

Lehman, H., Clark, E. A., and Weise, S. F. (1993) "Clarifying the definition of sustainable agriculture," *Journal of Agricultural and Environmental Ethics*, 6: 127–43.

Lowe, P. (1992) "Industrial agriculture and environmental regulation: a new agenda for rural sociology," *Sociologia Ruralis*, 32(1): 4–18.

Macer, D. R. J., Bhardwaj, M., Maekawa, F., and Niimura, Y. (2003) "Ethical opportunities in global agriculture, fisheries, and forestry: the role for FAO" *Journal of Agricultural and Environmental Ethics*, 16: 479–504.

McMichael, P. (ed.) (1994) *The Global Restructuring of Agro-Food Systems*, Ithaca, NY: Cornell University Press.

Medical Research Council (2000) *Report of a Medical Research Council Expert Group into the Potential Health Effects of Genetically Modified (GM) Foods*, London: Medical Research Council.

Neumayer, E. (2004) "The WTO and the environment: its past record is better than critics believe, but the future outlook is bleak," *Global Environmental Politics*, 4(3): 1–8.

Odgers, W. (2000) *GM Foods and the Consumer*, Canberra and Wellington: Australia New Zealand Food Authority.

Otero, G. (ed.) (2008) *Food for the Few: Neoliberalism and Biotechnology in Latin America*, Austin: University of Texas Press.

Pérez, M., Schlesinger, S., and Wise, T. A. (2008) *The Promise and the Perils of Agricultural Trade Liberalization: Lessons from Latin America*, Medford, MA: Global Development and Environment Institute, Tufts University. Available: www.ase.tufts.edu/gdae/Pubs/rp/AgricWGReportJuly08.pdf.

Pollan, M. (2006) *The Omnivore's Dilemma: A Natural History of Four Meals*, New York: Penguin.

Pusztai, A. (2001) "Genetically modified foods: are they a risk to human/animal health?," ActionBioscience, June. Available: www.actionbioscience.org/biotech/pusztai.html.

Roberts, P. (2008) *The End of Food*, Boston: Houghton Mifflin.

Royal Society (2002) *Genetically Modified Plants for Food Use and Human Health – An Update*, London: Royal Society.

Scialabba, N. E.-H. (2007) *Organic Agriculture and Food Security*, Rome: FAO.

Serageldin, I. (1999) "From green revolution to gene revolution," *Economic Perspectives: An Electronic Journal of the US Department of State*, 4(2): 17–19.

Sharma, D. (2005) *Trade Liberalization in Agriculture: Lessons from the First 10 Years of the WTO*, Brussels: APPRODEV.

Shaw, D. J. (2007) *World Food Security: A History since 1945*, Basingstoke: Palgrave Macmillan.

Soule, J., Carré, D., and Jackson, W. (1990) "Ecological impact of modern agriculture," in R. C. Carroll, J. H. Vandermeer, and P. M. Rosset (eds), *Agroecology*, New York: McGraw-Hill, pp. 165–88.

Stein, A. J., Sachdev, H. P. S., and Qaim, M. (2008) "Genetic engineering for the poor: golden rice and public health in India," *World Development*, 36(1): 144–58.

Tansey, G., and Worsley, T. (1995) *The Food System: A Guide*, London: Earthscan.

Thompson, J., and Scoones, I. (2009) "Addressing the dynamics of agri-food systems: an emerging agenda for social science research," *Environmental Science & Policy*, 12(4): 386–97.

Thrupp, L. A. (2000) "Linking agricultural biodiversity and food security: the valuable role of agro-biodiversity for sustainable agriculture," *International Affairs*, 76(2): 265–81.

UNCTAD/UNEP (2008) *Organic Agriculture and Food Security in Africa*, New York and Geneva: United Nations.

US Department of Agriculture (2009) *Food Security in the United States: Measuring Household Food Security*, available: www.ers.usda.gov/Briefing/FoodSecurity/measurement.htm.

Verbeke, W., Pérez-Cueto, F. J. A., de Barcellos, M. D., Krystallis, A., and Grunert, K. G. (2010) "European citizen and consumer attitudes and preferences regarding beef and pork," *Meat Science*, 84: 284–92.

Victor, D. G., and Runge, C. F. (2002) *Sustaining a Revolution: A Policy Strategy for Crop Engineering*, New York: Council on Foreign Relations.

WCED (World Commission on Environment and Development) (1987) *Our Common Future*, Oxford: Oxford University Press [Brundtland Report].

WHO (2005) *Modern Food Biotechnology, Human Health and Development: An Evidence-Based Study*, Geneva: WHO.

Williams, M. (2001) "Trade and environment in the world trading system: a decade of stalemate?," *Global Environmental Politics*, 1(4): 1–10.

Wilson, J. S. (2002) *Liberalizing Trade in Agriculture: Developing Countries in Asia and the Post-Doha Agenda*, Policy Research Working Paper 2804, Washington, DC: World Bank.

World Bank (2004) *World Development Report 2005: A Better Invesment Climate for Everyone*, Washington, DC: World Bank.

—— (2007) *World Development Report 2008: Agriculture for Development*, Washington, DC: World Bank.

WTO (1994) *Final Act of the Uruguay Round: Agreement on Agriculture*, available: www.wto.org/english/docs_e/legal_e/ursum_e.htm#aAgreement.

—— (2001) Ministerial Declaration: Adopted 14 November 2001, WT/MIN(01)/DEC/1, Doha, 20 November. Available: www.wto.org/english/thewto_e/minist_e/min01_e/mindecl_e.htm.

Zimmermann, R., and Qaim, M. (2004) "Potential health benefits of golden rice: a Philippine case study," *Food Policy*, 29: 147–68.

12 Persistent organic pollutants and pesticides

Peter Hough

Introduction

A number of international regimes have emerged over the last thirty years contributing to the global regulation of pesticides and other chemical pollutants. These developments bear testimony to the work of pressure groups and epistemic communities in highlighting the environmentally polluting effects of hazardous chemicals, which the regimes have helped alleviate. However, unlike the ecocentric restrictions that emerged in North American and Western European domestic pesticide legislation from the 1960s, these regimes were achievable only because they also satisfied anthropocentric values, given greater priority at the global level. It has emerged that human health and economic values are at stake, as well as the conservation of the non-human environment. Crucially, transnational business interests have come to favor worldwide regulation as a means of circumventing variable and sometimes more stringent domestic restrictions on chemical production and trade and so allow an unlikely consensus to emerge and permit the first steps of global governance to be taken.

What's your poison? Pesticides, POPs, and their environmental impact

The term "pesticide" refers to any substance used in the control of pests as defined by humans. Such pests include insects (hence the term insecticide), weeds (herbicides), and also fungi (fungicides). Pesticides may also be used in ways which fall short of killing pests. The term additionally covers defoliants used to strip trees and plants of their leaves, plant growth regulators, and substances which deter insects from certain locations (for example, mosquito repellents) or attract them away from crops (for example, through the use of pheromones). Natural pesticides, derived from plant extracts such as nicotine, and inorganic pesticides, derived from minerals such as arsenic, have been utilized in agriculture for many centuries and can be the cause of human and non-human poisoning, but it is the far more widespread use of organic pest control agents in the last seventy years in industrialized agriculture and public health campaigns that have had most environmental and human health significance.

Organic pesticides have their origins in World War II. The insecticidal properties of the original and still most notorious pesticide, diclorodiphenyltrichloroethane (DDT), were discovered by the Swiss chemist Dr Paul Muller in 1939, and it was quickly patented. A series of other chlorine-based compounds, the "organochlorines," were soon found to have similar properties, leading to the marketing of insecticides such as benzene hexachloride (BHC), aldrin, and dieldrin. A second branch of organic pesticides, the phosphate-based "organo-phosphorous" compounds, emerged as a side effect of wartime research into toxic gases by the German scientist Dr Gerhard Schrader. After the war Schrader put his research before the allied states and revealed the potential insecticidal application of the compounds. Parathion was the first major insecticide of the form to be marketed, and others, such as malathion, soon followed. Further branches of organic pesticides subsequently developed include carbamates (derived from carbamic acids), such as aldicarb, and phenoxyacetic (phenol based) acids, such as 2,4,5-T.

The most environmentally hazardous organic pesticides and some other organic chemical compounds created for industrial purposes have, in recent decades, come to be known as persistent organic pollutants (POPs). These are defined by the United Nations Environment Programme as: "chemical substances that persist in the environment, bioaccumulate through the food web and pose a risk causing adverse effects to human health and the environment" (UNEP 2009).

The proliferation of organic chemical pesticides, since the launch of DDT in the 1940s, has had a profound range of social, environmental, and political impacts around the world in a number of ways. Their use has undoubtedly helped increase crop yields as part of the "Green Revolution" in the last seventy years and has also assisted in the struggle against diseases spread by insects, particularly in curbing the considerable death toll attributable to malaria.

On the other hand, pesticides have also affected human and other life forms in a variety of negative ways. Field workers spraying the chemicals have been poisoned; food has been contaminated; accidental releases during production and transport have killed thousands; and flora, fauna, water, and the atmosphere have been polluted in many ways. Around 220,000 people per year are killed by acute pesticide poisoning, which does not include those fatalities that are more difficult to quantify as a result of cancers and other, longer-term ailments (Hart and Pimentel 2002).[1] Ninety-eight per cent of insecticides and 95 per cent of herbicides that are sprayed do not hit their target and, instead, can contaminate the air, water, and soil, with a variety of environmental consequences. Those pesticides that do reach their intended destination may still end up killing more than that target when they pass down the food chain and are ingested by other organisms. In the US alone, where restrictions on chemical use are among the most stringent in the world, it is estimated that, every year, between 6 and 14 million fish and around 5 per cent of the honeybee population are killed as a result of exposure to pesticides (Pimentel 2005). Globally, figures substantiating the environmental impact of pesticides are predictably sketchy, but certain well-documented cases give a hint at the scale of the damage. For example, forensic analysis has proven that at least 4,000 Swainson's hawks in Argentina were wiped out as a result of eating caterpillars that had been sprayed with a newly imported organophosphorous insecticide, monocrotophos, during the 1995–6 summer season (Goldstein *et al.* 1999). In Kenya hundreds of lions and vultures are known to have met their deaths between 2004 and 2009 as a result of exposure to a form of carbamate insecticides known as carbofurans, recognized as POPs. Carbofuran products, which are completely prohibited from use in the EU and highly restricted in the US, are designed to protect corn and other crops but, owing to their toxicity, are also fatal to other animal species. They are known to have been used by cattle herders, who lace animal carcasses and leave them as traps in order to eliminate mammalian prey (Howden 2009).

Aside from such "collateral damage" resulting from chemicals accidently missing their intended target or willfully being employed in ways for which they were not designed, the chemical properties of POPs mean that they can be an environmental hazard well away from the fields where they have been applied. Since they are so slow to break down and tend to be stored in fat, they can end up deposited in animals thousands of kilometers from where they were used. In a phenomenon known as the "grasshopper effect," chemicals such as DDT and carbofuran, after evaporating in the warmer climates where they tend to be employed, can be carried around the globe in the atmosphere or water in a series of "hops" of evaporation and deposition and then build up in food chains remote from where they were applied. Hence polar bears, at the top of Arctic food chain, have been found to be contaminated by POPs (Tenenbaum 2004).

The emergence of pesticide politics

The production and use of pesticides thrived from the late 1940s to the 1960s, when food yields soared and many tropical diseases appeared to be being brought under control, but then the rise of political ecology brought numerous side effects into focus. Pesticide-induced environmental pollution was, in many ways, the catalyst for the emergence of the whole issue area of environmental change on the international political agenda. The publication in 1962 of *Silent Spring* by the US marine biologist Rachel Carson, despite concerted corporate attacks on its scientific authenticity, is widely recognized as having helped fuel the take-off of environmental politics. The book's title alludes to a future world in which birdsong could no longer be heard, drawing on evidence that organochlorine use was damaging eggshells. It was this ecocentric message which prompted a backlash in the US and much of the West against what was undoubtedly a profitable and, in some cases, life-saving technology, although the book did also highlight human health hazards associated with organochlorine pesticide use (Carson 1962). The controversial spraying of the jungle defoliant Agent Orange (a trade name of the herbicide 2,4,5-T) by the US in the Vietnam War also served to heighten anxieties about pesticides. At that point the use of the chemicals even entered the world of "high politics," when, at the 1972 UN Stockholm Conference on the Human Environment, the Swedish prime minister, Olaf Palme, denounced the Agent Orange applications as "ecocide," prompting a diplomatic spat between the two countries. As with other environmental issues, the 1960s and early 1970s saw the whole area of pesticide production, trade, and use at the international level move from being a relatively unchallenged and heralded technological development to a highly politicized set of issues.

The rise in concern at the effects of organochlorine insecticides on wildlife since the 1960s has contributed to the banning of, or severe restrictions on, the use of DDT, dieldrin, and other notorious chemicals in most developed countries. The US government enacted legislation restricting DDT use in 1969 and then outlawed it altogether in 1972. Pesticides continue to arouse a certain amount of political controversy in the domestic political arenas of the developed world, but the phasing out of the most carcinogenic and polluting chemicals and their replacement with less toxic formulations, alongside the establishment of stringent consumer standards and health and safety regulations, has significantly reduced the environmental and health concerns. There have been some notable environmental benefits from these domestic legal changes, such as the return of sparrowhawks in the UK since the 1970s, after they had come close to disappearing. However, as the US figures referred to earlier indicate, there continue to be some significant pesticidal impacts on wildlife.

Since the 1960s, however, it has been transnational issues of pesticide use, production, and trade that have commanded most social, environmental, and political significance. The introduction into developing countries of Western agricultural technology in the 1960s and 1970s, known commonly as the "Green Revolution," opened up a massive southward trade in pesticides. Many chemicals withdrawn from domestic use in the developed world have continued to be marketed to the Global South, where regulatory standards tend to be much laxer. The monocrotophos used in Argentina that was referred to earlier was imported from the US, where it is prohibited. The response of many agrochemical firms to greater scrutiny of their produce by health and environmental groups in the North has been to redirect their goods to much less restrictive markets in the "industrial flight" and "race to the bottom" phenomena identified in Chapter 3 of this volume.

Chemicals were first legally restricted in a number of developed countries in the late 1960s and 1970s chiefly because of their documented effects on birds and other wildlife, but this, in itself, has never proved a sufficient basis for global rules to develop. Global regimes which have emerged in the governance of pesticides have only crystallized once vested industrial and governmental interests have also come to see some advantage in regulation on account of the consequent harmonization of trading standards.

It was the 1984 Bhopal disaster that served as the catalyst for a campaign involving numerous environmental and consumer activists aiming to regulate the global production, trade, and use of pesticides. It was led by the Pesticide Action Network (PAN), a global pressure group which had formed two years earlier. The world's worst ever industrial accident occurred at an Indian chemical plant owned by the US multinational corporation Union Carbide. Forty tonnes of the highly toxic chemical methyl-isocyanate (MIC), used in the production of the carbamate insecticide Carbaryl, was accidently released, killing over 2,500 people in the short term and countless thousands of others in the succeeding years through a range of long-term health effects and birth defects. The disaster served to highlight concerns over pesticide toxicity beyond that which had been possible in the countless smaller-scale disasters that had occurred previously. Bhopal also served to expose a clear international political economy dimension to the pesticides industry, since safety standards at the plant were found to be much laxer than at those permitted at the corporation's home base in Virginia.

Crucially, self-interest as well as compassion in the Global North came to favor the regulation of the pesticide trade in the 1980s and 1990s as governments came to see that domestic legislation was insufficient to protect their citizens. Pesticides profitably dumped on markets in the Global South can return to Northern consumers in their food imports from the same countries, or through long-range atmospheric pollution as a result of the grasshopper effect. Additionally, chemical firms needed to improve their reputations after Bhopal and came to see that global standards would be less costly than further domestic legal restraints on their industry, and might even be advantageous in the long run. Thus the powerful players in pesticide politics, the chemical companies and Northern governments, were gradually persuaded of the need for regulation, paving the way for the development of international law in the 1990s.

Contemporary global governance with regard to pesticides and POPs focuses on four areas: regulating permissible amounts of residual chemicals in traded food, regulating the export of certain pesticides, outlawing the use and production of the most toxic chemicals, and targeting a specific pesticide as part of the ozone regime.

Pesticide residues in traded food

The origins of global policy on pesticides can be traced back as far as 1963, when the Food and Agricultural Organization (FAO) and World Health Organization (WHO) co-launched a body intended to "protect the health of consumers and to ensure fair practises in the food trade" (CAC 1989: 31). The Codex Alimentarius Commission, the implementing machinery of the FAO/WHO Food Standards Programme, has a Committee on Pesticides Residues

(CCPR) which sets global standards for recommended maximum levels of pesticide traces in traded foodstuffs, initially intended to be no more than voluntary guidelines.

Environmental and consumer groups have long suggested that Codex standards are informed more by the latter of its two stated aims and cannot be relied upon to guarantee consumer safety, since the body is not impartial in its judgments and is motivated chiefly by the desire to harmonize national food standards to an agreed minimum in order to facilitate international trade. The membership of Codex is open to any member state or associate member of the FAO and WHO, which can then vote on a majority basis for the adoption of draft standards for food quality issues. The commission has always been far closer to the FAO than the WHO, owing to the latter's broader portfolio of responsibilities, and has attracted similar sorts of criticism to its closer parent of being over-influenced by transnational corporations linked to the food industry (Avery *et al.* 1993). Indeed, of the twenty-three "international non-governmental organizations" listed as participants at the thirty-ninth CCPR meeting in July 2007, all were business representatives (CAC 2007).

This concern for excessive corporate influence heightened with the creation of the World Trade Organization (WTO) and the sudden elevation of Codex's technical standards to quasi-international law. The 1995 WTO Agreements on the Application of Sanitary and Phytosanitary Measures and Technical Barriers to Trade cite Codex standards as the benchmark for determining whether state food standards are being used by members as an unfair barrier to free trade. This concern has yet to be realized, however. Food in the Global North generally still continues to be produced in accordance with national pesticide residue standards, since lowering consumer safety standards in democracies with active civil societies and a press is politically infeasible.

Codex standards for pesticides, though less stringent than the domestic standards of many developed states, are presently almost certainly sufficient to safeguard against significant risks to human health. Despite high levels of corporate influence, the CCPR's standards are drawn largely from the findings of the Joint Meeting on Pesticide Residues (JMPR), a respected WHO/FAO forum of scientists and academics without any corporate representation. JMPR recommendations on acceptable residue limits in foodstuffs, though less stringent than some domestic standards, are very much informed by the precautionary principle, with levels set much lower than are known to be dangerous to health.

As with many other environmental and health issues, there has been some breaking of the ranks on the appropriateness of the precautionary principle in spite of its apparent legitimization by all governments at UNCED in 1992. This was most notable in 2001, when the US delegation at the sixteenth session of the Codex Commission on General Principles led a walk-out in protest at attempts to develop further use of the principle in Codex standards, arguing that this would represent a "non-scientific" trade barrier. The US government and global chemical industry representatives have since focused on lobbying for a global harmonization of Codex Maximum Residue Limits (MRLs), but, to date, the right of states to fix their own – even more precautionary – MRLs has remained. Where Codex pesticide residue limits have been most influential is in providing a standard for developing countries lacking any MRLs of their own. Hence they have not leveled down standards with regards to pesticide residue in traded food and, despite extensive corporate lobbying and being co-opted by the WTO, have instead leveled them up and served to enhance public safety across the world. The precautionary principle has so far held sway. At present, the pesticide residues regime represents something of a "bootlegger and Baptist coalition"[2] (Yandle 1983), with its rules developed from principles emerging from an epistemic community committed to safeguarding human health and the economic interests of industry brought on board.

The methyl-bromide regime

An exception to the norm of global pesticide policy not being driven by environmental change is the regime which has emerged since the early 1990s that regulates releases into the atmosphere of the soil fumigant methyl-bromide. Methyl-bromide is used extensively in the farming of tomatoes and strawberries, particularly in the US. Concerns had been voiced for years about its environmental effects (the Netherlands government phased out its use in 1992), but it took the realization that the chemical posed a threat to human life for it to be made subject to any international regulation. The discovery that methyl-bromide was a significant ozone-depleting agent saw a global agreement concerning its use and production reached in November 1992 at Copenhagen as part of the Montreal Protocol on Substances That Deplete the Ozone Layer, the key treaty dealing with the issue of ozone depletion.

The Copenhagen meeting decreed that methyl-bromide production and consumption should be frozen at 1991 levels from the start of 1995, and in September 1997 the ninth Meeting of the Parties to the Montreal Protocol committed 160 governments to a timetable for a complete phase-out. In line with the "common but differentiated responsibilities" principle agreed upon at UNCED, developed countries agreed to end use of the chemical by 2005 after a series of intermediate cuts, while developing countries agreed to a deadline for elimination of 2015, following a freeze in 2002. As with other areas of environmental and humanitarian global governance, however, the US backtracked under the administration of George Bush Junior from seeming to support a complete phase-out, and has maintained a significant level of methyl-bromide use since 2005 by exploiting a "critical use exemptions" clause to the agreement far more than had been anticipated. The Californian strawberry industry, mindful of the costs of switching to alternative soil fumigants, lobbied hard for US delegates to argue that those alternatives previously agreed upon were not adequate for the West Coast climate – much to the irritation of most other Montreal Protocol parties (Gareau 2008). Hence methyl-bromide continues to be utilized, principally in the US, but also in eleven other countries. A global phase-out is still proceeding, albeit more slowly than was originally envisaged.

Prior informed consent in trading chemicals

Probably the most significant development in the global governance of chemical pollutants has been the 1998 Rotterdam Convention on the Prior Informed Consent Procedure for Certain Hazardous Chemicals and Pesticides in International Trade, which came into force in 2004. This sets out legally binding commitments constraining governments attempting to export chemicals banned in their own countries through the prior informed consent (PIC) procedure. The chemicals PIC regime stands as an example of how private governance (see Chapter 3 in this volume) can form the basis of more stringent consumer-focused regulation. The Rotterdam convention made legally binding Article 9 of the FAO's 1986 International Code of Conduct on the Distribution and Use of Pesticides, a voluntary set of safety standards for the handling and transport of pesticides.

PIC was initially resisted by displays of corporate power but, eventually, was able to overcome such vested interests. The relevant PIC provision in Article 9 was withdrawn during the lead up to the ratification of the FAO code in 1985, despite appearing on seven of its eight drafts in the face of strong UK and US persuasion, motivated by a chemical industry lobby alarmed at the prospect of restrictions on their trade. No national delegation officially requested the deletion of the PIC provision and thirty countries protested its removal, but it appears that covert pressure convinced delegates at the ratifying conference that the code as a whole would be at risk if a compromise over Article 9 was not accepted (Hough 1998: 113–20). Led by the Pesticide Action Network (PAN) and Oxfam, a campaign to reincorporate PIC into Article 9 of the FAO code and advance the principle carried on regardless of the 1985 ratification. The Netherlands became the first country formally to embrace PIC into domestic legislation in 1985, and the European Community made moves toward adopting the procedure for all its member states before eventually absorbing the whole FAO Code of Conduct, including PIC, into European law in the 1990s.[3]

The establishment of the principle of PIC as a binding international rule was sealed by the eventual support of the chemical industry in the early 1990s. The agrochemical industry's global political mouthpiece, the Groupement International des Associations de Fabricants de Produits Agrochemiques (GIFAP), announced in its 1991 annual report that one of its aims for 1992 would be to "continue to cooperate with FAO/UNEP on the implementation of PIC" (GIFAP 1991: 11). The reason for this apparent U-turn on PIC appeared to be a fear of the alternatives, such as an outright prohibition of the export of certain pesticides. The drafting of a bill in the US during 1991–2 proposing the introduction of export controls for pesticides raised alarm in the agrochemical industry and prompted GIFAP to take the extraordinary step of criticizing the bill on the grounds that it was contrary to the very article of the FAO Code of Conduct it had so vehemently opposed:

> A major concern … is the appearance of a draft Bill on pesticide export control in the USA which is very much at variance with PIC in the FAO Code, namely that this draft legislation is export rather than import control orientated.
>
> (Ibid.: 13)

GIFAP here saw an opportunity to ensure that any chemical trade regulations that did emerge would be based only on import rather than on export restrictions. In a choice between PIC and export restrictions of the sort discussed in the US Congress, the chemical industry came to accept the principle because it represented the lesser of two evils in the pursuit of their main goal of maintaining free trade. Thus, again, a pesticide regime came to be formed through a "bootlegger and Baptist coalition" of actors agreeing to cooperate to enforce norms in the name of differing values: safeguarding human health and maximizing economic returns, with the former the primary influence.

The Rotterdam convention obliges parties exporting any chemical restricted by their own domestic legislation to send decision guidance documents (DGD) to importing authorities detailing the basis of such restrictions. The process also ensures DGDs are automatically circulated to all parties for chemicals listed under Annex III of the convention. A Chemical Review Committee (CRC) considers proposals from parties for including new chemicals in the automatically triggered PIC list (Annex III). By 2008, thirty-nine chemicals, including twenty-eight pesticides, were contained in Annex III.[4] The CRCs consider the reliability of the evidence provided and the significance of reported effects in comparison to the quantities used and discerns whether any reported ill-effects could be prevented by the proper application of the chemical. The secretariat is able to take up reports from NGOs in addition to those from governments. This practice was established under the voluntary scheme following PAN pressure in highlighting health problems peculiar to developing countries resulting from the use of some pesticides. The contentious issue of whether the rules of the convention could be overruled by WTO provisions on free trade in the event of any clash was fudged by removing a get-out clause to this effect, which was supported by the US government. In its place a number of governments were permitted to include in the preamble a statement that the convention will not "prejudice their respective positions in other international forums and negotiations address-ing issues related to the environment and trade." There was some opposition to including the word "environmental" in the negotiations, but it was eventually agreed that PIC would be extended to any "chemical formulated for pesticidal use that produces severe health or envi-ronmental effects observable within a short period of time after single or multiple exposures, under conditions of use" (Article 2d).

Since the convention came into force, no new chemicals have been added to Annex III, as corporate and national interests have come to the fore and blocked the requisite "consensus" at the Conferences of the Parties. Even in the absence of the US – which has not yet ratified – uni-lateralism in less likely quarters has stifled progress since 2004. The Canadian delegation, much to the horror of that country's prominent environmental and human security activists, has led a small band of parties to the convention in blocking the addition of Chrysotile asbestos to the PIC list.[5] Chrysotile is the component of nearly all forms of the world's asbestos, a substance banned in sixty countries outright and considered by the WHO to be the cause of 90,000 deaths a year. It is also, however, a lucrative export earner for the Canadian government, a point reinforced by the Asbestos Cement Products Manufacturers' Association at the meetings.

Additionally, even for those chemicals listed in Annex III, whether PIC does lessen the problems associated with their trade is open to debate. The procedure provides for information to be supplied to importers but does not actually prohibit the trade in hazardous chemicals. Further, some have expressed concern that, far from empowering importing Global South countries, the PIC procedure has actually served to reinforce dependency, since the scientific assessments used are from the Global North (Barrios 2004; Karlsson 2004). The enshrining of PIC as a rule for the trading of hazardous chemicals is an important step forward for global governance but does not, in itself, represent the realization of environmental and consumer-focused safety standards comparable to those that have become established in many countries of the developed world since the 1960s.

The politics of POPs

Inspired by the progress achieved with the PIC regime, but also by its practical limitations, a global campaign aiming to eliminate the use and production of the most toxic and persis-tent chemicals worldwide emerged following the formulation of the Rotterdam convention. UNCED (Chapter 19, *Agenda 21*) raised the profile of a pressure group campaign, sup-ported by a WHO-based epistemic community, culminating in a treaty similar to the methyl-bromide convention, but for a range of chemicals, including notoriously hazardous pesticides such as DDT, aldrin, and dieldrin. After endorsement by UNEP's governing coun-cil in 1997, the Intergovernmental Forum on Chemical Safety, set up by UNCED, was charged specifically with the task of implementing the proposal, which it duly adopted as the chief of its "priorities for action" at its first meeting.

Once again the development of a new regime can be seen to have emerged from a lengthy process of pressure-group campaigning and UN agency-led epistemic cooperation. WHO expert committees have been at the forefront of developing global standards for measuring chemical toxicity since the 1950s, and their "Classification by Hazard Scheme," launched in 1975, is the key reference point for the FAO's "Code of Conduct on the Use and Distribution of Pesticides" and the Rotterdam convention. On the back of their success in getting the FAO code ready for signature, PAN in 1985 launched their "Dirty Dozen" campaign, calling for the outright prohibition of many of the same chemicals which subsequently formed the basis of a POPs regime.

Table 12.1 Chemicals subject to the Stockholm convention

Intentionally produced

Aldrin	Pesticide	
Chlordane	Pesticide	Use and
Dieldrin	Pesticide	production
Endrin	Pesticide	banned apart
Heptachlor	Pesticide	from
Hexachlorobenzene (HCB)	Pesticide	laboratory-scale
Mirex	Pesticide	research
Toxaphene	Pesticide	
Polychlorinated biphenyls (PCBs)	Industrial chemical	
Dichlorodiphenyltrichloroethane (DDT)	Pesticide	Use restricted to disease vector

Unintentionally produced

Polychlorinated dibenzo-p-dioxins and dibenzofurans (PCDD 'dioxins'/PCDF 'furans')		Use and production minimized with
Hexachlorobenzene (HCB)	Pesticide	the aim of
Polychlorinated biphenyls (PCBs)	Industrial chemical	elimination

Sixteen years later, many of the dirty dozen formed the basis of the International Legally Binding Instrument for Implementing International Action on Certain Persistent Organic Pollutants (POPs Treaty), which was signed by 127 governments at a diplomatic conference in Stockholm in May 2001 and entered into force in 2004.

Under Article 8 of the convention, a Persistent Organic Pollutants Review Committee appraises proposals to add new chemicals to the original twelve.[6] The Stockholm convention is explicitly linked to its UNEP sibling the Basel Convention on Control of Transboundary Movements of Hazardous Wastes and their Disposal, with measures calling on parties to minimize the generation and movement of waste POPs. The convention is an example of "soft international law" in that it is legally binding but contains no enforcement measures.

The production and use of the outlawed chemicals has long ceased in most developed countries, but their properties ensure that they remain a domestic hazard to their populations. Because of their slowness to break down and propensity to travel, sterility, neural disorders, and cancer in peoples of the developed world can be attributed to the use of POPs in other parts of the planet. The political significance of this is such that even President George W. Bush, shortly after his government's revocation of the Kyoto Protocol on Climate Change, in 2001 declared US support for international environmental cooperation on POPs. That the POPs regime is not fundamentally driven by ecocentric values is evidenced by the fact that the infamously environmentally unfriendly DDT is exempted from prohibition by governments signing up to the institution, who declare that they require the use of the chemical to combat mosquitoes in the fight against malaria. This qualification follows a concerted campaign by public health specialists. Again, rather than environmental values, the value of safeguarding human health and the coincidental satisfaction of corporate interests have formed the driving force for political action.

The chemical industry, represented at Stockholm by GIFAP's successor the Global Crop Protection Federation (GCPF) and other global lobby groups, again gave its backing to an agreement which constrains its freedom of action in order to prevent something more restrictive emerging. The industry's presence at the Stockholm negotiations was more low-key than at other conferences on global chemical trade issues, and it was largely receptive to environmental/consumer-group demands. The POPs pesticides were not worth fighting for, as they were by now rarely produced by the big agrochemical companies of the Global North; their patent protection had mostly expired, and cheaper generic versions were being produced by small companies in the Global South. Therefore a global ban on POPs could even serve the interests of the agrochemical giants, since it would give them an opportunity to corner the market in new, alternative, and patent-protected pesticides. Hence at Stockholm the chemical lobby concentrated on ensuring that the list of chemicals making up the POPs list be limited to the older organochlorine pesticides (Clapp 2003). The chemical industry and the US delegation at the negotiations of the Stockholm convention fought hard to ensure that the term "precautionary principle" did not appear in the final text, and it was eventually replaced with the more ambiguous compromise phrase "precautionary approach," which the industrialists hoped would open the door to less expansive "scientific" toxicity assessments (Olsen 2003: 99–100). The significance of such semantics is clear from considering the Bush administration's pronouncements on the principle previously accepted by the US government at UNCED: "the US government supports precautionary approaches to risk management but we do not recognize any precautionary principle" (Graham 2002). By 2008 the US had still not ratified Stockholm, the Bush administration's initial enthusiasm having been curbed by the inclusion on the list of furans and dioxins, which are significant by-products of the US's large chlorine industry.

Conclusions

The progress of global policy on POPs and pesticides fits well into the notion of a "middle ground" in environmental governance, not necessarily in direct confrontation with free trade and industrialization, as outlined in Chapter 3. Global rules have emerged dialectically from a dialogue between these rival interests, led by chemical corporations and environmental pressure groups, with governments somewhere in between and often divided themselves.[7] In this area of policy, free trade governance and the WTO have not trumped socially and environmentally driven governance, although there is still a possibility of this happening.

The regulation of pesticides became part of the global agenda on account of the action of pressure groups and epistemic communities coordinated by the United Nations. Powerful governments and business interests tried to resist this but were eventually persuaded, through fear of being exposed as immoral to their electorates/consumers, to come to the negotiating table. Pressure groups, led by PAN, have successfully helped put pesticides issues on the global agenda and advanced the values of environmental conservation and safeguarding human health. The rules that have emerged from this process are not, however, driven purely by social and environmental concerns and are "tempered" by the competing interests of the chemical industry, which generally has greater influence on the governments signing and ratifying the international agreements. Governments in international politics are still more likely to be driven by economic national interests than in domestic affairs, where consumer rights and ecocentric policies can hold them to account (at least in developed democracies). Global governance in the area of POPs and pesticides is as yet, therefore, limited in comparison with domestic environmental and health policy in much of the Global North and is insufficient to eradicate the occurrences of environmental pollution and human poisonings which still blight much of the Global South in particular.

The first steps taken in global pesticide governance may be small ones, but they are still significant. Norms once established cannot easily be erased. Unraveling agreements clearly made in the human and environmental interest is more difficult than preventing them in the first place, since the selfish pursuit of profit is more clearly exposed as such and reputation does count for something in the contemporary interdependent world. The precautionary principle cannot be wished away by the US or the chemical industry. Methyl-bromide is still going to be phased out, despite the increasingly desperate rearguard action fought by the US government. Codex standards are still based on precautionary calculations of human toxicity, even if they are being exploited by big business as a means of circumventing more stringent domestic standards. A strong global civil society movement centered on the "International Ban Asbestos" group allied to governmental pressure from the EU will probably eventually succeed in forcing the Canadian government into a corner and submitting to the inclusion of chrysotile on the Rotterdam convention PIC list. The POPs regime is currently limited in what it can do but, now in force, it can only be broadened and deepened. The Stockholm Convention Conferences of the Parties have discussed a working compliance mechanism to improve implementation, and five new chemicals are set for inclusion to the POPs list, thanks to concerted lobbying by PAN and many other groups present as observers at the review committee meetings and independent assessments by an epistemic community representing no vested interests.

The chemical industry has no direct interest in curbing its freedom to trade in pesticides as it chooses, but the Bhopal disaster and public fears of continued exposure to presumed obsolete chemicals brought them to a negotiating table laid by civil society actors. Once at the table, industry has been able to negotiate from a position of strength and further its own interests, but the fact that it has had to come to the table is still an important breakthrough in the development of global governance. Ultimately, the global governance of pesticides is in the interests of both sides at the table, even if their motivations for being there are different. Actors driven by different values can, nevertheless, reach mutually beneficial agreements. Just as bootleggers and Baptists supported US alcohol prohibition, environmentalists and the chemical industry have found themselves seeing global pesticide regulatory measures as means to very different ends.

Notes

1   It is worth noting, however, that a majority of these deaths are the result of suicides.
2   The term is derived from the days of alcohol prohibition in the US, when both the Church and the black market gained in different ways from the law.
3   EC Directive EEC2455/92.
4   List of chemicals subject to PIC procedure: *Pesticides*: 1) 2,4,5-T; 2) Aldrin (HHDN); 3) Binapacryl (Endosan); 4) Captafol; 5) dustable powder formulations containing a combination of at least 7% of Benomyl, 10% of Carbofuran, and 15% of Thiram; 6) Chlordane; 7) Chlordimeform; 8) Chlorobenzilate; 9) DDT; 10) Dieldrin (HEOD); 11) DNOC and its salts; 12) Dinoseb and dinoseb salts; 13) 1,2-dibromoethane (EDB; Ethylene dibromide); 14) Ethylene dichloride; 15) Ethylene oxide; 16) Flouroacetamide; 17) HCH; 18) Heptachlor; 19) Hexachlorobenzene; 20) Lindane; 21) Mercury compounds; 22) Pentachlorophenol; 23) Monocrotophos; 24) Methamidophos; 25) Phosphamidon; 26) Methyl-parathion; 27) Parathion; 28) Toxaphene (Camphechlor).
    Industrial chemicals: 29) Actinolite asbestos; 30) Amosite asbestos; 31) Anthophyllite asbestos; 32) Crocidolite asbestos; 33) Tremolite asbestos; 34) Polybrominated biphenyls; 35) Polychlorinated biphenyls; 36) Polychlorinated terphenyls; 37) Tetraethyl lead; 38) Tetramethyl lead; 39) Tris (2,3-dibromopropyl) phosphate.
5   India, Ukraine, Kyrgyzstan, Peru, and Iran also opposed the addition of Chrysotile at the third COP in 2006. The Russian government is a vociferous opponent of a ban but is not a party to the Rotterdam convention.

6   For example, among chemicals proposed for inclusion by the parties are Hexabromobiphenyl (HBB), Hexacchlorocycloheane (HCH, e.g. Lindane), Chlordecone, and Polycyclic aromatic hydrocarbons (PAH), which have been banned in Europe by the UNECE Protocol on Long-Range Transboundary Air Pollution since 2003.

7   The US government represents a classic case of "transgovernmental relations" when dealing with global pesticide issues, with the position of delegates at the Codex, PIC, and POPs regime meetings promoting international harmonization and less precautionary approaches to classifying chemical toxicity which are often at odds with the standards of the Environmental Protection Agency.

Recommended reading

Hough, P. (1998) *The Global Politics of Pesticides: Forging Consensus from Conflicting Interests*, London: Earthscan.

Johansen, B. (2003) *The Dirty Dozen: Toxic Chemicals and the Earth's Future*, Westport, CT: Praeger.

Selin, H. (2010) *Global Governance of Hazardous Chemicals: Challenges of Multilevel Management*, Cambridge, MA: MIT Press.

References

Avery, N., Drake, M., and Lang, T. (1993) *Cracking the Codex: An Analysis of Who Sets World Food Standards*, London: National Food Alliance.

Barrios, P. (2004) "The Rotterdam Convention on Hazardous Chemicals: a meaningful step toward environmental protection?," *Georgetown International Environmental Law Review*, 16(4): 679–762.

CAC (Codex Alimentarius Commission) (1989) *Procedural Manual*, 7th ed., Rome: Joint FAO/WHO Food Standards Programme.

—— (2007) "Report of the thirty-ninth session of the Codex Committee on Pesticide Residues," Beijing, China, 7–12 May, ALINORM 07/30/24-Rev.1, Rome: Joint FAO/WHO Food Standards Programme.

Carson, R. (1962) *Silent Spring*, Harmondsworth: Penguin.

Clapp, J. (2003) "Transnational corporate interests and global environmental governance: negotiating rules for agricultural biotechnology and chemicals," *Environmental Politics*, 12(4): 1–23.

Gareau, B. (2008) "Dangerous holes in global environmental governance: the roles of neoliberal discourse, science and California agriculture in the Montreal protocol," *Antipode*, 40, 1 January: 102–30.

GIFAP (Groupement International des Associations de Fabricants de Produits Agrochemiques) (1991) *GIFAP Annual Report 1991*, Brussels. GIFAP.

Goldstein, M. I., Lacher, T. E, Woodbridge, B., Bechard, M. J., Canavelli, S. B., Zaccagnini, M. E., Cobb, G. P., Scollon, E. J., Tribolet, R., and Hopper, M. J. (1999) "Monocrotophos-induced mass mortality of Swainson's hawks in Argentina 1995–96," *Ecotoxicology*, 8(3): 201–14.

Graham, J. (2002) "The role of precaution in risk management," remarks prepared for the International Society of Regulatory Toxicology and Pharmacology Precautionary Principle Workshop, Crystal City, VA, 20 June. Available: www.whitehouse.gov/omb/inforeg/risk_mgmt_speech062002.html (accessed 13 March 2008).

Hart, K., and Pimentel, D. (2002) "Public health and costs of pesticides," in D. Pimentel (ed.), *Encyclopedia of Pest Management*, New York: Marcel Dekker.

Hough, P. (1998) *The Global Politics of Pesticides: Forging Consensus from Conflicting Interests*, London: Earthscan.

Howden, D. (2009) "Kenyan lions being poisoned by pesticides," *The Independent*, 3 April: 29.

Karlsson, S. I. (2004) "Institutionalized knowledge challenges in pesticide governance: the end of knowledge and beginning of values in governing globalization and environmental issues," *International Environmental Agreements: Politics, Law and Economics*, 4: 195–213.

Olsen, M. (2003) *Analysis of the Stockholm Convention on Persistent Organic Pollutants*, Dobbs Ferry, NY: Oceana.

Pimentel, D. (2005) "Environmental and economic costs of the application of pesticides primarly in the United States," *Environment, Development and Sustainability*, 7: 229–52.

Tenenbaum, D. (2004) "POPs in polar bears: organochlorines affect bone density," *Environmental Health Perspectives*, 112(17): A1011.

UNEP (2009) "Persistent organic pollutants," available: www.chem.unep.ch/pops (accessed 7 July 2009).

Yandle, B. (1983) "Bootleggers and Baptists: the education of a regulatory economist," *Regulation*, 7(3): 12–16.

Conclusion: the future of global environmental politics

Gabriela Kütting

It is now time to draw conclusions from the conceptual and applied chapters in this book and ponder the future of global environmental politics, both as an academic discipline and as one of the biggest political challenges of the twenty-first century. The two are of course related, but they also exist independently of each other to a certain extent, as many of the chapters here have demonstrated.

There are several challenges that global environmental politics as an academic field has to face in the coming years, and the reader has been alerted to them by the conceptual chapters. While the study of global environmental governance is important and continues to occupy a predominant position in global environmental politics, many chapters here have shown that it is important to see governance attempts in perspective and not to forget their limitations. Global governance becomes a wider field when we include the importance of non-state actors, as Lucy Ford showed in Chapter 2. In fact, there are many governance forms that either do not involve states at all or are composed of a mix of state or intergovernmental actors and non-state actors. However, it is not only the actors but also the fields of action that have changed considerably in recent times. While until not so long ago attempts at regulating the causes of environmental problems focused on getting states to agree to certain targets, we now have the options of economic tools, such as cap and trade, for getting non-state actors involved in finding solutions to problems, and also taking into account new perspectives of how to conceptualize problems. For example, the concept of sustainable consumption, as explained by Doris Fuchs and Frederike Boll (Chapter 5), shows that including society and how individuals behave both as political and economic entities brings vital new dimensions to the field that become increasingly important, the significance of which had been overlooked for a long time. The same goes for ideas of justice and equity. While justice had for a long time been looked at in terms of fair burden-sharing between the states signing an international environmental agreement on a particular problem, it has become clear that justice or equity is a lot more than that, and global solutions to global problems need to be more accountable and respect the rights of all. Timothy Ehresman and Dimitris Stevis (Chapter 6) discussed a variety of issues and concepts related to international or global justice and equity, the main message being that the rights of communities have to be respected at the local, regional, national, and global level for legitimate solutions to environmental problems, particularly in the field of climate change.

Above all, the conceptual chapters have demonstrated how connected the political and economic, the theoretical and the practical, the individual and the institutional, the local and the global are. John Vogler on theories and concepts (Chapter 1) as much as Jennifer Clapp on global political economy and North–South issues (Chapter 3) connect in ways that are complemented by Lucy Ford's non-state actor emphasis, the focus on consumption and on justice. Shlomi Dinar, focusing on environmental security in Chapter 4, shows how the geopolitical aspect also has a huge bearing on how states perceive environmental problems. What all these chapters show together is that it is exactly this plurality of approaches that helps us conceive of global environmental politics as a whole, and such a plurality is needed for analyzing, interpreting, and finding solutions to global environmental problems. The academic field has become a lot wider in recent years, and this expansion will bring deeper and more fruitful academic analysis.

These gains in the development of global environmental politics are naturally complemented by how we as a global society approach these challenges to our planet, our lives, the lives of our children and their children, and ultimately all our livelihoods. Here, our case studies have given important clues. They are about some of the most pressing problems – some being particular issues, some being difficulties particular sectors are facing – and all vary in scope and complexity. First of all, the case studies show that a one-size-fits-all approach to global environmental problems clearly does not work, as each and every problem and challenge is different and needs a different solution. Yet it is also clear that all problems and challenges require solutions at the global level – solutions that have to be based on the current tools political scientists and policy-makers have at their disposal. Thus the global governance approach is of course still the predominant one, but it is often complemented by others. Peter Hough's study on pesticides and persistent organic pollutants (Chapter 12) illustrates the difficulties in the interplay between industry pressure and scientific standard-setting. It also shows that, with pesticides and other pollutants, a regulatory approach is possibly the only one that makes sense. When we compare POP regulation with the challenge of climate change, it immediately becomes obvious that curbing climate change is much more complex and far reaching – thus necessitating a different approach. While greenhouse gases can be curbed with a regulatory approach, the different nature of the industries causing the release of these gases makes a cap and trade approach a more politically acceptable solution, as discussed by Paul Harris (Chapter 7). At the same time, more sectoral environmental problems, such as those associated with marine pollution, forests, or agricultural production, very clearly show the importance of justice and consumption issues as parts of the solutions to the challenges posed. All studies demonstrate that environmental politics is strongly connected to political economy issues; thus, effective environmental governance will show an understanding of political economy in its widest sense.

In terms of who has the responsibility for meeting the environmental challenges of the twenty-first century, the resounding answer is all of us, in all political, social, and economic spheres. Political action cannot be a top-down approach, with governments telling their citizens what to do – it also has to be from the bottom up, with the citizens telling their representatives what they expect of them. The economy cannot become more sustainable solely by producers adopting more environmentally friendly production methods; there also has to be a rethinking of how and what we as people consume – and how we want our economy to be organized. Do we want an economy based on a concept of infinite growth, or do we want more of a steady state economy? Do we want environmental problems to become security threats and have them approached from this persepctive? Or do we see the roots of the problem in the organization of the neoliberal political economy? Can we achieve change through activism, and do we want to be active through non-state channels, or do we make the way we consume our political action? These are a lot of questions and they require a lot of thought. However, the environmental problems of the twenty-first century cannot be resolved through global environmental governance alone – their mechanisms, roots, and possible solutions are so complex that they require a wider angle and action on more than one front. It was the aim of the contributors of this volume to provide you with the tools to understand this complex web.

In fact, the strongest lesson for the future of global environmental politics as an academic field is that global environmental governance cannot be analyzed in isolation from the political economy of a particular environmental problem. This is something that virtually all case studies and most of the conceptual chapters have confirmed. So, what about the environmental challenges of the twenty-first century in general? Of course the biggest perceived challenge is that of climate change – although many of the problems discussed here are directly and indirectly related to it. Climate change is likely the most complex problem that global policy-makers have faced in human history. It is only with all the tools discussed in this book that global society can reasonably expect to tackle this existential problem.

Index

Lightning Source UK Ltd.
Milton Keynes UK
UKOW05f0336011117
311966UK00010B/274/P